Life, Liberty and the pursuit of Inequality

By Steve Wunsch

Table of Contents

1. The Pursuit of Inequality

Everyone pursues inequality. That is what we're doing when we work hard, or study hard, or practice the piano, or mow the lawn. We want to impress people. We want a better job that pays more money because we want to become richer than we were, or are, or than others are. We want to live in a better house in a nicer neighborhood where the rich live, because we aspire to be like them, and we long to have others aspire to be like us. That's what moving up means.

If you've been reading the news, you'd think there was something unholy about such thoughts, as if you were selfishly ignoring the societal need for equality by thinking only of yourself. Experts and politicians berate us with endless versions of the conventional wisdom that says, not only is inequality unconscionably unfair, the American dream is dying because of it. They beg us to help address the problem, and say we should feel guilty if we don't. Everyone assumes that countering inequality is imperative, on moral grounds, on efficiency grounds, on fairness grounds, and every other ground you can think of.

The president of the United States says so. [i] The mayor of New York says so. [ii] The chairwoman of the Federal Reserve says so. [iii] The IMF says so. [iv] The OECD says so. [v] The World Bank says so. [vi] The Pope says so. [vii] Democrats say so. [viii] Republicans say so. [ix] Right, left and center -- they all say that the biggest problem facing the country, the city, the world, the universe, is inequality.

But all those experts and leaders are wrong. Inequality is not only inevitable; it is a good thing. The founders of our nation assumed and accepted inequality as a fact of life, and gave us the right to pursue it as if it were the original and most important of all the rights in our Bill of Rights, indeed as if that was what was meant by our unalienable right to "the pursuit of happiness." [x]

The American dream is dying, all right, but not because of inequality. In fact the opposite is closer to the truth. It is our obsession with inequality -- the now nearly universal belief that inequality is our biggest problem -- that is killing us.

The first and most important point I want to make in this book is that, if the right to pursue inequality were not in our founding DNA, the United States would never have become a significant nation, much less the richest and most powerful country on earth. This right was central to the founding *as monopolies* of the industries at the center of early American capitalism, such as railroads, oil and steel. These New World monopolies formed largely without official protection of federal, state or city governments, and thus represented a significant departure from the way monopoly grants by the kings and parliaments of the Old World worked. Within a year of establishing the United States and the freedom to create our own monopolies, brokers on Wall Street were forming a price fixing cartel, culminating in the New York Stock Exchange's 1792 Buttonwood Agreement, which provided a model for the creation of many more monopolies over the next century. [xi] If we had not had the right to form such monopolies, none of them would have formed, and the soaring wealth, power and inequality of our country today would never have happened.

Second, I will show that we are dying economically because antitrust is both destroying old monopolies and blocking new ones, as it drains our wealth and power. For those that survive at all, antitrust transforms them back into Old World monopolies, as if patents from the king were still necessary, and puts redistribution at the top of their agendas, as a former SEC chairman says his policies "transferred billions of dollars from the pockets of brokers into the pockets of investors." [xii] Antitrust is thus a Trojan horse bringing concerns over inequality into the heart of American capitalism and thereby destroying it, starting with the stock market itself, but extending now to all of its children.

Third, I will show that attempting to address inequality through government policy, as antitrust does, can only cause economic failure and anger between groups of people. In contrast to those who argue that social peace and harmony depend on redistribution to counteract inequality, in fact such measures will not only not buy peace, they will actually do the opposite, namely cause civil war, at first figuratively, as they are doing now in the United States, but in the end fully literally, and across the globe.

Finally, I will show that a return of the people's right to pursue inequality is the only way to restore our country's economic greatness, which was always the essential foundation of our exceptionalism and our leadership role in the world. [xiii] But lest anyone misunderstand that by invoking exceptionalism I am calling for a more vigorously engaged American foreign policy, let me be very clear that I am calling for the exact opposite. We are in trouble in the first place because we have perverted our original founding principles into a grotesque denial of those principles and, second, because we have tried to foist those perverted principles and that grotesque denial on other peoples and nations. The escalating chaos and violence in the world today are not happening because the U.S. is not showing leadership, as some contend. They are happening because the U.S. *is* showing leadership, but of exactly the wrong kind.

Whether or not the United States is able to restore its economic greatness, it is imperative for the sake of peace and security in the world to restore the principles of our founding. We must demonstrate again that tolerance of inequality is the key ingredient that was embedded in our original unalienable rights. As the wealthiest and most unequal nation, and the one that is so visibly abandoning its own founding principle of tolerance for inequality, the United States has become a rallying cry for violent revolution at home and abroad. So the first order of business now is to show again that tolerance of inequality -- irrespective of its wealth-generating potential -- is where freedom begins.

2. From Freedom to Prosperity: The D.I.Y. Monopoly

In 1700 the most-free country on earth was England. By 1790 it was the United States of America. It is with some irony now and no doubt with some bitterness on the part of colonists at the time, that we fought the American Revolution against England essentially so we could establish the rights of Englishmen in the United States. [xiv] We knew the value of those rights, which boiled down to opportunity. Commerce was rampant in England, as what would later be called the Industrial Revolution took hold. People could work hard and escape poverty, as even the lower class English had begun to do, noticeably separating from the lower classes in the rest of Europe. [xv] And London speculators could gamble in lotteries or stocks or "projects," which promised quick riches. If only we could get out from under the restraints on our ambitions that being British colonies imposed. So we grabbed the bull by the horns, revolted, and severed those restraints.

Immediately upon independence, a few of our most ambitious and bold men in Philadelphia and New York were doing what London speculators had done with their freedoms 100 years earlier. They were gathering in taverns or coffee houses or on the streets to speculate in securities. Such crowds were flourishing before 1700 in London's "exchange alley," which by 1720 had developed all the functions of modern stock exchanges. [xvi] By 1790 our trading crowds were well on the way to the same functions and activities and, like London's, would eventually become stock exchanges.

Not that securities speculating involved all that many people, in spite of the perception during frenzies that everyone was involved. The inner circles of professionals may have numbered in the dozens or at most scores, [xvii] so actual speculators, including clients of the professionals, were probably not more than one percent of the population, although the percentage was higher in the neighborhoods where the activity occurred, such as "the City" or "Wall Street."

In any case, the general public viewed speculating with suspicion, as is often the case when public attitudes develop toward the "lucky" or "undeserving" rich. Not only did it tempt individuals to divert their energies from useful trades and occupations, it corrupted them to imprudently waste their families' savings. So the general public had every good reason to look down on speculation with self-righteous scorn.

Still, some couldn't help but want to give it a try, and it's not difficult to see why. Even the worst press of these iniquitous securities gambling dens, and the scandals surrounding their activities, had the effect of powerfully advertising the clearly true fact that the lucky, at least, and maybe also the skillful, bold, insightful, etc., could achieve the impossible dream shared by almost everyone, whether they admitted it or not, of getting rich quickly and without working.

In a funny way, its bad reputation was probably very good for the business of speculating, because it got the word out. Word-of-mouth gossip regarding the scandalous character of speculating probably caused information about its opportunities to saturate the entire public. Thus, even though the actual number and proportion of the public engaged in securities speculation was fairly small, it is likely that the number included almost all of those who could potentially be interested in it. In that regard, at least, the scandal was efficient. Even the moral superiority of the inequality argument served to spread the word to the maximum number of people to whom it might conceivably appeal.

The American version of securities speculation had a small but intensely devoted following, particularly in New York, where speculation had an unusually strong appeal, as we will learn in chapter 8. For this and related reasons, the industry these securities trading devotees in New York created gave rise to a new social and commercial structure that had not existed anywhere before, not even in London, which was its closest model. This structure, which grew out of the transformation by which trading crowds became stock exchanges, established the monopoly formation paradigm that is at the heart of American wealth and power. It unfolded roughly as follows, first in London and then in New York a century later, as New York perfected the model.

Speculating is the ultimate inequality engine, dramatically and quickly separating winners from losers. Some were so drawn to it that they devoted most or all of their time to the activity, and thus developed better ties to the inside circles of traders than those who still spent most of their time on outside occupations. One benefit of being a full or nearly full-time insider was that it provided more opportunities to gain better information than outsiders had. Well-connected insiders could more readily spot good trades and avoid bad ones. They could learn where the promising manipulative rings were forming and, equally or more important, where the scams and bad credits were, all of which enabled them to speculate more profitably.

But the most active traders in those early crowds also discovered they could go further in their wealth seeking than just trading and speculating profitably. They found that their status as insiders, itself, had additional value to outsiders that the insiders could charge for. So they became trading agents and information sources for outsiders, creating thereby an intermediation profession that reliably enhanced their wealth irrespective of the trading profits of either the insiders or the outsiders.

In time they solidified this position by forming club-like organizations that officially recognized the difference between insiders and everyone else, thereby formalizing the distinction between members and nonmembers of their trading crowds. The insiders agreed to honor the difference and to enforce it by refusing to trade with outsiders unless they charged them fixed commissions, a social protocol that effectively barred outsiders from being treated as insiders. The most powerful of these strictures was a requirement to not only refuse to trade with outsiders, but also to refuse to trade with other insiders who *would* trade with outsiders, thereby effectively banishing them from the "club," too.

These strictures worked to sharply define the difference between insiders and outsiders, or members and nonmembers. Thus the insiders in these early trading crowds naturally fell into building a monopoly for serving as brokers and dealers for speculators, creating thereby the first formal stock exchanges. So valuable was the status of being an insider or member of this particular club, both in terms of money-making potential and in terms of the larger commercial and social advantages that membership conferred, that members fiercely defended their new stock exchanges and often treated their obligations, rights and opportunities under their rules as superior to those of any government. This turned out to be important when governments tried to use their powers to shut down speculation and the exchanges by barring use of the courts to enforce trading contracts, or by banning public auctions.

The risk of hostile government action was a common danger to these early exchanges and always seemed to show up after a boom had turned to bust and moralistic public calls to rein in speculation proliferated demanding government action. Such anti-speculation backlashes occurred after busts in Holland following the tulip mania in 1637, in France after the Mississippi Bubble in 1720, in England after the South Sea Bubble in 1720, and in New York after the first American crash in 1792, which was a mainly New York affair.

The anti-speculation backlash also showed up after the 1929 Crash, which unfortunately led to the creation of the SEC. In today's terms, the commission aspect of these insider agreements amounted to a price-fixing cartel, and the refusals to trade with outsiders or with others who did amounted to boycotts. By the time the SEC was created, there were laws against such things, which caused no end of trouble for the exchanges.

But getting back to how they started, although the circumstances in each of the bubble and crash situations were different, only in America and only in 1792 New York did the exchange formation process emerge stronger after the bust than it was before or during the boom. This had the effect of immunizing not just New York's exchange, but America itself, from excessive government encroachment, an inoculation that lasted for a century and turned out to be the key to America's success. Exactly how it came about is a story we will explore in some detail in chapters 8 through 10. But one aspect of it is worth mentioning briefly now.

It was perhaps because traders in early America had Revolution and freedom fresh in their minds that they appeared to be more open and proud of their anticompetitive trading agreements, which were explicitly aimed at cartel or monopoly formation. In any case, these Americans were more likely than others who formed exchanges to advertise the existence and details of their agreements, as well as to sign documents evidencing them, at least one of which, the Buttonwood Agreement, had the proud look and feel of the Declaration of Independence. England may have had similar agreements a century earlier, but if so they did not survive, nor did any discussion of them or other evidence that they existed. In any case, America's stock exchange monopolizers were unusually open, proud and explicit about it and, therefore, it was America and New York, in particular, not London or others, that established the New World monopoly paradigm, creating for the first time in history a powerful commercial application of the club concept, one that was based not only on the social prestige of membership, as traditional clubs had been, but also this time on a formidable and ever-increasing economic privilege as well.

Some might ask, so what? Why should we care that these unfair inequality engines exist or achieve longevity, anyway? The answer to that is simple. For whatever reason, speculation and rising living standards appear to go hand in hand.

The countries we have been talking about -- Holland, England, France and the United States -- all had their turns as the wealthiest on earth, as well as the most unequal on earth, and there appears to be a more than accidental coincidence in the timing of their turns at speculation and their turns at wealth. Getting this one right may be critical to the wealth of the world's people.

The D.I.Y. monopoly formation paradigm spread far from its London and New York origins broadly into the economies of their respective nations, creating both vast wealth and vast inequality. But in spite of all the inequality the exchanges and their imitator monopolists created, such as, in the United States, Astor, Vanderbilt, Rockefeller, Carnegie and Morgan, the bulk of humanity that was left behind did quite well, too. From growth that had been too slow to notice from the year 0 to the year 1700 (about 0.02 percent per year in per capita output), world growth per capita suddenly showed up in measurable amounts for the first time in human history at 0.1 percent in the eighteenth century (technically quintupling from 0.02 percent to 0.1 percent) and then jumped in the nineteenth and twentieth centuries to 0.9 percent and 1.8 percent, respectively, [xviii] and was still surging upward in the twenty-first century in spite of being knocked back in the twentieth by two world wars and a global depression. [xix]

While economists, historians and social commentators are universally in awe of that surprising surge in growth, the general thrust and outlines of which are well known, there is no common agreement on what caused this "great enriching," as liberty guru and economist Deirdre McCloskey has called it. [xx] Personally, I am partial to McCloskey's thesis that the great enriching emerged essentially because of freedom, which she attributes not only to the English, but also to their North Sea neighbors, the Dutch, who shared similar traditions and principles.

> A big change in the common opinion about markets and innovation, I claim, caused the Industrial Revolution, and then the modern world. The change occurred during the seventeenth and eighteenth centuries in northwestern Europe. More or less suddenly the Dutch and British and then the Americans and the French began talking about the middle class, high or low -- the "bourgeoisie" -- as though it were dignified and free. The result was modern economic growth. That is, ideas, or "rhetoric," enriched us. The cause, in other words, was language, that most human of our accomplishments. [xxi]

I am also partial to McCloskey's articulation of how a change in the way ordinary people spoke of markets, innovation, trade and commerce was evidence of a sea-change in attitude about their own freedom and capacity to improve their circumstances, which she calls "bourgeois dignity," after which commercial activity was respected, whereas before it was not. The change reverberated down through history in an expansion of what McCloskey often loosely but poetically calls "human scope," but does not shrink from occasional attempts to quantify what that has meant to us in money terms.

> The idea of bourgeois dignity and liberty led to a rise of real income per head in 2010 prices from about $3 a day in 1800 worldwide to over $100 in places that have accepted the Bourgeois Deal and its creative destruction. [xxii]

But convinced as I am by McCloskey's thesis, not everyone agrees -- far from it. The above quotes come from a debate over the cause of the Industrial Revolution in which three other economists argue with McCloskey and each other about it. So, while everyone agrees the Industrial Revolution began a great enriching, no one knows for sure what caused it, as evidenced by the persistent disagreement on that front and the continuing existence of many conflicting theories.

It is my goal in this book to demonstrate that we now have the information to go beyond philosophies or opinions, or even iconic legal traditions of freedom -- Magna Carta, English common law, John Locke's rights, the Declaration of Independence, the U.S. Constitution, etc. -- to explain the appearance of the Industrial Revolution and America's economic success. We can now pin down exactly what it was about freedom that enabled it to work its wonders. While the icons may represent necessary background conditions, they may not by themselves have been sufficient to ignite the great enriching. But there is a specific institution that emerged that had not existed before, which caused the great enriching and the language changes heralding it to start "more or less suddenly," as McCloskey described its perhaps most significant clue. As outlined above, the original anticompetitive form of stock exchange, first in London (implicitly) and then explicitly in the United States, and particularly New York, is the only credible candidate to explain the onset of the original Industrial Revolution and its continuation in America. The evidence is old and sparse. But what is there is unequivocal, leaving no reasonable doubt that these two old exchanges were in fact the original trigger of the Revolution and, therefore, of almost all of today's wealth, since the overwhelming majority of it would not have been created at the old growth rates.

It is also important to note that along with per capita output, global population also perked up and exploded at the same time. And while it is difficult to disentangle whether the population growth triggered the output growth or vice versa, it is nonetheless certain that, in the degree to which economic growth enabled population growth, those two old exchanges can also be seen as the original triggering source of almost all of the people in the world today, most of whom would not be here if population growth had remained at pre-1700 levels. [xxiii]

Those exchanges were nothing like what we call stock exchanges today, which are required by regulators to be inclusive and undiscriminating in their membership and to compete fairly with many other exchanges. The original London and New York exchanges, in contrast, were the quintessential expression of the desire of humans to get rich by discriminating, both against nonmembers and against competing exchanges. As a result of their discrimination they were able to impose an unfair and exclusive monopoly that had no competitors. In what follows I will show that the opportunity to engage in that full and uncompromising monopolization is what drove the creation of these exchanges in the first place, and why they succeeded in igniting three centuries of explosive growth. Monopolization, far from restraining trade, as antitrust theory would have it, was actually the key to releasing all the unrestrained trade of which free human beings are capable.

The two key freedoms that allowed all that to happen are not listed in the Declaration of Independence or the Bill of Rights or the Constitution or the Magna

Carta or anywhere else. They are: the right to engage in unrestrained speculation, and the right to engage in unrestrained monopolization. They both rested on an implicit interpretation of the right to property or the pursuit of happiness that meant, among other things, that citizens could freely pursue inequality via speculation and monopolization. For over a century America thrived without any laws or successful efforts by government to restrain either of these implied rights.

This led to great wealth. But it also led to great inequality and an equally great backlash against it. Speculation is the human activity that most purely accommodates the desire to get wealthy without working, which, by definition, means wealthier than others, and in a manner bound to incite envy and anger, because it often involves luck or appears to be otherwise undeserved and, particularly when combined with monopolization, creates an endless succession of the world's wealthiest men, such as Astor, Vanderbilt, Rockefeller, Carnegie, etc. And monopolization of the securities speculating industry has proved capable of both structuring that industry -- the City and Wall Street -- to achieve as much inequality as possible for its clients (including that succession of world's wealthiest men), and of separately and even more reliably (if not as grandly) enriching the monopolists that created the industry. As a result, the industry got the reputation of conferring on itself another apparently undeserved privilege that, as the antitrust laws emerged, developed its own separate source of envy and anger.

Thus did the wealth-generating success of the rights to speculate and monopolize carry within them the seeds of their own destruction. Fortunately for America, her understanding of her founding freedoms proved capable of staving off that destruction for one full century or more before the clouds closed in, beginning in 1890 with the Sherman Antitrust Act and then, after the 1929 Crash and Depression, with the creation of the SEC in 1934. And fortunately for England, the Industrial Revolution was off and running and, in fact, over before anyone figured out what happened, or developed any Marxist theories about it. [xxiv]

But now, unfortunately, the freedom that allowed stock exchanges to germinate and to create in their wake three centuries of rapid progress is coming to a close, as worldwide government, led by the U.S., sets itself up to snuff out inequality. While the world waits for some nation or nations to provide the practical and spiritual guidance America once did and Britain did before her, the people of the world will increasingly find themselves in a dangerous place where neither wealth nor borders nor armies can protect them. And it could be a long wait. A hundred years ago no one predicted that two world wars sandwiching a global depression would wipe away millions of lives and trillions in treasure over a period exceeding three decades. We may fancy ourselves smarter now, able to engineer our way around inflations, deflations and depressions, able to cooperate past conflicts and steer clear of atrocities like genocide. But the fact is that none of these improvements is real. Every one of the problems that led to the horrors of the twentieth century is still with us, ready to bubble up and explode again, as before, in disputes over inequality.

The first sign that these problems are in store is evident now in the dearth of jobs across the wealthy countries of the West, which due to concerns over inequality are increasingly unable to employ their citizens. This is true even in America, as we will explore next.

3. Where Do Jobs Come From?

The JOBS Act is a piece of work. It was passed because of a spreading recognition that our unemployment problem in the United States may be caused in part by a lack of new business formation, particularly through IPOs, and that this may in turn have been caused by mistakes made by the SEC in the design of today's electronic stock market called the "National Market System" or "NMS." The existence of the JOBS Act means that, whatever good stock exchanges used to do for us by way of capital formation and jobs, they don't seem to be doing it now.

That the nation may be suffering an employment deficit due to a dearth of IPOs, and that the SEC may have caused the problem, is a possibility raised by a former NASDAQ official named David Weild in a series of alarming Grant Thornton-sponsored white papers he co-authored arguing that, "Over the past several years, the IPO market in the United States has practically disappeared." [xxv] Weild's arguments caught the attention of legislators on Capitol Hill and provided the catalyst for assembling several previous bills that had been languishing into the JOBS Act, for which efforts he became known as "the father of the JOBS Act." [xxvi] While there had been many laws since the creation of the SEC in 1934 authorizing and directing the SEC to reform the markets, the JOBS Act is important as perhaps the first to be based on the worry that the SEC, perhaps while acting on those previous reforms, may have done something wrong. So wrong in fact that it might be causing the American economy to falter visibly enough to get Congress's attention.

The fear underlying the JOBS Act is that an SEC reform called decimalization killed the incentive to bring new stocks public. The reform brought minimum increments for stock trading, or "ticks," and consequently bid-offer spreads that dealers earn when trading, down to a penny from a minimum of an eighth, or twelve and a half cents, but practically speaking a quarter, or twenty-five cents, in the micro-capitalization sector of the NASDAQ market where IPOs were born. This reform, which is one of several related market structure reforms that are generally thought to be responsible for introducing high-frequency trading, or HFT, to markets, may, the thinking goes, have killed the economic incentives for investment bankers to bring small new companies public. That is because investment banking firms are also trading firms that make a good deal of the money they earn from new companies not just from their IPO fees, but from secondary trading in the few months after an IPO occurs. As a result of these concerns, the SEC is now being forced by the JOBS Act to conduct a Tick Pilot to see if wider ticks could help restore IPOs, new companies and jobs. There is no need to go into any detail on the pilot or the conflicting views on it, since the problems go far beyond anything the JOBS Act or the Tick Pilot contemplated, and decimalization or tiny ticks in general are only the smallest part of them.

As CNBC reporter John Harwood explained on the NBC evening news (1/18/15) as background for President Obama's upcoming State of the Union, the middle class has been falling behind for forty years. Decimalization is only fourteen years old. Is it possible the problem with jobs began forty years ago in 1975 with the SEC's National Market System itself? I believe that case can be made, which I will outline below and in chapter 12. Not that the problems Weild highlighted did not occur when he says they did, beginning about eighteen years ago in 1997. But those problems are only intensifications of the general problem with capital formation evident in economic statistics showing a struggling middle class beginning, as John Harwood said, about forty years ago.

Decimalization began in 2001, long after NMS and fully four years after the problems Weild spotted in his studies. Ironically, Weild, who brought the problem of the missing IPOs and their possible connection to missing jobs to the public's attention beginning in November 2008 with *Why are IPOs in the ICU?* is also the person who demonstrated in those same studies that decimalization came after the problem and, thus, couldn't have caused it. While decimalization was potentially very harmful to investment banking revenues and IPOs, the IPO market had already collapsed prior to the time decimalization kicked-in in 2001. The same can be said for a variety of other reforms that, while they were also potentially harmful to IPOs, nonetheless did not arrive on the scene until well after the collapse in IPOs highlighted by Weild showed up. [xxvii] IPOs collapsed beginning in 1997 right after the SEC and the Justice Department instituted a series of antitrust-based market structure reforms that forced electronic trading onto the NASDAQ market, the best known of which was the Order Handling Rules. And almost all of the collapse in IPOs had occurred by the end of 1999, which was before any of these other reforms hit. Weild, who had been a NASDAQ official in charge of bringing IPOs to market, made this chronology very clear in that first study and all of its subsequent updates over the next several years.

But as Weild's critiques gained traction on Wall Street and in Washington, and particularly in a Congress looking for explanations for the decline in new company formation and jobs, the original market structure explanation for the problem gave way to a focus on decimalization, presumably since that was easier to understand and explain to constituents and the press. As the JOBS Act took shape with Weild's encouragement, the remedy for the problem with IPOs became synonymous with that experiment called the Tick Pilot to try to reverse the harm that penny ticks were doing to banker spreads. In one sense this was understandable, since it seemed that, whatever the cause of the problem, it was not unreasonable to assume that wider ticks might restore some banking revenue and thus potentially solve it. Nonetheless, Weild and his co-authors remained clear, as they had from their first papers, that decimalization -- while not helpful -- did not cause the IPO crisis.

Here is how they put it in a January, 2014 letter to an SEC committee that was in charge of investigating the effect of decimalization and whether and how to do a Tick Pilot to address any problems that decimalization may have caused:

> Over the past 6 years, we have studied in great detail the structure of our stock markets and the causes of the decline in IPO activity and exchange listings. In 2008, in *Why are IPOs in the ICU?*, we uncovered two previously unrecognized and highly disturbing facts: first, that the small IPO market in

the United States, defined as IPOs raising less than $50 million, declined abruptly in 1998 and never recovered; second that this decline in the small IPO market took place a full two years before the introduction of one-cent trading increments and three years before the much-criticized Sarbanes-Oxley Act of 2002. In 2009, in *A wake-up call for America*, we documented the percent change in the number of listed companies for seven major global stock markets. We showed that the U.S. listed stock markets (excluding OTC) were losing companies every single year from its peak in 1997, while the other major markets all enjoyed increased listings. By year end 2012, the United States stock market had experienced 15 consecutive years of declines in listed companies: a 44% reduction in the population of listed companies from 1997 to year end 2012, to levels not seen *before* 1975. [Emphasis in original] xxviii

As was made clear in all of Weild's and his co-authors' white papers from 2008 through 2014, there was a crisis in IPOs, but decimalization did not cause that crisis. This was made clear in all of the white papers in graphs as well as through cogent accompanying explanations of why it was in particular the decline of the smallest IPOs that mattered most to capital formation, as we will discuss in detail in chapter 12. The point here, though, is that we should beware of even the most cogent critiques of government, because even they can be perverted by the political process into excuses for government that neutralize their effect.

By the time the JOBS Act was signed on April 5, 2012 at a White House ceremony by President Obama attended by members of the President's Equity Capital Formation Task Force, xxix Weild's original market structure critique and explanation for the decline of IPOs had been forgotten and in its stead all hopes were pinned on the Tick Pilot's potential to widen spreads in micro-cap stocks. Weild bought into that strategy, as did Wall Street's lobbying group, the Security Traders Association. Even the SEC, however embarrassed it might have been for whatever errors on its part had led to the decline in IPOs, seemed relieved to be able to confine them to perhaps having paid too much attention to the market in big stocks and therefore having inadvertently neglected the market in small stocks. On all sides, it became popular to pronounce that "one size does not fit all," a phrase that let the SEC off the hook for its errors and at the same time put it even more firmly in charge of market structure going forward by forcing it to administer the Tick Pilot.

Neither the JOBS Act nor the Tick Pilot will produce anything useful. It is now both a scapegoat and an excuse for the SEC to increase its role in the design and oversight of market structure, the very role that Weild's original report implied was the cause of the problem with IPOs, since the SEC created the market structure that led to the decline in IPOs. In the degree to which the Tick Pilot locks the industry and its participants into accepting the SEC's role, it is the paradigm for the destruction of the American economy at the hands of antitrust regulators that I examine in this book, a paradigm that could be described as follows. *Give the agency that is killing us ultimate power, and participate in a "democratic debate" led by that agency in order to fix our problems.* Some might call this, accurately, working with the fox to design a better henhouse.

As we will discover, democratic debate itself is the core problem. The JOBS Act is important only because its very existence demonstrates that a lot of people in the Congress and the Administration as well as on Wall Street recognize that something is terribly wrong with the stock market. But the JOBS Act will not solve the problem, nor will the Tick Pilot. So let's step away from the JOBS Act for a minute and have a brief look at the real issue.

The IPO collapse the JOBS Act recognizes has roots, not in decimalization (although that is not unrelated), but in what is essentially an SEC redistribution policy based on antitrust law, which in turn has roots in our inequality obsession. This is a complicated story. But the bottom line is that as a result of the SEC's antitrust-based electronic trading reforms, IPOs and capital formation have indeed disappeared in the United States and our economy, and the jobs it could otherwise create, are on the ropes as a result. Moreover, this is a problem that appears to be "specific to, or more pronounced in, the United States" and almost certainly began much earlier than 1997, as one study demonstrating our faltering labor market "fluidity" suggests. [xxx]

Even worse, we appear to be stuck with the problem, as we are stuck with the SEC. Neither the JOBS Act nor any other policy that it would be possible to adopt through normal democratic channels has any chance of reversing the damage or preventing its continuation and intensification. That is because the inequality obsession, of which antitrust and the SEC application of it to the stock market are a part, is untouchable by political and academic discourse, as if honest discussion of it were subject to a tribal taboo. This has the effect of making antitrust untouchable, too and, with it, the SEC. And this is in spite of the fact that antitrust, according to academic theory, should have nothing to do with either inequality or redistribution, as we will discuss. But leave that inconsistency between antitrust theory and practice aside for the moment.

The real problem is that it is difficult to conduct an honest debate when all the key terms and concepts under debate are little more than unsupported conventional wisdom slogans, and thus are never actually up for debate. This is how the JOBS Act, which would seem to have something to do with jobs, was passed in the first place.

> AngelList co-founder Naval Ravikant, who spent six months lobbying for the JOBS Act reforms, recalls: "It ended up being a giant dog's breakfast of different bills combined together, and then some genius, probably some congressional staffer, said "How are we gonna get this thing to pass? Oh--let's say it has something to do with jobs. Jumpstarting Our Business Startups! JOBS, JOBS!" And then, what congressperson can vote against something called the JOBS Act? It was a miracle."" [xxxi]

Thus did an unusually insightful and thorough analysis of a problem caused by the SEC become a government program to support the SEC. Decimalization and related market structure errors by the SEC are now used as excuses to increase the SEC's power to make further similar errors with more rules, aided and abetted to that end by such silly exercises as the Tick Pilot and a "holistic review of market structure," which is the currently most popular buzz-phrase used by SEC supporters both inside and outside the agency to describe its mission going forward.

Weild himself still sounds hopeful that something useful will come out of the pilot, presumably because, as he told Larry Tabb in a recent interview, the IPO problem has already cost 10 million or more jobs. [xxxii] Nonetheless, he worries it will be too short and that it will not try to use a large enough tick size to test the concept. The latest studies he and his coauthors have done for the OECD have shown that the tick must be at least one percent of the value of the trade to elicit support for IPOs, which is twice the nickel tick the pilot will test. Weild says they would have to test "at least a dime" to get meaningful answers, and would have to extend the pilot for far longer than the planned one year. But as one might expect from the "father of the JOBS Act," he says the pilot could still be useful "if it's structured properly."

That is wishful thinking, in my opinion. In the first place, the pilot won't be structured properly, as Weild is apparently beginning to realize. And secondly, it would still be harmful even if it were structured properly, because that would only further increase the power of the SEC by making it appear as if the SEC were in competent control. For my money, Weild had it right the first time, or as right as he dared go. But even the courageous title of his and Kim's 2009 paper, "*Market structure is causing the IPO Crisis*," did not go far enough. Since the SEC is the author and controller of market structure and the creator of HFT, what they really meant was *the SEC is causing the IPO crisis*. But even they couldn't go that far. Note that their balancing of candor and discretion did not earn Weild or Kim a seat on the SEC's panel of 17 experts on its Equity Market Structure Advisory Committee. Neither did inequality critic and Nobel Prize laureate Joseph Stiglitz get a seat, reportedly because he, like Weild, has been critical of HFT. [xxxiii]

The real underlying problem, as noted in my 2012 book, *Nature's God*, is that the SEC is committed to defending HFT at all costs, because HFT is the final stage of its baby, the National Market System. Reviews of market structure will not only not solve this problem, they will dig us deeper into the same hole, because "such discussions organized by the SEC are how we got into the mess we are in today." [xxxiv] Those who still believe the path to a better market lies in working with the SEC suffer from a naive optimism that is no longer justified, if it ever was. As we will learn in chapter 12, the SEC is now constitutionally opposed to capital formation. So working with SEC puts these naive optimists in the position of unwitting accomplices in the destruction of the U.S. capital markets. Such perspectives can explain the otherwise inexplicable fact that neither father-of-the-JOBS-Act Weild nor Nobel laureate Stiglitz were deemed expert enough by the Commission to be on its panel of 17 experts. [xxxv]

With the SEC in charge, the JOBS Act and all of the SEC's future machinations will only cause the further destruction of jobs in America. As our founders would have understood, now that capital formation and private sector jobs are an official program of government via the JOBS Act, America's days as the world-beating creator of new industrial categories, new technologies and jobs are numbered if not already over. This is what happens in the quagmire of democratic debate, not just in the stock market, but in general, which we will discuss next.

4. The Per Se Trap

To get a handle on this vast problem that encompasses all aspects of our economy, we will start with a general review of the taboo on honest discussion of inequality, with brief reference to how the stock market instance of it fits in. We will look at how our most mistaken viewpoints are exacerbated by or filtered through the biggest error of our time, which is antitrust. Later we will drill down on the stock market instance of this antitrust error, and how it is both the most important and the best example of the taboo on honest discussion of matters relating to inequality. In that analysis we will discover how innocent or even patriotic sounding terms and concepts like "democratic debate" or "national conversation" are actually stalking horses for redistribution and have stock market analogues, like "public comment period" and the lately fashionable "holistic review of market structure." But first we need to get a broader picture of how the inequality obsession gives rise to the errors of antitrust, which is the larger category under which the stock market mistakes fall.

The general backdrop for this problem is our fixation on what is called "political correctness." Under the spell of this delusion, we seem to have forgotten the importance of being honest, either with each other, or even with ourselves, when it comes to our understanding of and observations about the world around us. The dishonesty is always rooted in a hidden requirement to believe that inequality is wrong or evil and that, consequently, failing to address it via redistribution is likewise wrong or evil. This is dishonest because the opposite is clearly the case, as history has demonstrated over and over, especially in the horrors of the twentieth century where socialist and communist experiments resulted not in justice or fairness, but in mass atrocities and tens of millions of deaths. But we ignore those histories, because we are hell bent on resurrecting the same policies under different names and slogans today. It is as if we were hypnotized into following the conventional wisdom, unaware that we are lapping up and regurgitating tired platitudes as if they were pearls of new insight, mesmerized into believing we are thinking for ourselves when we are really only spouting standard solutions that have redistribution to address inequality as their true agenda.

The core values of that agenda are treated as per se verities, truths that can go unspoken because they are so obvious, but for that reason can also be used as the final nail in an argument that closes off alternatives. Often mere words or phrases do the work: "the one percent," "the 99 percent," "the rich," "the poor," "fairness," "level playing field," "small business," "diversity," "inclusion," "equal pay for equal work," "glass ceiling," "gay marriage," "LGBT," "racism," "prejudice," "high-frequency trading," "HFT," "average investor," "long term investor," "little investor," "dark pool," "insider trading," "front running," "manipulation," "conflict of interest," "rigged," "conspiracy" and, of course, "Wall Street."

Some of these are recognizable by almost everyone, while some are recognized only in a particular field. Some promote positive images for downtrodden groups, while others incite indignation or anger at the better off groups, implying that the better off are the cause of the condition of the downtrodden. But all share three main properties. One, they imply a view on inequality as our core driving problem that is assumed to be in need of a solution. Two, they imply the active involvement of government to provide that solution. And three, they inspire conflict between groups of people. Behind each word or phrase is a group that claims an implied right to government help to improve its members' positions in the world. Inequality is thus the hidden driver of every policy debate, and all the debates turn on the role and size of government.

The way government helps downtrodden groups always involves discrimination. Either government itself discriminates in favor of those downtrodden groups, such as through favorable tax rates or affirmative actions or entitlements or other benefits, or it passes laws that bar private parties from discriminating against them or at all. This is where political correctness comes in, which is inimical to the ethos that pertained at the nation's founding when the stock exchanges formed essentially by engaging in private acts of discrimination that had pursuit of inequality as their goal. None of those acts would have been legal under antitrust laws, and none of them would have been possible if modern political correctness principles that deny the right of discrimination had been around. Not surprisingly, government and political correctness always run parallel to and support each other when it comes to addressing inequality between groups. Their joint efforts to block private acts of discrimination cause great dishonesty and pretense amongst our people, as if we were no longer human beings. Discrimination is a powerful and valuable human faculty, perhaps the most valuable in practice when it comes to the pursuit of happiness. Forcing it underground is the greatest sin of both our government and political correctness.

Today's focus on group rights, with government both engaging in discrimination itself and at the same time banning private acts of discrimination, is profoundly different from the way the founders of America thought of the world. They had a great appreciation for the traditions of English common law, which gradually established precedents for the rights of individuals to their lives, their liberty and their estate, as John Locke phrased it, [xxxvi] or to life, liberty and the pursuit of happiness, as Thomas Jefferson put it in our Declaration of Independence. These were not group rights that could be claimed by virtue of being a member of a group. These were rights that inhered in the individuals themselves, as individuals. The founders could scarcely have imagined how the common law concept of stacking precedent upon precedent could somehow have been perverted to replace the right to property with the right to equality. But they would have noticed that something was wrong when group rights began to replace individual rights.

They would surely have noticed that the new Supreme Court lodestones of diversity, inclusion and equality are in terminal conflict with the right to property. You cannot both protect an unalienable right to property and make property redistributable by government to accomplish other goals such as diversity, inclusion and equality. The founders would certainly have seen that even the common law, indeed even democracy itself, could be perverted to tyrannical ends if they were applied in service of equality rather than to protecting property.

18

But somewhere between the founders' time and our time we switched principles and today everyone seems not to notice. We ignore the massive alphabet soup of antitrust agencies designing and administering all of our industries, and just assume they must be necessary, or at least that they have been since passage of the Sherman Antitrust Act in 1890. No one gives a thought anymore to the possibility that the Sherman Act was all along and still is incompatible with our unalienable rights to property and the pursuit of happiness. Senator Sherman and his supporters were working against the backdrop of the hated robber barons, who became unbelievably wealthy with their trusts and monopolies, so surely a law was needed, right? And even if there were some kinks and incompatibilities between the Sherman Act and our rights as individual Americans, you'd think by now they'd have worked all that out and be getting the hang of it, right?

Wrong.

Robert H. Bork opens his 1978 classic, *The Antitrust Paradox: A Policy at War with Itself*, with the following arresting assessment of the state of antitrust at that time:

> One reason for the stifling solidity of received opinion about antitrust, why counterarguments make so little headway, is that most of us accept our first principles and even our intermediate premises uncritically, as given, because we assume that they were established theoretically and confirmed empirically by legislators and judges long ago. Discussion begins from there. What we all "know" is wrong. We are working from an intellectual base that does not exist . . . It is *not* true, as we trustingly assume, that these ideas were ever demonstrated theoretically or confirmed empirically. In that sense, the intellectual history we rely upon is false, in antitrust as in so much else of the law. [Emphasis in original] [xxxvii]

Thus begins Bork's description of the confusion in antitrust that gave rise to a policy of declaring certain practices illegal *per se*, that is, regardless of any defense or reason that might be offered for their adoption by the accused party. A price fixing conspiracy by competitors, for example, is a violation regardless of why the competitors agree to fix prices, even if their actions appear to be for a greater good, or appear to be consistent with other antitrust considerations.

To pick a recent example, if Apple and book publishers feel that an Amazon "monopoly" threatens traditional book publishing and distribution with cut-rate prices, and they adopt a common price fixing agreement in response, then they are guilty of violating antitrust per se, regardless of the merits of any of their arguments or justifications. Those justifications could include, as they have in this case, the special importance of books, or of information, or of informed debate to democracy itself. No matter: if price fixing occurred, then it's a per se antitrust violation.

Antitrust jurisprudence fell into the per se policy due to what Bork describes as the fundamental problem with the law:

> Because antitrust's basic premises are mutually incompatible, and because some of them are incorrect, the law has been producing increasingly bizarre

results. Certain of its doctrines preserve competition, while others suppress it, resulting in a policy at war with itself. [xxxviii]

While the per se policy provided an understandably desirable shortcut for confused judges in the early days of antitrust, the confusion remains today in spite of the per se crutch and its apparent, but unjustified, legal precision. The result is an overall antitrust policy that continues to produce seemingly arbitrary settlements and industry structures. Apple, for example, is still fighting its loss in the book distribution battle and it is unclear whether Apple and the settling publishers that participated in its price fixing conspiracy, or Amazon and its ultra-cheap pricing, are more in tune with consumer interests. [xxxix]

The answer to that question would have interested Bork, who died in 2012. Bork argues in *Paradox* that both congressional intent and antitrust theory are on the side of the consumer, full stop. Bork explains, for example, that the common belief that a monopoly's excess profits that were diverted from "consumer's surplus" should be considered in evaluating the legality of mergers, or redistributed to aggrieved consumers if an antitrust violation occurred, is incorrect. Distribution among different consumers or even between consumers and monopolies should have nothing to do with considering the legality of monopolies, and any redistribution should only be to effect greater efficiency from the consumer's perspective, not to deliver punishment or a more fair distribution of wealth. [xl]

The point is critical and serves to underscore the sincerity of Bork's belief in the wisdom of antitrust, if properly applied, as well as his belief that, for all its inconsistent and confused history, it actually could be properly applied. The big problem with this view, however, and this is a problem that Bork did not appreciate, is that conventional antitrust wisdom defines both consumer welfare and the overall efficiency of the market very narrowly, as if the only thing that mattered were price competition from multiple competitors in the same product, competition that will produce the best immediate price to the consumer. Antitrust and all of its per se prohibitions are devoted to making sure that this narrow type of consumer welfare and efficiency are not restrained by monopolists acting to block it through such monopolizing acts as price fixing agreements.

But consumer interests can also be served by monopolies and monopolization in ways that antitrust does not and cannot accommodate. If, rather than focusing solely on competition by multiple competitors *within* each product, there is competition among monopolists for the consumer dollar *across* industries, the consumer and society generally may benefit in ways and to degrees that are substantially more significant than they can through narrow price competition within each industry alone. In other words, while antitrust contemplates a certain kind of efficiency that results from multi-party competition within each industry, there is another perhaps much more important kind of efficiency that could be realized if competition across industries facilitated by monopolists seeking to extract maximum prices from consumers were allowed.

These two types of efficiency from the consumer's perspective would almost always, by definition, be in direct conflict, with one aiming for lower prices and the other aiming for higher prices. Antitrust favors and at least nominally requires through its per se policies the within-industry competition that produces the best price, sometimes called "perfect competition" or "Pareto Optimal" efficiency. The other kind of efficiency would discover consumer preferences among multiple competing industries or product choices seeking to extract higher prices from consumers. This kind of efficiency is ignored by antitrust and forbidden if it involves monopolization, which its most effective realization inevitably would. Even if Pareto himself were to come back from the dead and pronounce the superior value of such preference discovery competition among industries, the antitrust per se policy would still forbid it.

Further, and perhaps much more important, individuals who are consumers often have interests other than their consuming interests, such as to be employed, or to move to a better job, or to get a raise, or to not get laid off, or to save, or to be wealthy, and these interests can also be in conflict with their interests as consumers. These values could easily be far more significant than the values antitrust strives for, as well as far easier for the individual to see that, with respect to them, his interest does not lie with antitrust. Saving a few dollars, or even as little as only a few cents, on purchases of gasoline or stocks, for example, would obviously be insignificant compared to having a good job or being able to retire comfortably when the time comes. But antitrust, and particularly its per se policy, can give no quarter to individuals interested in these other factors if they are in conflict with their interests as consumers in the best prices of "perfect competition," even though a rational individual would willingly give up this interest in order to obtain those other benefits. If monopolization can lead to new industries with many more jobs and the greater potential for individuals to earn more money and to save and invest their wages and become wealthy, well that's just tough luck, as far as antitrust is concerned.

Several other benefits that might spring from this currently forbidden type of competition immediately come to mind.

First, it would manage itself naturally through the truly free market, with no need for armies of bureaucrats, lawyers and industry experts figuring out what efficiency means or which violations are per se and which are up to judges' discretion, with all the confusion, conflicts and corruption such a process inevitably entails. No need for policies at war with themselves, to use Bork's terminology.

Second, there would be a better chance that capital will be allocated to the industries and products that are more highly valued by consumers. Equally important, capital will be naturally drained from industries and products that, relatively speaking, lose their appeal, not because antitrust regulators decide it is time to attack them or force artificial competition into them, but because consumers tire of them. This would lead to a constantly modulating marketplace where monopolists learn what consumers really want by discovering what they will pay for it. The result is a consumer-oriented selection where the mix of products is constantly changing to reflect changing consumer interests and relative demand.

This is in effect the difference between Schumpeterian *creative destruction* and the inevitably arbitrary regulatory destruction of antitrust, which targets industries primarily for their political vulnerabilities on the redistribution landscape (never mind what purists like Bork have said about redistribution not being a legitimate part of antitrust). If, for example, industries can be portrayed as enriching monopolists who are gouging the public with their price fixing conspiracies, those industries and their products are toast in terms of consumer satisfaction, because trustbusters will kill their quality by commoditizing their products, regardless of what the public wants. This kind of competition is what the robber barons called "ruinous competition" and occurs when perfect competition runs profits all the way down to zero, a presumed benefit to consumers that they seldom appreciate. A good example is the stock market today with its multiple competing exchanges and razor thin margins, accompanied by low-cost electronic high-frequency trading that nonetheless leaves the public annoyed, confused and angry about the unfairness of it all.

In contrast, with monopolies and monopolists on the case trying to find out what consumers want by discovering what they will pay for it, the mix is more likely to reflect at all times what consumers truly prefer than it is under the artificial and arbitrary price destruction dictated by antitrust. Moreover, when tastes do change or innovation occurs, the changing mix in response will be both more swift and less disruptive than under antitrust. Monopolists who want to keep their monopolies will have to be not only quick to innovate, but careful to make new technologies compatible with old, still popular ones. Without antitrust, therefore, consumers will not arbitrarily be left stranded in abandoned technologies, and transitions between new and old products and technologies will be less traumatic.

Third, with the option of trying to maximize price through monopolization, businesses can focus, at least sometimes, on a different kind of strategy for serving the consumer. Rather than trying solely to reduce price to meet the within-industry competition mandated by antitrust, in some situations where monopolization instead of competition is possible, such as in network industries, businesses will have the option of focusing on product improvements instead. This is in effect the opposite of the commoditizing competition that, as noted above, is so annoying to consumers because it degrades product quality. Improved quality, in contrast, will enhance the ability of providers to draw dollars from other industries, which is in itself an attractive form of efficiency from the consumer's perspective.

In addition, the focus on improving product rather than cutting price can lead to the formation of multiple coordinated networks of related products and services that are in aggregate very pleasing to the consumer and moreover very compatible with the other product and service networks the consumer wants to deal with, because a key consideration for each monopolizing product segment will be compatibility with the other successful segments. All in all, if the monopolization option is allowed to establish advantages where they can be found, the overall mix of products and services may feel far better organized to suit consumer interests in simplicity, innovation, compatibility and stability than an antitrust-managed environment whose only option is to force multi-party price competition on each industry, separately.

Fourth, network industries are often "natural monopolies," which tend to naturally eliminate competitors until there is only one left standing. Consumers in such industries would often prefer to have a single provider connecting all the customers or destinations or nodes of its network. It is actually inefficient and often downright frustrating to consumers of the services of such industries for antitrust to perpetually block the true Darwinian competition that would produce a single winner in the marketplace. It may sound strange to talk of antitrust as blocking competition, since its nominal primary goal is to promote competition. But this is in fact what happens when a winner is forced by antitrust to give up its advantages to competitors. [xli]

In an even stranger and more confusing twist, such industries are often considered to be "deregulated," an idea developed by conservatives such as Chicago school academic, author and judge, Richard Posner, meaning that they are not regulated as public utilities, which is presumed in government and academic circles to be the only sane alternative to antitrust for regulating natural monopolies. [xlii] (No one in such circles has ever contemplated, out loud anyway, the alternative of letting natural monopolies be monopolies, naturally, which is my preferred alternative and the main theme of all of my books, including this one.) The terminology is confusing because it implies that antitrust regulation means lighter regulation or even no regulation, compared to utility regulation, although it is usually a more intrusive rather than a less intrusive form of regulation. This confusion may have played a part in causing conservatives to believe that antitrust is a free market policy, as we will discuss in the next chapter. For now just note the absurdity of calling an industry "deregulated" when it is effectively controlled in all of its structures, goals and operations by the government via antitrust, which is by any honest measure a very serious form of regulation, indeed.

Examples of how frustrating such perpetually no-win competitions managed by antitrust can be would include stock markets, where the directness and simplicity of centralizing trading on a single market are obvious. Stock exchanges are classic network industries benefiting from network effects. The more people use them, the more liquidity begets liquidity, and thus the more functional and satisfying they become. They are in this sense one of the most natural of all natural monopolies, and present the choice referred to above of whether to regulate them either as public utilities, on the one hand, or as deregulated industries with multiple competitors under antitrust, on the other. The SEC chose the multi-competitor deregulation approach in its reforms of the NYSE, a choice that was made in the course of writing the Special Study Report in the early 1960s that set the stage for all of the market structure changes over the last fifty years, such as the National Market System. Interestingly, the official in charge of that study, Ralph Saul, who seems fully versed in network effect concepts and the natural advantages of concentration, said in a 2001 interview that he regrets having chosen the competition alternative. If he could do the study over again, he would opt for the utility approach instead, rather than "developing competing institutions just to get at the hegemony of the New York Stock Exchange." [xliii]

But that is all water over the dam at this point. As investors and traders are discovering in the SEC's multimarket deregulation imposed on them since 1997 in NASDAQ "OTC" stock trading and since 2007 in NYSE "listed" stock trading, the bizarre results of having many competing exchanges instead of one can be confusing, not to mention scary and off-putting. The bizarre results now include the Flash Crash of May 6, 2010, [xliv] high frequency trading (HFT) and regular charges that the markets are unfair, two-tier and rigged, all of which are examples of antitrust-induced product degradation.

Worst of all, while trading costs are down, that benefit may have been purchased at the price of the granddaddy of all unintended consequences. The destruction of Wall Street's revenues may have killed off the healthy IPO market that was essential to new company formation, innovation, and jobs in the U.S. economy. This was the strange effect that David Weild pointed out that led to the JOBS Act and Tick Pilot, as discussed in the previous chapter. But forget all the structural problems and unintended consequences in the big picture. What about consumers? Under antitrust, consumers do not have the option of seeing competition result in what they may very well prefer: a single stock exchange, in this instance. How is that consistent with consumer welfare? Similar stories could be told about other deregulations, such as airlines, electric utilities, telephones and computer software in which monopolists were busted. It's not that lower costs aren't beneficial from one perspective. It's that ignoring the value to consumers of the integrated service of the unified network that had to be broken up to produce the cost reduction is short-sighted, and may in fact be ignoring what consumers really want.

Fifth, capital will be energized and effectively cheaper if businesses have the monopolization option, because the potential returns will explicitly include the brass ring reached so famously by such men as Astor, Vanderbilt and Rockefeller, each of which is generally considered to have had a brief run as the world's wealthiest man, and one of which, Rockefeller, is considered to be the wealthiest person in world history. All of these men beat out kings and queens and other beneficiaries of inherited wealth, and built their fortunes from modest beginnings on monopolization models. Without antitrust, therefore, not only would such grand success stories still be possible, but returns would no longer be artificially truncated just when success was at hand. So stock could be sold to investors at higher prices or for a smaller percentage of the company, a form of efficiency not allowed under current law, but one that would probably be more important to the economy than all of the antitrust efficiencies combined. One effect of this efficiency is that it will make it easier for founders to hang on to dominant positions in their companies, which, as we will see in chapter 12, is critically important to creating jobs.

Sixth, capital will no longer be required to create multiple redundant networks, as it plays out its required competition fate under antitrust. We will no longer necessarily have to suffer flash crashes from dozens of "stock exchanges" being unable to coordinate price discovery; dropped calls and slow data when multiple telecom networks are required to compete with each other; or travel delay nightmares whenever the airlines cannot coordinate their services around a storm, etc. Being freed up from having to build multiple redundant networks may be another efficiency that is worth more than all the efficiencies of antitrust combined.

Seventh, if monopolies were allowed, it would become possible to benefit from natural free market solutions to many of our most perplexing domestic and international problems. While jettisoning antitrust would not necessarily solve all of them, it just might. Compared to the environment we have now, in which every one of the most important industries is perpetually in crisis, an antitrust-free

24

environment in which the competition can actually produce a winner wherever consumers would actually prefer that result, might solve more problems than we think.

For example, America would no longer have to unilaterally disarm via antitrust when an industry it invents, or at least wins the first successful monopoly in, dominates world commerce in that category. Examples of industries we have squandered away an early American advantage in due to antitrust would include oil, electricity, telephones, steel, automobiles, air travel, big computers, little computers, computer operating systems, computer chips, and computer software. Would we have had to suffer the volatility and geopolitical instability occasioned by the energy crisis if oil markets had not been broken up by antitrust? Would OPEC have gotten off the ground? Would we have had to bail out GM and Chrysler (twice)? Would Detroit have gone bankrupt? Would we be worrying about running out of oil, or be desperately searching for renewable energy sources? There is no natural stewardship of resources when there is no ownership of them by single entities, i.e., by monopolies. Nor is there any natural sense of responsibility that a monopolist that owns an industry would feel reputation-bound to honor, lest he lose the monopoly privilege to some new competitor that sprang up to exploit his weakness. Such senses of stewardship and reputation-bound responsibility are impossible to instill when each competitor is desperate to survive the competition that antitrust imposes. So instead we have to develop coercive and artificial competition policies and environmental policies and fuel-efficiency policies and carbon emission policies, etc., to force multiple players to conform to our ever-changing perceptions of the national interest. All of these problems might very well solve themselves if antitrust were not around.

This list is not even close to complete, but will suffice for the moment. The point isn't to play planner and figure out the rules that will produce the best results, but simply to suggest that there may be other types of competition that antitrust does not allow but that may be very pleasing to consumers or otherwise very valuable to individuals in our society when they are not acting in their capacity as consumers. Why not recognize the value of having a job and the wealth to consume, rather than always worrying only about how low prices can be? The benefits of antitrust, even if they are more than theoretical, might be relatively minor compared to the values we are forgoing by skipping monopolization.

Imagining such potential values merely requires us to think outside the box, to avoid for the moment, in our imaginary scenarios at least, the principles and prerogatives of the alphabet soup, and to accept instead the basic set of individual rights that Americans began with, which implicitly came with the right to monopolize. Consider, for example, the following two short descriptions of what an antitrust-free economy looks like.

First, we should always keep in mind that the antitrust laws did not come into existence until 1890, about a century after America's founding. While the rapidly growing wealth of monopolists like the robber barons created growing discomfort in the same era that Karl Marx was developing his redistributionist theories in Europe, the economic growth in the United States in the century before antitrust was stellar, enabling the U.S. economy to rapidly grow from nothing to being the largest in the world, [xlv] just as our monopolists mentioned above did in terms of their personal wealth. Antitrust theorists have neglected to address how the U.S. grew so fast and became the greatest economic show on earth with all those monopolists around. If monopolies are so bad, how did that happen? Do they actually believe we could have done even better under antitrust?

But that was a long time ago, and the reader could be forgiven for not necessarily seeing the relevance of that experience to today's economic institutions. So our second example of what free-wheeling monopolization might look like without antitrust is today's fast moving world of social media technologies, where products come and go at blinding speed, tiny nothings become behemoths overnight, and then disappear or meld into something else the next month. The youngest consumers dominate the field, including the notoriously fickle teen and even pre-teen populations. And perhaps due to the rapid turnover of products even without regulatory intervention, antitrust hasn't gotten much of a toehold yet.

Both of these examples illustrate the fundamental fact that competition among and between monopolies creates new industries, which are the main source of growth in jobs, incomes and wealth. These are categories of consumer interest that antitrust's narrow view of consumer welfare has no room for even in theory and, because of its per se policy, cannot legally take account of anyway. Trustbusters are effectively trying to provide value within each already-created industry, separately, while ignoring the potential value that monopolization could provide by maximizing the creation of new industries and jobs across the economy.

Once you get to thinking about such things you realize that there is actually no limit to how far we might go again without antitrust. Trade balance, Federal deficit, tax inversions? These perennial or new problems may seem farfetched in terms of what getting rid of antitrust might solve, but they're really not. If you just think about the vigorous economic expansion that accompanied the robber barons monopolization, or that which accompanied the most recent imitation of it -- the tech boom of the 1990s, which came before the antitrust-based stock market deregulation that destroyed the IPO market -- it is not at all difficult to imagine solving such problems by jettisoning antitrust. Not only were economic growth and productivity growth and jobs growth unbelievably powerful during these periods, deficits were non-existent or disappearing, and American business was a great source of pride at home and jealousy abroad, both for those directly involved in creating these businesses and for those Americans consuming or manufacturing and selling their products. Against such boisterous economic backdrops, which were filled with justified patriotism and pride, it is much harder to imagine the cloying cynicism and desperation that gave us the tax inversion wave or the budget and trade deficits of the current era. We were producing products that were in high demand, both at home and abroad, and we had no need to coddle the consumer via antitrust to get them sold.

One of the most enduring excuses for intervention is the "tragedy of the commons," which sometimes goes by the name of "public goods" analysis. This is the theory that there are some problems so big -- and incentives so wrong -- that only government can solve them. Unless government steps in to prevent overfishing by private fishermen, for example, the incentives of the individual fishermen will cause them to catch as many fish as possible and potentially threaten the overall population of fish they all depend on to the point where everyone will be worse off. The theory is that no one is big enough or powerful enough to impose discipline on fishing except the government.

But the reality is that we have no idea what problems might be solved if we didn't break up or retard our monopolies. From space exploration to "infrastructure" to "basic research" to universal health care to delivering the mail and education; from drug research to protecting our technology industries against foreign hackers and theft of intellectual property; from money laundering to protecting the security of online banking and credit card use to preventing dangers to our citizens from identity theft, i.e., "Cyber Security" -- we now rely mostly or solely on government to play the primary role of regulating all participants in all of these large network industries so as to make them behave in accordance with the presumed public good provided by that network, and to protect us from foreign intrusions or other bad actors. Because of government's universally dominant and thoroughly intrusive role, we have no idea what private industry might be able to accomplish to solve these alleged public goods problems. We have no idea, in other words, how those industries might behave or perform if a modern Astor or Vanderbilt or Rockefeller ran them. Therefore, the presumed fact underlying public goods analysis is demonstrably false, namely that there are some problems that are too big for anything but government to solve. Unless we were to let monopolies run again, we simply have no basis on which to conclude, as public goods and tragedy-of-the-commons analysts do, that only government can solve the big problems. Who knows, maybe even a fishing industry monopoly could solve the overfishing problem better than government.

In any case, it is obvious that a consumer that doesn't have a job will not be doing much consuming -- or enjoying life, for that matter. But these are interests that antitrust has very little ability under traditional theories to give any credence to, except through the limited effect on employment of the restraint of trade theory. Antitrust has no ability to contemplate the far larger job-creating value that monopolization can engender through the creation of new industries. Given the potential, and seemingly actual, benefits of an antitrust-free economy, where did we go wrong? Since monopolization was allowed prior to 1890, and we were doing so well with monopolies back then, catching up to and roaring past the great economies of the world, why did we give up the original interpretations of our rights to property and the pursuit of happiness that allowed monopolization? Why in the world did we buy into Sherman's jealousy-based complaints about the robber barons? The answer, it appears, is that everyone was complaining about inequality back then, too. Sherman was not special or original; he just went with the flow. [xlvi]

Again, Bork can help us understand these things, partly because he understands so much about antitrust, and partly because what he doesn't understand tells the whole story.

> The model outlined addresses the total welfare of consumers as a class. It says nothing of how shares of consumption should be allocated through changes in the distribution of income. Yet all economic activity has income

effects and, in particular, restriction of output by the exercise of monopoly power has income effects not taken into account by weighing only changes in allocative and productive efficiency. If the reader will look once more at Figure 4 [not shown here] he will see that at the competitive price, P1, there is a large area under the demand curve that lies above the market price. This area represents the amount above the actual price that consumers would be willing to pay rather than go without the product; it is generally called the "consumer's surplus," perhaps on some notion that the consumer gets surplus value for his money. Those who continue to buy after a monopoly is formed pay more for the same output, and that shifts income from them to the monopoly and its owners, who are also consumers. This is not dead-weight loss due to restriction of output but merely a shift in income between two classes of consumers. The consumer welfare model, which views consumers as a collectivity, does not take this income effect into account. [xlvii]

Several points must be made about this passage. First, it is a clear statement that antitrust should not worry about redistribution, because, after all, monopolists are consumers, too. In other words, purists should not care whether the consumer's surplus is in the monopolist's pocket or the consumer's pocket, as long as the correct judgment has been made about the tradeoff between allocative and productive efficiency such that there has been no counterproductive restraint of trade that would result in an unnecessarily inefficient allocation of overall economic activity. Bork maintains that it is relatively easy to figure this out, although I have my doubts. But either way, note also that if there were any non-purists around who wanted to treat the which-pocket-should-the-surplus-reside-in question as a matter of class warfare, Bork has described both sides in ways that would make that interpretation easy enough to adopt. He has done this by talking of consumers under the welfare model as being a "collectivity" or "a class" that would share whatever benefit they could derive from antitrust as a group, not as individuals. What Bork fails to grasp is that there is no conceivable practical way for consumers or anyone else to judge how much the fight over consumer's surplus is worth to them as individuals. But because it is set up as a battle between opposing classes, those who want to pitch it as a giant inequality problem pitting consumers against monopolists have a lot to work with, Bork's statements about the inappropriateness of redistribution notwithstanding.

This is just another instance of Americans today being treated not as individuals with rights that are simple and easy to understand, such as the original unalienable rights the Declaration of Independence spoke of, but treated rather as members of groups or classes that must depend on government to get their fair shares. Whether or not there are judges around who can juggle "allocative" versus "productive" efficiency or "dead-weight losses" versus "consumer's surpluses," etc., treating individuals as members of groups is going to make competition policy an eternally fraught topic leaving everyone perpetually mad at someone else, whether they be members of the opposing class, or judges or regulators thought to be improperly interpreting or implementing the law.

5. Where the Right Went Left

Bork is of course one of the most admired conservatives of his generation and, coming from the ultra-conservative Chicago school, where antitrust-based deregulation was born, is entitled to give as credentialed a rendering of the value of antitrust as can be given from a conservative perspective. But how did conservatives like Bork buy into antitrust in the first place? Why did they not reject it out of hand as they would any other big government intrusion into the operation of the free market? Why did they accept it at all? The answer may lie in the fact that it is possible to portray antitrust as a seemingly never-ending parade of American-sounding themes and capitalist-sounding themes, such as freedom, free markets, innovation, competition, democracy, deregulation, survival of the fittest and many others. Such concepts, words and phrases no doubt contributed to antitrust having always had a very good reputation on the political right as, in Bork's words,

> a law that became and for a long time remained the politically potent symbol of the virtues of free and unregulated markets. [xlviii]

But none of this changes the fact that antitrust is, first and foremost, an intervention. So the question remains for these conservatives who, like Bork, are presumably no pushovers for cheap jingoism and certainly, over time, have thoroughly explored the matter: How could it not be obvious that tens of thousands of bureaucrats and lawyers is an intervention? How could it not be obvious that we're not talking about "free and unregulated markets" here when antitrust alters all of our most important industries drastically, pushing their structures far away from what they would have been or were during their natural course of evolution and operation? Never mind what antitrust does, pro or con; how did free market conservatives, of all people, come to see it as anything other than an intervention?

Of course it is possible that conservatives are as drawn as anyone to the power and glory of intervention, and have simply glommed on to the seeming symbols of freedom, patriotism and capitalism offered by antitrust as an excuse to engage in it. They would be aided in this cynical endeavor by many editorialists, even those on the Right, who sing the praises of antitrust. In a typical and well-put articulation of the Nanny State view, for example, but coming from a source that would avoid that term like the plague as applied to themselves, and a source that would also no doubt agree with Bork's characterization of antitrust as a symbol of free and unregulated markets, the Financial Times of August 13, 2014 carries an editorial in defense of antitrust as the law that protects the rights of Englishmen "to take your custom elsewhere." Leading off with Nobel Prize-winning economist James Tobin's famous line that "It takes a heap of Harberger triangles to fill an Okun gap," [xlix] FT first summarizes Tobin's point and then immediately takes issue with it:

> He meant that the big issue in economics was not battling against monopolies but preventing recessions and promoting recovery. After the misery of recent years, nobody can doubt that preventing recessions and promoting recovery

would have been a very good idea. But economists should be able to think about more than one thing at once. What if monopoly matters, too? [l]

Another economist, Robert Kuttner, begins a more detailed analysis of these issues and the difficulty of balancing them as follows:

> The point of Tobin's quip is that little allocative efficiencies do not compensate for big, Keynesian inefficiencies of insufficient purchasing power, low growth and high unemployment. At the same time, Tobin's deliberately and splendidly mixed metaphor--triangles and gaps-- underscores that standard analysis lacks a common metric for assessing in the same conversation the interaction of these two conceptions of efficiency. If a Keynesian intervention reduces allocative efficiency by distorting market prices, but appropriately stimulates demand, standard market economics is literally unable to calculate *a priori* whether the trade-off is worth the candle. [li]

Clearly no one is sure enough about any of these issues that we should be basing major interventions on their inevitably contested opinions. And this acknowledged confusion arises only from comparing the presumably big "productive" efficiency of economy-wide Keynesian stimulus to the presumably smaller "allocative" efficiency that comes from stacking up even a great many antitrust enforcements, the aggregated efficiency improvement of which comes from totaling all those little recovered dead weight losses or Harberger triangles that the separate industry monopolizations had been allegedly depriving us of. And of course Kuttner probably did not mean that "a Keynesian intervention *reduces* allocative efficiency by distorting market prices," at least not directly, but only that if the Keynesian focus results in forgetting about antitrust, it would have that effect, which was the FT's point.

But that clarification aside, there is an even much bigger but hidden and unacknowledged confusion problem. Addressing via antitrust the presumed little allocative inefficiencies (the little Harberger triangles compared to the big Okun gap), works against and in the opposite direction of the allocative efficiencies that monopolization could promote, as described in the previous chapter. In addition, allowing monopolization could easily power growth sufficiently on its own to close any Okun gap without artificial stimulus. In the age before either Keynes or Okun, such as when the robber barons were active, it was not automatically assumed, as it is now, that productive efficiency comes only from wise government decisions about how fast to push the economy via stimulus. Nor was it assumed that allocative efficiency came only from busting monopolies and recovering those dead weight losses, since those esoteric antitrust theories were many decades away from even being thought about. Allowing monopolization, in other words, could solve both the triangles and the gaps problems -- and without intervention. The real problem with standard analysis is not the lack of tools to compare the importance of Harberger triangles and Okun gaps, as Kuttner and Tobin lamented, but that there are no tools at all for considering the value of monopolization to either allocative or productive efficiency. Monopolization is the king of all efficient allocation forces in an economy, and the drive to monopolize may push the economy as fast or faster than any Keynesian would dare to. Thus, monopolization could easily handle on its own both the triangles and the gap problems, because the allocation benefits of monopolization plus the production efficiency benefits of monopolization may well be larger than all the Harberger triangles and Okun gaps put together.

First, as regards allocation, as discussed in the previous chapter, there is the consumer preference allocation that could come from allowing monopolizers to compete and thus to discover the price that consumers would pay for an industry's products. Second, there would be the allocation of activity to new industries that we didn't know could exist until monopolization discovered them. Third, there is the allocation efficiency achieved by the most important of these newly discovered industries, namely the one called a stock exchange, the value of which is often extolled by economists precisely for its capacity to allocate capital in an economy. And finally in this short but by no means exhaustive list of the potential allocation efficiencies of monopolization, there is the potentially better organization of resources and economic activity that could be accomplished through maximizing both the number of desirable industries and their ability to work together in a coordinated fashion, as well as to gain other benefits like the previously mentioned stewardship and better service through reputation maintenance, all of which would come from allowing monopolizers to seek to own whole industries and to keep them for as long as they can.

To drill down on the most salient example, and it is the one on which all of the main arguments in this book are based, what about Wall Street? It is commonly acknowledged that the primary role of Wall Street is to allocate capital to its most efficient uses through the capital allocation process that occurs via IPO issuance, trading, price discovery, etc. What if Wall Street didn't exist? It is my contention that, but for monopolization, Wall Street would not exist. Not just the physical location or exchanges we have become familiar with, but capital allocation itself as an industry was created only by virtue of the monopolization that attended the creation of the London and New York stock exchanges. What if those monopolizations had never happened? Then how much allocative efficiency would we have enjoyed? And what if they are destroyed by antitrust now, as I believe they have been? How much allocative efficiency can we expect in the future? Even with all its acknowledged confusions due to conflicting types and definitions of efficiency noted by Tobin and others, the Harberger triangles versus Okun gap argument is a triviality compared to the real allocation efficiency we would have missed out on without the original Wall Street from 1792 to 1997, and are almost certainly missing today.

And as to productive efficiency, the last few decades of the nineteenth century exhibited perhaps the greatest sustained growth in our nation's history. Does anyone really believe that we could have done better than what the robber barons did if we had had Keynesians around then to tell us what to do?

What is most notable ideologically about this feckless argument over triangles and gaps is that it is basically just one team of socialist doodlers versus another, between those who favor big Keynesian interventions and those who would give more weight to lots of little antitrust interventions. But as the FT editorial asks, why shouldn't economists be able to do both? If you accept either side of the argument in the first place, the FT implies, you should be on board for an all-intervention-all-the-time policy. Economists should merely be figuring out the appropriate weights among the intervention possibilities, with those determinations presuming at all times the inappropriateness of the free market. The very existence of the argument over triangles and gaps presumes that all sides and nuances of this particular democratic debate are legitimate because they presume the wisdom and necessity of intervention.

Conservatives come down mostly on the side of antitrust, even if they, like Bork, formally disavow the appropriateness of deciding through antitrust whether the consumer's surplus should be redelivered to consumers through antitrust enforcement, or left with monopolizers by declining to enforce. Their deliberations are more pure, they imply, than those crass interventionists who would intervene to accomplish redistribution. The only thing that should matter, they say, is the efficiency that comes about by preventing monopolizers from restraining trade. Having established that presumed per se value, the doodlers then go after each violator, industry by industry, antitrust action by antitrust action, dead weight loss by dead weight loss. But don't be fooled by these conservatives' attempts to reestablish their bona fides on the sanctity of property by asserting they don't care whether the surplus is owned by the monopolist or the consumer, that it would be inappropriate for antitrust to take action just to effect redistribution. The reality is that almost all public support for antitrust action, and therefore the political support for it, comes from precisely such motives, impure or not. So in practice there is nothing pure or free market about saying it shouldn't be so, when it is obvious to anyone with eyes to see that it is so. Antitrust is all about redistribution, pure and simple, regardless of what Bork has to say about the matter.

But much more important than those relatively technical questions, these conservatives completely ignore and foreclose the option of letting the free market find new industries. No one knows in advance which industries will stick, which ones consumers will flock to and want to see expand and which ones they will let fall by the wayside, which are essentially allocative efficiency questions. And no one knows in advance how intensely consumers will demand a new industry's product nor how much its existence will cause increased demands for other industries' products, which are essentially productive efficiency questions. It is an absurd arrogance to think that antitrust can help with these critical processes, or indeed do anything but destroy them. The kind of allocation that discovers which industries consumers desire and in which proportions, and with how much intensity, are far more important efficiencies than can possibly come from just lowering the price to increase trade in existing industries, if for no other reason than that the antitrust variety of efficiency mostly sticks with the existing industry array, while monopolization will turn up new industries we didn't know we needed or wanted.

The grand irony here, and it is a triple irony, is that while the academics and editorialists argue over one form of intervention or another on efficient allocation grounds, which assumes antitrust, they miss entirely the fact that monopolization, which requires no intervention and no antitrust, is valuable primarily for its allocation effects. And the best example of that in history is the creation of the allocation industry itself in the form of the stock exchange, which is not only known as the capital allocation engine supreme, but was itself created through the allocation-by-monopolization process it now administers -- or would if not for antitrust.

In spite of all the unknowns, some recognized, such as by Tobin, but most not recognized, we not only have the massively interventionist antitrust enterprise wading in with huge distortions all across our economy, but we have the entire conservative community cheering them on, as if antitrust were a free market policy. Although Bork, Kuttner, Posner and Tobin are all considered conservative, free market economists, they are all pushing what amounts to a Nanny State policy selling inherently conflicting and contested notions of efficiency, the intellectual arguments over which are really nothing but excuses for intervention and redistribution, no matter what they say.

The big question here does not concern the fact of universal intervention, which is too obvious to be in dispute, but how it is that conservatives like Bork could so thoroughly buy into such policies, however they were justified. How and why did they come to believe that antitrust was a free market policy? How did the FT come to think that English traditions of the freedom "to take your custom elsewhere" should trump John Locke and the right to accumulate and keep property? The short answer of course is that monopolists are not deemed as having the right to keep any property gained through monopolization if regulators believe they should be deprived of it to create a more perfect or fair or efficient market or to serve other goals they gin up. Fair enough, if you believe in such theories. But whether you do or not, how is this even conceivably consistent with an unalienable right to property, and how did conservatives, usually the most ardent defenders of that right, miss the error?

We dwell here on the conservative errors regarding antitrust, because they are at the root of the errors of the entire society. In fact, it is the very reputation of conservatives as free market people that enables them and the rest of government's supporters, including liberals, to fool us all into accepting their pro-government policies. Understanding how conservatives were fooled on antitrust will give us a model for understanding how our country and much of the world were fooled into policies that are not only at war with themselves and destroying their respective economies, but are generating wars, themselves, real wars.

6. Heroes, Villains and the Father of Fascism

It is common for conservatives to revere President Theodore Roosevelt, [lii] who did so much to launch the antitrust enterprise politically, in spite of his clearly left-leaning Square Deal [liii] and Progressive Movement politics. While to a man conservatives blame most of the leftward tilt in modern America on President Franklin Delano Roosevelt's New Deal, they seldom note that trustbuster Teddy was probably the more naturally interventionist of the two and the real socialist in the family. [liv] Having only jealousy of the rich robber barons to work with, and without the massive government spending excuses of world wars and depression that virtually forced Franklin to move left, Teddy's instinct for downward redistribution was probably more pure than Franklin's. In any case, coming earlier, Teddy's signature policy of busting trusts with his Big Stick was certainly more seminal than Franklin's New Deal in terms of what pushed America in the socialist direction.

Teddy was eager to strong-arm monopolies via antitrust into government oversight. This policy, whether it restrained big companies or broke them up, or brought them under government's wing under antitrust oversight, looked little different than the unified government policies known a couple decades later as national socialism in Germany and fascism in Italy, both of which also harnessed their national champions into operating as government-protected and therefore effectively as government-run monopolies. So Teddy's Big Stick was arguably the model not only for Franklin's alphabet soup, under which, for example, the banking and Wall Street monopolies were forced to submit to being run by agencies like the SEC, but also for the dictatorships in Germany and Italy that adopted similar policies at about the same time.

The focusing fact here is that Teddy, more than Franklin or the dictators, was the progenitor of such policies. While left-leaning Americans remember fondly Franklin's "I welcome their hatred" comment when speaking of the bankers and moneyed mob that hated him, [lv] it was easier for Franklin to say such a thing because by then it reflected little more than the common populist wisdom that all bankers were evil, largely due to the socialist pioneering that Teddy had done before him. And who can forget the ultimate extension of this anti-banker view in Hitler's vilification of the international Jewish financiers who were supposedly conspiring in 1939, according to Hitler, to start a second world war? [lvi] Hitler's hatred of bankers was more extreme than Franklin's or Teddy's, but was clearly no more than an extension of the same moral sentiment. In Hitler's case, it ultimately provided the justification for his "final solution" in the Holocaust, as well as the Nazi's pseudo-scientific eugenics policy, which was also at its core nothing but an extreme form of redistribution.

There has always been a militaristic and nationalistic component to Teddy's reputation that appeals to many hard-right conservatives. From San Juan Hill and the Rough Riders to his launching of 40 antitrust lawsuits to start busting the 318 trusts, or about 40 percent of the economy, [lvii] that existed when he took office, the image of TR as the courageous and bold defender of freedom and American interests was unmistakable. So imagine what the American model must have looked like in the 1920s as Mussolini and Hitler were gathering their thoughts, both on theories of government and on how best to appeal to the screaming masses. Gazing across the ocean was the enormous and fast-rising industrial might of the United States, the might that had helped win World War I, where business had been rapidly and forcibly yoked to the national interest by warlike Teddy [lviii] and his successors. [lix] The fact that Mussolini got history's nod as the inventor of the unified government model now known as fascism, where industries were all forced by their government to pull in the same direction, was almost certainly due to his successful public relations that switched the name of the label on TR's Square Deal policy to his own. The same historical disregard was shared by Hitler, whose PR was apparently also not as good as Mussolini's, since history mostly refers to his own *national socialism* (Na-Zi) [lx] adoption of the same unified government policies as fascism, the term associated with Mussolini.

Viewed from a distance, Mussolini's fascism, Hitler's national socialism, FDR's New Deal and TR's trusbusting looked the same. They were all unified government policies that aimed to control business in the public interest or national interest, depending on which leader's terminology you prefer. And the great irony is that, instead of resulting in the ordered world their sponsors promised, these unified government policies all resulted in industrial chaos, leaving social and geopolitical chaos in its wake, where, in William Butler Yeats' famous phrase from *The Second Coming*, "Things fall apart; the centre cannot hold."

The main point of my 2012 book, *Nature's God*, was that the natural pursuit of monopolies by private interests creates order, while overriding the natural pursuit of monopolies via antitrust causes chaos. My main point here isn't just that history has missed these subtleties; it is that conservatives have missed them. This is particularly ironic in Bork's case, because by the time he wrote *Slouching Towards Gomorrah* two decades after *The Antitrust Paradox*, Bork was very sensitive to the dangers of chaos in the world, and took the title of this second book from *The Second Coming*. [lxi]

Unfortunately, there does not appear to have been any recognition by Bork in the years after either book that antitrust itself causes chaos. In fact, conservatives like Bork have become the most effective defenders of modern socialism in America, the vanguard of which is antitrust, precisely because of their unequivocal support for this chaos-inducing policy. As a result, antitrust is still perceived, in spite of all evidence to the contrary, as a chaos-calming and freedom-based policy, and even though it has been wielded by demagogues and dictators pursuing various forms of patriotic nationalism that resulted in acknowledged chaos, as Bork alludes to with his reference to *The Second Coming*. The fact that Bork, of all people, did not make the correct connection between antitrust and chaos is a very bad sign. And similar errors made by almost all conservatives explain why TR, perhaps our original socialist, is a revered conservative icon.

I will never forget getting a call from someone I didn't know who put this view in stark terms. He had read my 2013 "trilogy" of articles on TabbFORUM outlining how antitrust and the SEC were destroying IPOs in the stock market and, thereby, jobs and economic prospects, and he apparently thought I had made a good case. [lxii] But this realization caused him great anguish, as if I had killed his first-born child. He needed to talk, hoping to explain the free market roots of antitrust to me, which was a big part of his own worldview. He started filling me in on Teddy Roosevelt's role and the need for competition, but sounded quite tentative, as if he feared he was not telling me anything I hadn't already heard. My articles had opened his eyes to something he hadn't considered, however, and so he did his best to reconcile this new information with his deeply held beliefs.

Since I had not mentioned Teddy Roosevelt in this particular series of articles (although I have elsewhere), [lxiii] he apparently was hoping against hope that a discussion of TR's role in antitrust, filled as it is with aggressively patriotic American symbols, would help him or me understand what one of us was missing. But his anguish only deepened as I described my view of his favorite Roosevelt. He was apparently hoping that I would identify with his view, so common among conservatives, that TR's credentials as a hard right conservative were as solid as FDR's credentials as a liberal socialist. He was disappointed that I put them both in the liberal socialist camp. But as this fellow realized that my perspective on his icon was at least consistent with my view of the real roots and flaws of antitrust, as described in the articles, he apparently also realized that he would not be able to reconcile his new understanding of antitrust with his old view of his hero, which was too deeply ingrained to imagine changing.

At the same time, I realized that, curious and intellectually open as he was, the gap that remained between a simple intellectual grasp of my points on antitrust and his ability to embrace those points over his icon's dead body was insurmountable. Further, I realized that he was probably typical of the readers I was reaching with my iconoclastic views and differed mainly in his willingness to consider -- in spite of everything that his personal history with the symbols of American patriotism told him -- that I might be right.

The TabbFORUM debates are just a subset of the debates over stock market structure and regulation that occur throughout the Wall Street industry at practitioner and academic conferences, regulatory roundtables, SEC and Congressional hearings, comment periods on regulatory rule filings, etc. All of these could be characterized as part of the democratic process in which the issues are hashed out in public in a so-called "national conversation" or "democratic debate," to use left-leaning author Thomas Piketty's favorite term for it. [lxiv] The idea is to figure out what the rules of the road ought to be, and especially what kind and amount of redistributive effects those rules should have. Although many of the purists in these debates believe they are arguing only over technical structural questions having nothing to do with redistribution, they are, like Bork, fooling themselves on this issue. As long as the main proposer of reform in the stock market, for example, the SEC, repeatedly references redistribution images such as level playing fields in support of its proposals, then redistribution is the main object of the proposals, however technical and separate from that question some of the debaters would prefer to think of them.

As I first noticed during my unique experience arguing for a fixed time auction in the 1980s and 1990s, many debaters are not really open to rational argument, but are instead fixed in their positions as if they constituted religious doctrine and were fundamental to their faith. They truly believe in the wisdom, moral value and efficiency of the SEC's downward redistribution policies of the antitrust-based National Market System, and accordingly add their voices reflexively to the chorus of calls for more reform. [lxv] Although such beliefs are often couched within and camouflaged by recommendations with respect to specific technical adjustments to structure presented as efficiency improvements, they all add weight and effect to the presumed need to combat inequality via redistribution.

For example, regardless of any opinions regarding the previously discussed Tick Pilot the SEC is conducting under the JOBS Act to determine the potential efficacy of wider ticks, the mere fact of commenting on or opining on any of the issues presumes the SEC should remain in charge of market structure. This assumption is tantamount to concurrence with the overall redistribution goal of the SEC's general electronic trading reforms, regardless of the commentator's opinions on any particular issue or structure. Thus although it may appear that the issues are being hashed out and adjusted in response to rational debate, that is not in fact what is going on, because the regulatory imperative of keeping the SEC in power drives the market structure bus.

Although self-interest might be what is causing the seemingly disingenuous debate, since anyone who wants to have or keep a job in the industry in some capacity must be on the SEC's bus, my experience tells me that that is not the case, at least not primarily or explicitly. As in many matters of faith, the most fervently faithful do not know and could not explain in rational terms how they came to their beliefs, apart from simply retelling their religion's founding narrative and pointing out its sacred objects, to use terms borrowed from Jonathan Haidt, an author we will discuss in the next chapter. The founding narrative in the market structure debates recounts the SEC's selfless struggles to overcome evildoers on Wall Street to establish the electronic National Market System, and the sacred object is Cost Reduction. Any arguments that might threaten this narrative are instinctively rejected, mostly before even being heard. So the debaters are sincere in their faith, but not really engaging in open debate, however much their apparent participation in the reform exercises would seem to indicate otherwise.

The result is an 80-year squeezing out of the revenues and prerogatives of Wall Street, leading to, as mentioned, drastic reductions in IPOs from where they were in the 1990s before the latest reforms kicked-in in 1997. And even though revenues are down dramatically and so, naturally, are trading costs, (nearly to zero, by my reckoning), [lxvi] there is still nevertheless a relentless drumbeat for more reforms to knock them down further. Although costs are negligible now, the desire to blame Wall Street for even negligible costs is such a core element of debaters' belief in downward redistribution systems that they are perpetually willing to complain loudly, in spite of the lack of any noticeable or measureable cost to speak of. It is apparent that even if costs were actually zero, the complaints would keep on coming as the mob fixes on what they see as per se violations or advantages of HFTs that would, by definition, cause no harm if they caused no cost. Almost everyone who participates in the debates -- traders, industry leaders, regulators, market structure consultants, populist authors, congressmen, senators, editorialists and others -- cheers the SEC on to further action, buttressed now by aggressive efforts to criminalize previously normal market behavior, as entities such as the Justice Department, the FBI, and state attorneys general weigh in.

But if the debaters would ever step back and listen to what they are saying, they would see that the debate is bound to take the market structure to a dead end or worse. It is always alleged, for example, that reforms are needed to restore investor confidence because things are terrible. But it is never noticed that the conviction that things are terrible on which reform is premised is a constantly renewing view requiring additional reforms. The reform agenda, therefore, is bound to generate many more years of projected reforms and completion horizons before the reforms are implemented and will continue long after there are truly, literally, no costs or other evidence of terrible things that can be identified, or any victims found to attach them to. Consequently, by their own terms and process, the reformers have set things up such that there will never come a time when the pending reforms on which confidence allegedly depends will be completed. Therefore, confidence will never return.

The trajectories of stock market deterioration we have seen for decades are therefore the ones we will in all likelihood continue to see, because nothing in the debate pattern has changed or is likely to change. No matter what is said in the debates and hearings, or what new rules or structures come out of them, confidence will continue to fall, revenues to brokers and dealers will continue their decline, the alleged crisis justifying reform will be forever renewed, and the capital markets will continue their slow deaths. The reality is that the democratic process of debate is not capable of producing the successful conclusions its existence presumes and the debaters nominally always strive for. Instead, the debaters fix their positions on heroes and villains, never noticing that the goals, processes and effects of antitrust would look the same, whether Teddy Roosevelt, Franklin Roosevelt, Benito Mussolini or Adolf Hitler is in charge. And all of them achieved their political success because of the appeal of redistribution to address inequality.

In the stock market structure field, this is an appeal that underlies the popularity of several books, such as *Dark Pools*, by Scott Patterson, and *Flash Boys*, by Michael Lewis. Although both of these purport to tell us something new about the evil shenanigans of Wall Street professionals, particularly high-frequency traders, neither of them does, and both of them rely on and apparently receive support from readers who already believed in the need to spread the advantage of trading from HFTs to the little guys. [lxvii] These books achieve their popularity essentially by saying that inequality (i.e., unfairness) is a problem in need of reforms that effect downward redistribution (i.e., fairness). In other words, they are popular because they restate conventional wisdom, albeit with lots of detail.

Such books as *Dark Pools* and *Flash Boys* give intellectual sophistication to theories that supposedly demonstrate the problems of inequality by doing nothing more than describing current operating practices of markets and their recent histories. But these descriptions reveal nothing new to knowledgeable market practitioners. They thus present a false picture on two levels. Number one, they imply we are learning something new about how markets operate. And secondly they imply we are seeing new proof that markets are "rigged," to use the term

Michael Lewis made famous on 60 Minutes with regard to *Flash Boys*, but that Scott Patterson had used in the same way in his earlier book, *Dark Pools*. But these books tell us nothing new, or at least nothing that was not already common knowledge among experienced practitioners. And they provide no new smoking gun. Nonetheless, the overall effect on the average reader is to stroke his feeling of righteous support for redistribution remedies that he was probably already in favor of, such as any or all of the SEC's new rules or its holistic review of market structure.

Beyond market structure in the larger sphere, there are many similar new books, some of which are also quite popular, that rely on the same methods to imply the moral imperative of redistribution remedies, such as progressive taxation. Although non-economists like me can learn plenty of new things about the operating mechanics of inequality and its history from these books, I do not get the impression that knowledgeable economists are learning anything new from them. In any case, these books also seem to rely for their popularity on readers who already believed in their conclusions before turning the first page. And they have a certain sameness of belief and coverage that imparts an echo chamber character to them all, as if their authors were working in concert to lead their witnesses to conclusions they already had, and were merely coaching them on how to convince the judge and jury. As such, the books' authors are both free riding on the preexisting moral sentiment regarding inequality and on each other to persuade their readers. Just as Michael Lewis and Scott Patterson are very complimentary to each other as authors, and often tell much the same tale about rigged markets, Thomas Piketty and Joseph Stiglitz tell much the same story, as do books by Branko Milanovic and Angus Deaton, albeit with different coverage specialties. [lxviii] While each of these books is fascinating in its own way, bottom line is they all reach the same conclusion: inequality should be countered by government policy.

While I have enjoyed all of these books, my hands down favorite is Thomas Piketty's magnificent contribution to our understanding of inequality: *Capital in the Twenty-First Century.* The book is rich in wide-ranging detail, and complex economic principles are laid out patiently, allowing even non-economists to grasp what causes inequality and what it looks like. But like the others, this book relies for its popularity essentially on the appeal of redistribution as a remedy for inequality. And like them, it gives the impression that there might have been some economic rationale offered amidst all the complexity to show why inequality was harmful or redistribution was justified on economic grounds; Piketty, after all, is an economist. But this impression is an illusion.

In 577 pages of dramatic and frightening descriptions of the supposed problem of inequality, Piketty never once offers a reason why inequality is bad for the lower classes that allegedly suffer from it. Instead, he relies upon the implied assumption that everyone else thinks inequality is as unjust as he does and, therefore, believes as he does that the non-rich must suffer unjustifiably from jealousy or a sense of being abused or exploited, particularly if the rich do not deserve their wealth.

In this book, I focus not only on the level of inequality as such but to an even greater extent on the structure of inequality, that is, on the origins of disparities in income and wealth between groups and on the various systems of economic, social, moral, and political justification that have been invoked to defend or condemn those disparities. Inequality is not necessarily bad in itself: the key question is to decide whether it is justified, whether there are reasons for it. [lxix]

While the jealousy, sense of exploitation, and consequent potential for social upheaval are certainly real, Piketty never demonstrates any actual economic harm that occurs to the middle or lower classes as a result of either the existence of the rich or their capital. In fact, he says the opposite on several occasions, such as when recognizing the great growth created by the Industrial Revolution.

The best available estimates suggest that global per capita income increased by a factor of more than 10 between 1700 and 2012 (from 70 euros to 760 euros per month) and by a factor of more than 20 in the wealthiest countries (from 100 euros to 2,500 euros). [lxx]

Piketty describes several economic forces that push inevitably toward inequality, which he characterizes as "laws" of capitalism. These laws are similar in effect to the natural forces described by others, such as Vilfredo Pareto and his 80-20 rule. The most important of his laws of capitalism, according to Piketty, describes the relationship between the rate of return on capital, which he designates "r," and the rate of general economic growth from which wages derive, which he designates "g." The law, r > g, says r is generally greater than g, which causes inequality.

The central thesis of this book is precisely that an apparently small gap between the return on capital and the rate of growth can in the long run have powerful and destabilizing effects on the structure and dynamics of social inequality. [lxxi]

The gap between these forces (r - g) is likely to widen substantially in the twenty-first century, by Piketty's predictions, which will lead to the rich getting richer at a faster rate than working people can and, thus, cause inequality to get worse and worse, potentially to socially destabilizing degrees, as it did during the Ancien Régime that preceded the French Revolution in 1789 and during the Belle Époque that preceded World War I in 1914.

Whenever the rate of return on capital is significantly and durably higher than the growth rate of the economy, it is all but inevitable that inheritance (of fortunes accumulated in the past) predominates over saving (wealth accumulated in the present). In strict logic, it could be otherwise, but the forces pushing in this direction are extremely powerful. The inequality r > g in one sense implies that the past tends to devour the future: wealth originating in the past automatically grows more rapidly, even without labor, than wealth stemming from work, which can be saved. Almost inevitably, this tends to give lasting, disproportionate importance to inequalities created in the past, and therefore to inheritance. [lxxii]

And so the impending conflict between undeserved wealth (such as from inheritance) and "wealth stemming from work" is painted by Piketty in dire terms, likely to overwhelm the good things that Piketty acknowledges have happened for the lower classes, such as, as noted, that humanity has been getting richer over time, by factors of from ten to twenty-five since 1700, regardless of the ebbs and flows of inequality. Piketty also is impressed that the recent "emergence of a "patrimonial middle class" owning between a quarter and a third of national wealth rather than a tenth or a twentieth (scarcely more than the poorest half of society) represents a major social transformation." lxxiii But these hopeful and dramatic improvements for everyone hardly seem to matter, overwhelmed in Piketty's view by the fact that the rich are still getting richer faster than the middle class or the poor, and are likely to see their advantage increase as the twenty-first century progresses.

If your goal is to ignore the good things that have happened for the lower and middle classes over time in order to focus fear on "the failure of the French Revolution" as we head again toward record inequality, it seems you can do it very well with Piketty's third law of capitalism, r > g. But you can also do it, as Piketty acknowledges, with Pareto's 80-20 rule, or the power law, albeit not as well, in Piketty's opinion. Still, given the similarity in effect of their different ways of describing inequality, I was somewhat surprised that Piketty seemed anxious to find fault with Pareto, the only material explanation for which appeared to be rooted in a philosophical difference. Piketty wants us to believe that inequality is a problem that must and can be addressed, while Pareto is more comfortable with it, and not so sure it can be addressed even if we try. Piketty seems to try to undermine Pareto's position by noting, "the Italian Fascists adopted Pareto as one of their own and promoted his theory of elites." Piketty also seemed happy to report, "Fascists would naturally have been attracted to Pareto's theory of stable inequality and the pointlessness of trying to change it" and that "Pareto, shortly before his death in 1923, hailed Mussolini's accession to power," lxxiv as if Pareto should have known then what was coming. But Piketty saves his most biting attack on Pareto for his skills as an economist:

> When we say that a distribution of wealth is a Pareto distribution, we have not really said anything at all. It may be a distribution in which the upper decile receives only slightly more than 20 percent of total income (as in Scandinavia in 1970-1980) or one in which the upper decile receives 50 percent (as in the United States in 2000-2010). In each case we are dealing with a Pareto distribution, but the coefficients are quite different. The corresponding social, economic, and political realities are clearly poles apart. lxxv

But isn't the fact that the Pareto distribution happens in all these different places in varying degrees why it is called a "rule" or "law?" I have always heard the 80-20 rule described as a loose law or a rule of thumb. The general tendency of "network effects," which is a modern term for what Pareto was describing, to show up in many different places, such as in wealth distributions, or the number of peas in peapods, or the number of people in cities, is the very reason Pareto's discovery was monumental. Modern network scientists invariably grant Pareto hero status for being the first to recognize the universality of network effects. They do not seem hung up the way Piketty is on the law's inconsistencies. Instead, they are simply awed by its general universality in nature. It seems too obvious to have escaped Pareto that the precise steepness and consistency of the distribution can vary from place to place and from time to time, just as Piketty says it does with respect to his own means of describing inequality, which in his more generous moments he doesn't seem to mind acknowledging point to similar or identical phenomena as Pareto distributions or Pareto coefficients do.

> When we study inequality in historical perspective, the important thing to explain is not the stability of the distribution but the significant changes that occur from time to time. In the case of the wealth distribution, I have identified a way to explain the very large historical variations that occur (whether described in terms of Pareto coefficients or as shares of the top decile and centile) in terms of the difference r - g between the rate of return on capital and the growth rate of the economy. [lxxvi]

Will r > g ever be called "Piketty's Law?" Will his next book mention the existence of the network science field and its potential contributions to economic and inequality sciences? In particular, will monopolies and the processes that create them, which, in my view, are network formation processes that tend to generate power law distributions -- not to mention some of the wealthiest people of all time -- be incorporated into the future Piketty explanation of inequality? We can only hope.

As noted earlier, Pareto is also known (and probably best known) for the concept of Pareto Efficiency or Pareto Optimality, which is used among other things to identify conditions of perfect competition, i.e., situations that are so thick with competitors that no monopolist can increase price by restraining supply and thereby create those dreaded dead weight losses or Harberger triangles. And the Pareto Principle, or the 80-20 rule, is thought to be the first and still the most popular articulation of what a power law distribution or "Pareto distribution" looks like, which modern network scientists would recognize as a sign that there are network effects about, driven by a powerful discriminatory force in nature they now call "preferential attachment" or, literally, "rich get richer." [lxxvii] Thus Pareto is famous both for major contributions to our understanding of the forces that create monopolies and for the mathematical underpinnings of the policies that prevent them. Given my interest in monopolies, this is a fascinating combination of talents. But Piketty is not impressed. Instead, he treats Pareto as an insignificant eccentric, as if the power law was an obscure mathematical construct of no importance compared to his own laws of capitalism, and as if it were mostly just curious that Pareto had such a strange fascination with it. And Piketty ignores entirely the modern network science field, which, given his interest in inequality, and the science's focus on *rich get richer*, I found strange.

Another Piketty belief worth mentioning again at this point is his faith in democratic debate to decide how we should address inequality with progressive taxes and similar policies. The reader already knows that I am skeptical of democratic debate, and it appears that Pareto was, too.

In his later years Pareto shifted from economics to sociology in response to his own change in belief about how humans act. He came to believe that men act nonlogically, "but they make believe they are acting logically." [lxxviii]

I do agree with Piketty that horrible things are coming as a result of inequality. But while he sees the need for redistribution to head off the violence and conflict that inequality will otherwise cause, I do not see any possibility of democratic debate being able to resolve inequality, either through redistributive taxes or anything else, such as SEC policy. In fact, such debate is what we are effectively engaged in now, and it is producing only increasing anger and frustration, as well as some violence. Rather, I believe that restoring a tolerance of inequality, which I see as the essence of the unalienable rights embedded in the founding of America, is the only way to deal with inequality short of the conflict and more serious violence that may ensue if nothing is done. It's not that our founders knew what would happen if freedom were followed as our guiding principle -- quite the opposite. But they had faith in that principle nonetheless, and would never have thrown freedom overboard for a promise of redistribution or anything else that merely sounded good, like efficiency, fairness, level playing fields, low trading costs, or fear of a dead weight loss.

But the lack of equal opportunity today convinces many that, whatever the founders had in mind, some government help is in order now because things aren't working out as the founders hoped. Thomas Byrne Edsall highlights what he considers a new and welcome willingness of even Republicans to recognize inequality and its roots, as he approvingly quotes a new analysis by Michael Gerson and Peter Wehner:

> Many conservatives fail to see the extent to which equal opportunity, a central principle of our national self-understanding, is becoming harder to achieve. It is a well-documented fact that, in recent years, economic mobility has stalled for many poorer Americans, resulting in persistent intergenerational inequality. [lxxix]

Equality before the law is not enough, these people say, unless it produces equal opportunity, too, as demonstrated by mobility.

The founders would not have made this mistake. The freedom to form an association or club automatically involves the freedom to block others from joining your club, thereby deliberately blocking their mobility and some of their opportunities, as shown by the history of the formation of the New York Stock Exchange, where the very purpose of exercising such rights could be, and in fact was in the NYSE's case, to produce inequality. Those who think our national self-understanding included equal opportunity or mobility or equality of anything other than our unalienable rights are simply confusing the nineteenth century and the twentieth century. While it is true that leaders like the Roosevelts did usher in a vision like the one these Republicans and Edsall prefer to remember, it had nothing to do with the original vision of the founders of America.

Attempts by government to address inequality with pro-active redistribution programs like the SEC's National Market System and other affirmative actions to help discriminated-against or excluded groups can only destroy both true opportunity and mobility, because such policies destroy the economy's ability to produce jobs, as the SEC's NMS has done. *This* is what has resulted in the "well-documented fact that, in recent years, economic mobility has stalled for many poorer Americans." Unfortunately, the kinds of redistributionist policies these Republicans and Edsall would favor are at least close cousins of the very SEC policies that have caused the mobility and opportunity problems they describe. Such policies are the opposite of those that were in place as the prosperity created by the New York Stock Exchange was launched, which enriched Americans of all classes for most of two centuries.

Three quarters of a century before Karl Marx's *Communist Manifesto*, the founders had already thought up the antidote to his tempting interventions: the freedom to pursue self-interest, i.e., the freedom to try to be unequally better off than others if you could pull it off. Our only real chance to head off the horrors now is to blow off the redistributionists, from Marx to Sherman to Piketty, and to reinsert the tolerance for inequality that America's founding gave to humanity -- at least for a while.

Dislodging settled reputations is not an easy thing to do. Thus it seems that Marx will remain the Father of Socialism and Communism, and Mussolini will retain his title as the Father of Fascism. TR will have to settle for Trustbuster with a Big Stick. Pareto, too, will probably keep his principles, distributions, coefficients, laws and rules, even though he might have been more worried by the end of his life about where humanity was headed than about mathematics or economics. Piketty will probably be remembered for his fascinating but morally misguided writing, as is Marx, at least by those who recognize his guidance behind the millions of deaths perpetrated by demagogues in the name of Marxist theories in the twentieth century, or who can see that the basic principle underlying Marxism is theft.

7. Whistleblowers Everywhere

In Jonathan Haidt's seminal 2012 work, *The Righteous Mind: Why Good People are Divided by Politics and Religion*, we learn that all of us are, or act as if we are, self-righteous mini-politicians trying to appear good or admirable to our presumed audience of friends, family, co-workers and the public generally, as if we wanted them to vote for us in an election. The positions we adopt are less the result of the dispassionate analysis we think they are, and more the result of the pattern of opinion we perceive would be popular at the moment as justifications for the actions and positions we take without thinking. Seeing how this "pattern matching" works, according to Haidt, can help you understand "how illogical people become when they disagree with you." [lxxx] It can also help explain what Pareto meant above when he said men act nonlogically, "but they make believe that they are acting logically." They are just being instinctive pattern matchers rather than rational analyzers. But what pattern are they attempting to match?

As I first described in *Dark Pool Comment Letter* and mentioned above, I had a unique vantage point from which to observe theoretical errors in market structure debates because of the technical difference between the fixed time trading of a single price auction and the continuous trading of normal markets. [lxxxi] I discovered that many of those I was arguing with held the view that electronic trading per se would cause the trading costs of intermediation (i.e., those costs occasioned when professional Wall Street traders interpose themselves profitably between public buyers and sellers) to disappear. I tangled with this view because, as I argued, while it was possible for such trading costs to disappear in a perfectly designed single price auction operating at fixed times, it was not possible -- theoretically or in practice -- for them to disappear in any form of continuous trading. To me, this was important. To many of my opponents, it was irrelevant. To me, this was critical to understanding why the single price auction was an improvement on current continuous trading practice. But my opponents didn't care. Although in my mind the debate was over fixed time versus continuous trading, in their minds it was over electronic versus non-electronic trading. Since they believed that electronic trading would in and of itself remove all trading costs, they dismissed my arguments out of hand as moot, since they believed that, once the SEC had finished mandating its electronic trading reforms, trading would be free anyway. In other words, since The Millennium was coming soon anyway, why worry anymore about such details as continuous versus fixed time trading?

I thought then and still do that it is not possible to eliminate the trading costs of intermediation in any form of continuous trading. I believe this is demonstrable both in theory (because as time passes, even in milliseconds or microseconds, there will always be some who are faster than others to the good trades) and in practice (as the empirical fact of continuing, if only very small, profits to HFTs shows). So although this was an open and shut case in my view, with virtually a priori proof on a theoretical level, and plenty of empirical proof in the form of intermediaries' profits even before the advent of HFTs, many of my debating opponents didn't see it that way. Since all of us debaters at least pretended that we were arguing primarily or solely as far as this issue was concerned on theoretical or empirical grounds only, the fact that many very capable, intelligent, rational and otherwise open-minded people would nonetheless stubbornly stick to what appeared to me to be incorrect theoretical or empirical positions was what triggered my realization that something other than rational debate was going on.

The pattern they were matching was, in one dimension at least, the popular belief that trading could and should be free of intermediation, i.e., free of Wall Street's traders' ability to make a profit, a belief cultivated since the 1960s in SEC and academic studies and hearings and rules like NMS, the preamble for which called for "an opportunity, consistent with the provisions of clauses (i) and (iv) of this subparagraph, for investors' orders to be executed without the participation of a dealer." [lxxxii] But this was really too complex a background to be used for pattern matching, which must be quick and instinctive, and the above debating history occasioned by my single price auction experience illustrates that quick and instinctive it was not. Electronic trading was the best-sounding rationale they could come up with for this incorrect view, in spite of the fact that continuous trading theory then and HFT experience today, prove that intermediation is bound to remain a fact of life in continuous trading, regardless of how electronic it was. But because this view reflected the popular SEC and academic views of the time that trading on screens would automatically let buyers naturally meet sellers without intermediation, they went with it. This was a good example of pattern matching: kneejerk opinion first, flimsy rationale second. But why was it so readily available? What was the bigger, readily match-able pattern that led so easily to this conclusion? Although I didn't think of this at the time, in recent years I recognized the pattern.

These were whistleblowers.

While few of them would have formally identified themselves as such, at least not back then, the overwhelming tenor of the debate and the participants' positioning of themselves in it was that of people who wanted to be perceived as knowledgeable practitioners who were able, by virtue of their expertise, to inform the public and regulatory authorities of the evil deeds going on behind the scenes on Wall Street, and who could credibly advocate for rules that would effectively reform such practices so they would no longer occur, and/or would punish the evildoers.

Haim Bodek is the most visible recent example of a market structure whistleblower, and one who proudly claims the label. In a series of interviews in the Wall Street Journal and articles on TabbFORUM, and in books both by and about him, such as the previously mentioned *Dark Pools*, by Scott Patterson, Bodek has hammered on the evils of high frequency trading and how some HFTs are in cahoots with exchanges and the investment banks who own them to mislead investors and other traders with their complicated order types so they can take advantage of them. Bodek has accordingly demanded that the SEC engage in various reforms to level the playing field between HFTs and non-HFT investors, and he has provided massive detail on what to do about the problem. Bodek himself is a former HFT who implies now that he has given up the riches he might have made with his expertise in order to become a whistleblower advocating reforms to improve the markets for others by pointing out how they are "rigged." [lxxxiii] The details of his recommendations are voluminous and complex and quite interesting if you have the time (and mostly available on TabbFORUM), but irrelevant to the points I want to make.

Scott Patterson openly embraces Bodek's cause in *Dark Pools* and makes similar points in his coverage of other people throughout the book, which puts him into the same whistleblower category. Patterson and Bodek form the same basic pattern that Michael Lewis and his own self-sacrificing hero, Brad Katsuyama, form as joint whistleblowers in the much more famous *Flash Boys* book by Lewis, as well as in the 60 Minutes episodes highlighting the book's release, which first brought to the general public's attention the charges by all of these whistleblowers that the U.S. stock market is "rigged." And 60 Minutes is not alone, as almost all of the news media appear to be in sync with the whistle-blowing ethos, both in their presentation of the stories and in their editorial positions. The overwhelming undercurrent of the story is that there is something very rotten on Wall Street, that it's called or at least has something to do with HFT, and that the SEC had better get on the case before investor confidence disappears entirely.

In terms of pattern matching and whistle-blowing as an example of it, this is a pattern as old as the SEC's eighty years, during which it has always been the SEC's mission to investigate and reform the rottenness on Wall Street before investor confidence disappears entirely. So the apex or target of all this whistle-blowing is the SEC, as well as other regulators, such as the Justice Department, the FBI and the New York attorney general's office, which are all now aggressively elbowing to get in on the SEC's act. But while each whistleblower tries to make his revelations sound new, they seldom are. In fact, I can't think of a single one that was not common knowledge at least among sophisticated practitioners. Not that they don't make interesting reading or point out real, if tiny in their effect, infractions. The reality nonetheless is that investors have never had it so good. Individual investors and even, with only slightly more effort, institutional investors, can easily bring their trading costs down to negligible using only simple market orders, the most standard and easiest to use order type there is. It is simply not true, as alleged or implied by all the whistleblowers -- and by the SEC and other regulators -- that investors are being harmed by HFT.

The important point here is that democratic debate is somewhere between counterproductive and useless. For all the whistle-blowing and market structure hearings, seminars, white papers, roundtables, rule filings, concept releases and comment periods initiated by the SEC in the Federal Register, and in on-line forums such as attend every article and editorial in newspapers like the Wall Street Journal and New York Times, and on TabbFORUM, there is still no chance whatsoever that market structure will improve as a result of it. Evidence that any minds are ever changed by the discussions is virtually nonexistent, and in any case there has never been any sign that the general trend toward market destruction has ever been arrested or even slowed down as a result of them.

Furthermore, the recent ratcheting up of the stakes, as federal and state attorneys general have filed criminal charges that threaten jail time for trivial infractions such as spoofing, will only further accelerate the market destruction, because it is the very impression that all this whistle-blowing is projecting that is undermining investor confidence by convincing investors that Wall Street is, indeed, rotten. While HFT versus HFT spoofing may look under the microscope like fraud, front running, manipulation, lack of transparency and several other dastardly deeds, how is preventing one HFT computer from fooling another HFT computer going to convince a retail investor that he is safe? [lxxxiv] And if it won't, how is highlighting this previously unknown problem going to improve confidence?

The reason we are so off track is obvious, if we combine the lessons learned in Robert Bork's and Jonathan Haidt's books, as well as Pareto's insight. It is that the discussants -- from the whistleblowers and market structure experts right up through the regulators and prosecutors -- are not truly able to discuss or see things rationally, because they are essentially bound by their tribal or religious beliefs on the matters under discussion, to borrow Haidt's terminology. Although they think they are engaged in rational investigations and analysis, they are really not. Instead they are driven by pattern matching instincts to form opinions against a backdrop of confused and conflicting per se beliefs that lock them in to one view or the other based primarily, but in hidden ways, on the redistribution effects of the issue.

Thus even the most complicated and esoteric questions, from maker-taker rebates, payment for order flow, and Hide Not Slide order types and the details of the Tick Pilot or spoofing in the stock market, to Harberger triangles in antitrust and first mover advantages in network industries, are affected by the magnetic pull of the redistribution effects of the structure or theory or infraction in question. The participants probably don't know or understand this and certainly don't explicitly acknowledge it, which is part of the reason why debate is confused at best, as Bork pointed out in the beginning of *Paradox* and Haidt provides a theoretical framework for understanding. We think we know what we are talking about and what our premises are and where they came from, but we really don't. So we swerve back and forth on the redistribution landscape with arguments meant to impress, but in reality full of sound and fury, signifying nothing.

And "we" includes almost everyone. On the upper end of the sophistication scale, there are pundits, Nobel Prize winners and billionaires. On the lower end are retail investors and even many who are too poor to own stocks at all, but have heard the market is "rigged" and is somehow harming them. They are all sure the market structure has run amok [lxxxv] and the SEC should conduct a holistic review of market structure and do something about it. For the SEC, this is all good news. The holistic review and the Tick Pilot are just two among dozens of ongoing justifications for continuing its comprehensive investigation into how to change market structure for the better.

8. The Last Word

Debates over market structure had nothing to do with how stock exchanges formed in the first place. Pursuing better markets was not part of the process. Pursuing inequality was. For the founders of Wall Street, that meant making money through antitrust violations. Fortunately, there were no antitrust laws then. And there was certainly no SEC. Nor were there any rules against front running, insider trading, manipulation or price fixing, whether of commissions or spreads or ticks or anything else, or conspiring with one or more other people to do any of these things.

A remarkable book called *Wall Street*, published posthumously in 1991 five years after the death of its principal author, tells this whole story through meticulous research and references all the materials that one would need to be familiar with to definitively reach the above conclusion, namely that markets did indeed form essentially around the opportunity to engage in what would later be antitrust violations. Authors Walter Werner, a professor of corporation law at Columbia University Law School, and his law student, research assistant and co-author, Steven T. Smith, set the matter to rest, in my opinion, confirming an intuition I had formed at least by 1997. [lxxxvi] But until I read *Wall Street* in 2013, I didn't have any solid evidence to back up my intuition. The fact that it was possible through reverse engineering from the characteristics of today's "membership organization" to reach the probable conclusion that these stock exchange structures that had formed long ago were *actual* violations (or would have been if antitrust had been around back then) did not by itself prove the case. It only provided strong circumstantial evidence for it. But *Wall Street* proves the case beyond any reasonable doubt.

It is possible, however, to miss the rather technical and understated evidence on antitrust violations in the book amidst an even bigger blockbuster claim that Werner highlighted over and over, namely that speculation was the key not only to Wall Street's success as a business, but also to the effectiveness of its critical capital allocation role. As the Foreword written in 1990 by Werner's widow says in a touching parenthetical anecdote,

> Walter was to conclude that "speculation," as a memo scrawled on a yellow pad a week before he died, says, "is the essential native genius of Wall Street." [lxxxvii]

This statement, presumably his last word on the subject, was significant because it implies a direct conflict with federal regulatory policy, which from the outset was designed to restrain speculation. Among other histories of the era that covered this ground is one published in 1975 by none other than Walter Werner: *Adventure in Social Control of Finance: The National Market System for Securities.*

> The Exchange Act, in the President's words, was also intended to implement a "national policy to restrict, as far as possible, the use of . . . exchanges for purely speculative purposes. Senator Fletcher, who introduced the bill in the

Senate, declared that the law was "made necessary by the needs of the entire American public that the operation of securities exchanges shall never again intensify . . . or help precipitate a business depression," and the law's purpose was "to make the stock markets places for investors and not places of resort for those who would speculate or gamble." [lxxxviii]

Werner was eminently qualified to write such histories. Before being a law professor, he was a Director of Policy Research at the SEC who worked on the SEC's Special Study Report in the early 1960s, which set the stage both for the National Market System (NMS) and for the abolition of fixed commission rates. Prodded by Werner and others on such issues, and particularly on the need to end fixed commissions, which Werner was reportedly the first to raise at the Commission, [lxxxix] the SEC gradually became primarily an antitrust enforcer focused on market structure reform, but with a continuing anti-speculation mission styled as investor protection. And Werner was clearly familiar with the origins of stock exchange structure and the conflict with antitrust long before he wrote *Wall Street*, as evident in another passage from that 1975 paper describing the membership organization's similarity to "other private clubs."

> The association determined both the limit on the number of memberships or "seats" and qualifications of members. It could summarily reject--and often did--applications of brokers possessing the highest character and business qualifications. There was no right of appeal. Actions of the association, like those of other private clubs, were final. Such arrangements among other businessmen would later be classed as illegal price-fixing agreements and boycotts. The nation's securities markets grew up, however, virtually free from government restraint of every kind, including antitrust laws. No one, including brokers barred from association membership, questioned the right of self-selected securities businessmen to organize their associations, to operate their exchanges as they saw fit, to agree on uniform commission rates that each would charge for his services, to choose the persons they desired to join their associations, and to exclude others on any basis they saw fit. These practices were universally accepted as within the rules of the game. [xc]

Such passages indicate that Werner was clearly aware of the strange circumstance that we have now banned practices that were freely allowed when markets formed, and that would seem to have been most critical to market formation. Werner did not, however, either in that 1975 paper or in *Wall Street*, explicitly reach my conclusion that the conflict between antitrust and stock exchanges means that it is antitrust that is misguided, not stock exchanges. In fact, his earlier writings, as well as the views he reportedly held while at the SEC, suggest he may very well have been completely at odds with my conclusion. Nonetheless, the facts Werner unearths in *Wall Street* leave no doubt that antitrust is poison to market formation and to capital formation, an ineluctable conclusion compelled by Werner's history which drew credibility at least partly in my view from his apparent reluctance to reach it. By the end of his life his policy views, his legal views, his market structure views, etc., all appear to have given way to his obsession with getting the history right. This, he appears to have done, as confirmed implicitly by the absence of any challenges on that front from even his most fervent critics.

Walter Werner was, as mentioned, perhaps the first person at the SEC to suggest ending fixed commissions. And his work on the two-year, six-volume Special Study Report, delivered in the fall of 1963, which set the stage both for ending fixed commissions and for NMS, would indicate he was anything but antagonistic to antitrust. Indeed there are many other examples of his writing and thinking after leaving the SEC, such as the 1975 paper referenced above, that indicate he was always pushing the SEC to take more aggressive action, not less, to reform the markets along antitrust lines.

So I will endeavor to make clear that what I am saying is not necessarily what Werner, or Werner and Smith, have said. The two issues that matter to me are speculation and antitrust. In my opinion, markets must be free of regulation of either speculation or antitrust, as they were at the time of their founding, which *Wall Street* clearly demonstrates. But since the case in *Wall Street* is made primarily or solely by just telling the unvarnished ancient history of market formation, it is less clear what the authors think about the policy implications of their findings. Indeed, there are certain passages toward the end of *Wall Street* that seem to accept on the face value of conventional wisdom that regulation has been a net positive for markets.

> For almost 150 years, United States securities markets were virtually unregulated, and now extensive modern laws, regulations, and administrators are involved in smoothing securities trading. A close look at these regulations, however, reveals that their purpose and effect is to strengthen securities markets by improving investor confidence. [xci]

As to antitrust, it is not even clear what the authors think about the absence of antitrust at the time of the founding of markets, much less what implication they might draw from that absence then for policy today. There is, for example, no comment about monopolization being the "native genius" of Wall Street, or anything similar, although I believe their history could have as easily led to that conclusion as it did regarding speculation.

Nonetheless, I will also make clear that my arguments do not depend at all on Werner's, or Werner and Smith's, opinions on these issues, or anyone else's, for that matter. My arguments depend solely on the history their research reveals being correct. Their opinions on policy, then or now, do not matter to my case. As long as *Wall Street* is a correct portrayal of history, the conclusions I draw from that portrayal will stand.

Wall Street focuses primarily, indeed almost exclusively, on the period from 1790 to 1840, digging into the details of how the markets actually formed, and letting the facts speak for themselves. Amazingly, this had not been done before with anything like the attention to detail or persistence that Walter Werner brought to the task in the last decade of his life. This enabled him to come up with original and overlooked materials that required reconsideration of several old myths about the period. Interestingly from my perspective, the myths tended to have the effect of covering over the importance of speculation and monopolization at the market's founding. Werner's use of the new evidence to bust these myths, therefore, had the effect of revealing and restoring the truth, which is that speculation and monopolization were critical to the founding of the markets.

Although I go in the direction of questioning antitrust with that information, it is also possible to go in the opposite direction, which Werner seems to have done, at least in his earlier days. In the 1975 paper, for example, he highlighted the harm to investors that resulted from the SEC's failure to regulate fixed commissions.

> Investors were directly harmed. SEC failure to supervise exchange commission rates and the odd lot differential resulted in excessive public costs for transferring ownership of securities. The cost was enormous on any scale, whether measured against earlier rates, profitability of the securities commission business, price of an exchange seat, compensation of registered representatives, portion of nominal commission retained after directed give-ups or the savings investors have realized from negotiated rates. A prominent economist has suggested that fixed minimum commission rates cost investors more than all the benefits conferred on them by the SEC. [xcii]

But while he was consistently on a conventional consumer welfare mission in his writings prior to *Wall Street*, and was unrelenting in his explicit criticisms of SEC failures to engage in market structure regulation on the investor's behalf, Werner's final work was different. *Wall Street* only obliquely references the errors of modern regulation, and mostly only by implication in a few footnotes that support its myth busting. For example, one of the myths that Werner and Smith bust is that early public corporations did not need or benefit from securities trading markets.

> Too many corporate historians have misread the significance of early securities markets in the maturation of the corporation. Some have focused on corporations and treated early securities markets as institutions that have affected them, but not greatly. Others have denigrated early securities markets because of their large speculative components. [xciii]

Why have historians missed the importance of trading markets and, especially, of speculative trading markets, to early American corporations? Because, as we learn in a footnote to the above passage, they may share the common wisdom against speculation underlying laws such as the Securities Exchange Act of 1934 that created the SEC.

> 11. For example, a description of the early investment market in securities can be found in Margaret Myers, *The New York Money Market.* 1:10-16. Myers' description is skewed insofar as it downplays the central importance of the speculative influence. Myers' views were in step with views of securities market functions current at the time of her work. The gambling variety of speculation was discouraged, and Congress attempted to outlaw "unnecessary, unwise and destructive" speculation in the Securities Exchange Act of 1934." [xciv]

Thus *Wall Street* was different in several ways from Werner's earlier writing, and potentially represented a change in his thinking. It was different, as mentioned, because of the almost complete absence of the unrelenting explicit criticisms of the SEC for failing to engage in market structure regulation. Such criticisms were the hallmark of his previous writing and included, as in the above example demonstrating investor harm from fixed commissions, Werner's charge that the SEC had failed to oversee fixed commissions, which, in his view, it was supposed to do, and which it later claimed, incorrectly according to Werner, it had been doing, as it swung simultaneously into justifications for both abolishing fixed commissions and for launching the National Market System, an impetuous response in which "inaction swiftly became over-reaction." [xcv] Secondly, because even the implicit and softer criticisms that remain in *Wall Street* were in support of the myth busting, they pushed in the opposite direction of the earlier explicit criticisms. That is, they pushed away from an embrace of antitrust, rather than toward it.

But probably the best evidence of a potential change in Werner's thinking is his use of the term, "native genius," which, as mentioned, appeared in the handwritten note on the yellow pad written a week before he died. In his earlier writings the term was always used with sarcasm, although then it was "natural genius," not "native genius," while in *Wall Street* it was heartfelt and genuine, as it was on that yellow pad. The term apparently originated with Congress at the SEC's suggestion, as described in the SEC's 1936 Report on Trading in Unlisted Securities Upon Exchanges. As Werner discussed the situation with all due sarcasm in another paper, published in 1984:

> In 1936 the agency submitted a detailed report recommending that unlisted trading be confined to issues satisfying new statutory criteria for a "properly functioning" exchange market. Congress amended section 12(f) of the Exchange Act to provide for these criteria and stated national policy with respect to the structure of trading markets. That policy, which remained the norm for thirty-five years, was "to create a fair field of competition among exchanges and between exchanges as a group and the over-the-counter markets and to allow each type of market to develop in accordance with its natural genius and consistently with the public interest." The policy failed to point out, however, that a major attribute of the NYSE's "natural genius" was its anticompetitive restraints, and the "natural genius" of the regional exchanges was their ability to provide members with a method for avoiding NYSE restraints. [xcvi]

The foibles and misdirections set in motion by the passage figure in the repeatedly-referenced "multiple trading" embarrassment of the SEC in its first foray into market structure regulation in which the SEC adopts and then rescinds a policy meant to preserve and foster competition by regional stock exchanges when the SEC discovers to its horror that, instead of saving the regionals, its policy would have put them out of business. The regionals, it appeared, had no "natural genius" to work with, since they could not exist without the NYSE's price discovery and thus could not meet the Commission's new test inspired by the "natural genius" passage of being "properly functioning" markets. Thus, the Commission would have been forced buy its own new policy meant to support the regionals and highlight their "natural genius" for competition -- to withdraw their licenses to operate. As to the NYSE, its "natural genius" was simple and direct, which was to thumb its nose at federal competition policy. This whole embarrassing "multiple-trading" experience, according to Werner, was what caused the SEC to shy away from its responsibility to be a market structure regulator all the way up to 1975, and then, as mentioned, caused it to tumble impetuously into simultaneously ending fixed commissions and launching NMS, a responsibility for which, according to Werner, it was unprepared. And worst of all, according to Werner, NMS was a policy that was probably not even necessary once fixed commissions were ended. In any case, Werner had many good reasons to use "natural genius" sarcastically and appears to have always done so in his writing prior to *Wall Street*.

But the use of the term, or its slightly changed derivative, "native genius," in *Wall Street* is for the first time sincere and not sarcastic. By extolling the role of speculation in capital formation, and by identifying the embrace of that role by Wall Street as the secret to its success, Werner appears to have finally found a version of competition and a use of "native genius" that he is comfortable with. The natural or native genius Werner is referring to this time is not in praise of any scheme of antitrust-style, multi-party competition mandated by Congress or the SEC, but rather to its opposite, a dominant new NYSE built on "unrestrained speculation."

> One crucial characteristic of these early New York securities markets was that while customers of all stripes and predispositions bought and sold securities, the trading market was dominated by speculators. The markets might have evolved differently if the NYS&EB [the New York Stock & Exchange Board, the original name of the NYSE] had fallen under the control of older, conservative members who discouraged time bargains, or if the New York legislature had insisted on "reform," but by 1840 there was no turning back. At that point, the New York securities market had realized its ultimate native genius: its capacity for unrestrained speculation. [xcvii]

I must emphasize again that it does not matter to the case I make against antitrust whether Werner changed his mind on the issue or not. The only thing that matters is whether he is correct on the history of Wall Street, as I believe he is. While I am not a historian, Walter Werner, by the end of his life, certainly was, and by all accounts of the first order. Even people who disagree vehemently with his implied policy recommendations for today have yet to take issue with any aspect of his historical accuracy.

One typical review of *Wall Street* was highly respectful of Werner as a researcher and historian, but clung to the conventional wisdom, un-persuaded by what the reviewer took to be Werner's policy implications. Louis Lowenstein, a colleague of Werner's at the Columbia University School of Law, cuts to the chase in the title of his book review: *Is Speculation "The Essential Native Genius of the Stock Market"?* [xcviii] Lowenstein is skeptical, as implied by the title, which free rides fully on conventional anti-speculation wisdom as it implies that Werner is driven by an eccentric, perhaps off-the-wall conclusion. By the end of the review in support of this conventional wisdom, Lowenstein provides elaborate multiple-page analyses of why the particular nature of securities requires heavy regulation to protect against the abuses that are so clearly revealed in Werner's history.

Nonetheless, Lowenstein admired Werner as a former colleague and finds much to praise in *Wall Street* as history.

> Werner was a historian and this book is the product of roughly a decade's research. The development of Wall Street in its early days had for years been his primary professional interest. Werner died before the book could be finished, and Smith, a student who had helped with the work, saw it to conclusion after graduation. Smith obviously brought much to the finished product, but it does not diminish his contribution in the least to note that Werner's was the dominant influence.

Moving on the to the nub:

> Werner would not have tried to reform the stock market in 1790, and he held fast to these same laissez-faire views almost 200 years later.

This statement interestingly leaves out Werner's decidedly non-laissez-faire crusade to reform the stock market while at the SEC in the 1960s, and his persistent advocacy of such reforms in his written works at least up until the appearance of *Wall Street*. It is possible, of course, that Lowenstein was unaware of Werner's previous history and work. But in any case his review quickly runs into a much bigger problem when Lowenstein launches a lengthy argument with Werner over something called the "inherence thesis."

> The thesis of *Wall Street*, called the "inherence thesis," is that a stock market on some meaningful level, and speculation, have been with us from the beginning. True, the authors say, there are short-lived price distortions, but "intelligent speculators" sooner or later bring prices back into line. Those who from time to time would reform the stock market need to look at the process as a whole, not just the injuries occasionally inflicted on a gullible if otherwise innocent public. The authors' affection and respect for the stock market, even its excesses, are consistent with the neoclassical economics so much in fashion at the present time.

> The problem with this line of attack is that the inherence thesis *Wall Street* talks about has nothing to do with "short-lived price distortions" or bringing "prices back into line." While the implications of the history revealed in the book might sound consistent with such a thesis, it seems that Lowenstein missed Werner's real meaning of "inherence." We'll come back to that in a minute. But note first how Lowenstein draws immediate implications for current regulation based on his own views on speculation, volatility and such fundamental values as "income streams."

> There are, however, a growing number of skeptics, this reviewer included, for the Werner and Smith analysis would be too simple by half. What is there about stocks that attracts so much speculative interest? Why are stock prices so volatile, much more so than the underlying income streams they are supposed to represent, as Werner and Smith themselves recognize? Even in the 1790s, the press and the public were critical of the trading frenzy that

from time to time afflicts the nation. And for more than half a century now, the federal government has regulated the trading of stocks much more closely than real estate and other assets. The authors fail to demonstrate why we must regard the stock market as existing in some Thoreau-like state of nature, and if not, how much intervention is desirable. My own answer to these questions would not be so free-market as Werner and Smith's, but it is difficult to fully engage the debate because they ask us to accept their conclusion on faith, relying solely on history. What was, or even is, must be. One should not do that without first exploring the nature of the stock market, and trying to see why it is that the market is now, and, as Werner and Smith document so well, has always been, a hotbed of manic-depressive pricing, manipulation and outright fraud. Only by examining the important differences between stocks and tangible commodities can we address the question of whither, if at all, we might go with regulation.

There is no question whither Lowenstein wants to go with regulation.

The issues are particularly important today [the review came out in January, 1992, just after *Wall Street* was published], as financial markets go global. We in the United States, with our much better developed system of securities regulation, will need to convince our major trading partners of its desirability, or else face a race to the bottom in which either financial markets gravitate elsewhere or our own set of rules are seriously diluted. The conventional economic theory is that in a well-functioning market, speculation provides protection from risk for those who need to hedge and helps the "real" buyers and sellers by smoothing price fluctuations. It is, therefore, a good thing. A combination of four distinct factors, however, make the stock market quite unlike any other.

Lowenstein then goes on for many pages laying out his own thesis on why stocks are different and require, therefore, more regulation. Whether he is right or not, his passion for his own regulatory theories appears to have caused Lowenstein to miss the main implication of Werner's history. Not only was the stock market not something that has "been with us from the beginning," as Lowenstein incorrectly says Werner claimed, the American market was new and different, a unique wealth-generating engine that came into existence for the first time during the unbridled, unregulated, laissez-faire century that was Werner's sole focus in *Wall Street*.

While Werner, Smith, Lowenstein and others, including me, might have different views on what should be done now as policy matters, none of us can any longer escape the facts of history that Werner laid out, and are so at odds with the conventional wisdom on regulation "today," whether in 1992 or 2015. Even Lowenstein, who embraces that conventional wisdom fully, is hard pressed to find fault with the book as research and history.

The weakness of *Wall Street* is that we are asked to accept the authors' laissez-faire views on faith. On the other hand, the considerable strength of the book is that their "inherence thesis" can be regarded as peripheral. Werner and Smith have fashioned a very readable account of the early years of the stock market. The book focuses on the 50-year period from 1790-1840, and reflects a simply stunning amount of research in the periodical and other literature of the day. Werner poured over correspondence at the New York Historical Society and issue after issue of the *New York Daily Advertiser*, the *Daily Gazette*, and the *New York Courier*. The result is impressive. Speculation, Werner and Smith contend, "has [now] come of age . . . and is as legitimate and necessary as the securities markets themselves" (pp. 77-78). While I would draw a different conclusion, *Wall Street* is a wonderfully detailed and interesting history of the early days. For those with an eye to the past, it is well worth the voyage.

Although Werner and Smith do make clear that the markets of today and the markets of old were always full of bubbles, frauds and crashes, they do not dwell on what modern regulators should or should not be doing about it, other than by saying, mostly through the unstated implication of their history, that they probably shouldn't be so worried about such things. We always recovered fine and grew very fast even when there were no regulators, invariably rising higher in booms than we lost in busts.

> Typically, following a cyclical upswing and crash, securities markets are left in a stronger position than before the upswing. They take two steps forward, one step backward. As Stedman observed in 1905: "Each succeeding era of speculative enthusiasm will leave after its recession the values of honest securities higher than they lay where the preceding wave had flowed and ebbed." [xcix]

It is legitimate, of course, to argue over what current policy should be. But now, after *Wall Street*, the argument must be framed differently. Before thinking about what policy should be today, we have to think first about what policy should have been back then. It may be that America's early days of market formation are only an interesting "voyage" for those with "an eye to the past," and it is now time to apply some serious adult regulation to what those misguided founders did. But we can no longer pretend that this would not be an about face of monumental proportions, a 180 degree change in ideological and practical terms. We can no longer pretend if we believe in the principles of modern regulation that whatever led to those old markets was not flat out wrong and misguided. If modern regulatory principles are sound, then applying them back then should have led to even better results, at least in theory. But if Werner and Smith are right about the history, then it is also true that if our markets then had been regulated as they are today, following the conventional wisdom of Lowenstein and almost everyone else, they would never have formed in the first place. *Wall Street* compels us to think about *that*.

If we think circumstances are different now and that the two eras call for different regulatory regimes, then we should just say so and say why. But Werner and Smith make no such claim, nor does Lowenstein. They do not say that either securities or securities markets or corporation finance or any other significant market structure factors are different now than when they began. In fact, they say the opposite:

United States corporate history demonstrates that the line of development from the corporate system of 1790 to today is direct and continuous." [c]

This view is repeated several times, and it is a contention that Lowenstein does not challenge. The authors argue that the continuous evolution of markets ruled out the so-called "erosion doctrine" [ci] that supposedly saw a loss of control by owners of corporations and a transition to manager control as corporations went from being privately financed to being publicly financed and traded on markets. This erosion doctrine was one of those speculation-denigrating and markets-denigrating myths that Werner and Smith bust in *Wall Street*.

Thriving securities markets, however, grew in tandem with the public corporations they served. These markets fostered the separation of ownership and control, which has existed as long as stock markets have existed, and which is *inherent* in corporations with publicly traded shares. [cii] [Emphasis added]

This is where the "inherence thesis" comes into play. It had nothing to do with whether or not speculation did or did not distort prices, or how long it took for "wrong" prices to correct, but rather was a theory of Werner's that showed the inevitably symbiotic relationship between public corporations and trading markets, a relationship that *Wall Street* demonstrates was continuous from the beginning of markets to today. The inherence thesis ruled out any view that modern securities or securities markets are different with respect to any important structural aspect of them, including any greater or lesser penchant for speculation or implied need for more or different regulation as a result. And it also ruled out any view that public corporations had existed before markets did, as historians had incorrectly imagined. One implication of this particular busted myth is very significant, which we will explore shortly.

Even Lowenstein does not contend that *markets* are different now compared to the past. He says that *securities* are different at all times because of their inherent volatility and, thus, "make the stock market quite unlike any other." Thus Lowenstein believes that stock markets should always be regulated heavily, not because they are different now, but because they are different, period. Therefore, merely putting our original markets in an irrelevant "voyage" to the past, as if they could have happily and productively been completely laissez-faire, while separately arguing that modern markets should be heavily regulated, does not answer or deal with the questions raised by Werner's history, even as it highlights, however accidentally, the importance of those questions. And the most important of those questions is this: If modern-style regulation would have prevented the formation of markets and the reaping of their value to corporations in need of capital back then, why should we not assume that it would have the same effect of killing capital formation now?

As it turns out, this is in fact the case, which we will explore in some detail in chapter 12. But a brief mention here of two examples will help frame the issues raised by Werner's history: the NASDAQ spread-fixing scandal and the Libor rate-fixing scandal. Both of these ushered in capital formation mini-monopolies that were effective re-energizations of the Wall Street monopoly that had been banned. And each of them is almost certainly responsible for billions if not trillions of dollars of value added to the world's wealth. Both of them snuck through by the luck or skill of monopolizers whose "rigging" was not noticed by regulators, for a time, anyway. The NASDAQ spread fixing and other antitrust violations created the high tech companies in the 1980s and 1990s that led to the American high tech advantage. And the Libor standardization of interest rate fixing enabled the acceptance of financial processes by millions of people, such as for buying houses, among many other things. Just as stock exchanges would not have existed at all were it not for the laissez-faire environment that enabled them to form, these are just two recent examples of other things we would be missing if regulators could always suppress a laissez-faire environment. How many companies like Microsoft, Intel, Apple and Amazon would not exist today if the NASDAQ dealer market had not existed? And how many families in homes now would not be in those homes if Libor fixes had not standardized and thereby facilitated borrowing for mortgages?

Werner's history presents this conundrum to us in stark terms. It says to the Lowensteins and other supporters of regulation: *Since nothing material has changed between then and now (as even Lowenstein does not dispute), if we should be regulating capital formation to death now, there is no reason that we should not have done so back then, too. If we had done that, there would never have been any markets in the first place.*

The only way to answer this challenge from the Werner history is to confront directly, not how markets should be regulated today (although that may be an end result), but how we believe they should have been regulated back then. Unless regulators and their defenders can present a theory of how they would have created capital value equal to that created by the NYSE between 1790 and 1890, say, or NASDAQ between 1980 and 2000, or all the economic betterment based on Libor fixes, gold fixes, silver fixes, currency fixes, swap fixes, etc., we are left with laissez-faire as the only possible means to allow such market formation benefits to materialize. Werner's history compels us to think not just of the scandals, the booms, the busts and messy parts, but also of the value that was created anyway. Unless the regulators can show not only how they would have saved us from the messy parts, but also how they would have created the value that came with them in spite of those messy parts, the regulators, in the light of Werner's history, can only be seen as net destroyers of value.

9. Big Bang

Werner and Smith do not dwell on the anticompetitive roots of exchange formation. They simply tell the story. Like the fact that only roughly half of the early securities trading community in New York at the time made the cut to get into this particular club. [ciii] Like the fact that certain documents, such as the Buttonwood Agreement of 1792, [civ] which the NYSE claims to be its founding document, but also a 1791 "broadside" [cv] (a single sheet, one-sided newspaper-like format popular for advertising opinions or events, and meant for public display on walls or posts), were clearly concerned with extracting oaths of loyalty to their conspiracy from signers. They were required to agree not only to abide by their price fixing agreements and to favor the other signers in their stock trading negotiations, but also to not trade with non-signers, effectively shunning them from direct access to the exchange.

It was the shunning aspect of this oath, the most anticompetitive of all the early exchange features, in my opinion, which, by requiring both the public and other professionals to go through exchange members, became the basis of the membership organization. Not only did this oath thus underlie the structure of the club known as the membership organization, which became the dominant form of exchange, it inspired by its very anticompetitive example all those subsequent self-made monopolies and trusts, which were all based on similar conspiracies to discriminate in favor those on the inside of the conspiracy and to discriminate against those on the outside of it. By requiring nonmembers to go through members, these anticompetitive oaths on Wall Street thus created the basis for great wealth for their members and the nation, wealth which lasted and grew magnificently, antitrust attacks notwithstanding, for a couple of centuries after they were sworn.

That the Buttonwood Agreement was a price fixing cartel was known by many who had heard of this strange agreement claimed by the NYSE as its founding document. But most people in modern times were probably more impressed by its old date than by any substance within it, an impression no doubt fostered by the NYSE's public relations people who were naturally more interested in being perceived as venerable than as anticompetitive. Prior to my own interest in antitrust, this was certainly the case with me. And even after I was familiar with antitrust and the cartel aspects of Buttonwood, I found that the overwhelming reaction to it if you brought it up (as I sometimes did) was something like, "Oh that: well, that was just a price fixing agreement," as if their "just" and their dismissive tone for "price fixing" relegated the Buttonwood Agreement to the insignificant status of an anachronistic throwback to a primitive time before the exchange knew any better. What was not understood until *Wall Street* described the surrounding social, as opposed to trading, issues, was that the formation of this particular club was far more deliberately exclusionary than people today fully grasped even if they did know it was a cartel. But in spite of the fact that the book has been available since 1991, few appear to have read or absorbed these points and, consequently, the market structure debate is still in 2015 as benighted on these issues as if the book had not been written.

The important point revealed if not explicitly made by *Wall Street* is that the history of the social environments in which these exchanges welled up in places like New York, Philadelphia and Boston, as well as a century earlier in London, demonstrates that *the primary impetus to exchange formation in all these cities was the opportunity to get rich by engaging in anticompetitive conspiracies.* It is obvious, by thought experiment, that if antitrust laws or the SEC or any of these other regulators had been around in the eighteenth or nineteenth century, the exchange that formed on Wall Street would never have happened, nor would any others have formed anywhere else.

Moreover, another aspect of the history is equally intriguing. The reason that New York beat the other contenders for being the dominant world market, such as London, Philadelphia and Boston was, in all likelihood, that New York was better at being anticompetitive than they were. It was in any case more explicit about the anticompetitive intent of its organizing, as implied by advertising the terms in broadsides and by proudly and openly signing the Buttonwood Agreement. And so strong were its membership commitments that the exchange was able to set up and enforce its own rules requiring, for example, the honoring of even the most speculative leveraged derivatives trades, even as the state of New York was trying to banish such trading (and perhaps shut the exchange) by barring use of the courts to enforce speculative contracts. The other cities with exchanges had tried this, too, but it seems that New York's exchange was better able to weather these Nanny State storms, probably, once again, because of the city's greater penchant for speculation, which would have given its members greater incentives to honor their anticompetitive oaths and rally 'round their exchange.

Or perhaps it was because they had revolution and freedom fresh on their minds. And Wall Street's connection to those events and sentiments may have been more significant than history has remembered. Boston and Philadelphia, of course, are better known than New York in American Revolution lore. But the first blood shed in the series of conflicts that became the Revolution was shed only a few blocks from Wall Street on January 19, 1770 in The Battle of Golden Hill. The dispute involved a "Liberty pole," such as

> the Sons of Liberty (or "Liberty Boys") in New York City sometimes erected . . . to symbolize their displeasure with British authorities . . . After the New York Assembly finally voted to comply with the Quartering Act in December 1769, Alexander McDougal issued an anonymous broadside entitled "To the Betrayed Inhabitants of the City and Colony of New York". In response, on January 17, 1770 British soldiers sawed down a Liberty pole. The "red coats" also posted their own handbills which attacked the Sons of Liberty as "the real enemies of society" who "thought their freedom depended on a piece of wood". On January 19, 1770, six weeks before the Boston Massacre, Isaac Sears and others tried to stop some soldiers from posting handbills. Sears captured some of the soldiers and marched his captives towards the mayor's office, while the rest of the British soldiers ran to the barracks to sound the

alarm. A crowd of townsfolk arrived along with a score of soldiers. The soldiers were surrounded and badly outnumbered. Another squad of soldiers arrived and the officer gave the order "Soldiers, draw your bayonets and cut your way through them." More soldiers and a group of officers arrived to disperse the soldiers before the situation got totally out of hand. Several of the soldiers were badly bruised and one had a serious wound. Some of the townsfolk were wounded and one had been fatally stabbed. [cvi]

Hostilities continued the next day.

A second eruption came the next day on Nassau Street, "when a large party of seamen, fed up with the loss of jobs to military personnel and vowing to revenge the death of a fellow Jack Tar the day before, came to blows with some soldiers. A month later Sears and the Sons of Liberty put up a fifth pole, another great mast (some 80 feet) carried down from an East River shipyard. Well sunk and ironclad at its base, this one survived until October 1776, cut down only after British forces regained Manhattan. [cvii]

Thus the battle of the broadsides started by Alexander McDougal was what set off the Golden Hill dispute. McDougal went on to serve as a "major general in the Continental Army, and as a delegate to the Continental Congress. After the war, he was president of the first bank in the state of New York and served a term in the New York State Senate." [cviii] After (or during) the Revolution, nearby King Street, a block south of Golden Hill and three blocks north of Wall Street, was renamed Liberty Street. [cix] And roughly at the same time or shortly thereafter, the brokers, dealers and auctioneers of Wall Street were trading under the Buttonwood Tree or in the Tontine coffee house, and issuing another broadside, this time advertising their intentions on exchange organization and their plans to meet "at the coffee house" to sign oaths evidencing them.

Whether steeled by patriot ardor or merely more clear than others on what freedom meant to them and how to defend it, New York apparently had a better ability than other cities to resist regulatory encroachments after the nation's first securities boom and bust. And of course their resolve, from whatever source, would be rewarded in proportion to the value of that "native genius" for speculation that Werner and Smith thought was unique to New York.

During the New York securities markets' formative years, significant markets also existed in Philadelphia, Boston, and to a lesser extent elsewhere. As early as the 1790-1792 boom and bust, securities prices varied among cities, and dealers surmounted significant transportation barriers in order to arbitrage. Already, however, it was New York that set the pace and the prices for the other markets to follow. The large volume of trades executed by speculators made New York the nation's leading trading market. [cx]

Werner and Smith wonder if it might have been Boston's "heritage of frugal Puritans" or Philadelphia's "Quakers, who eschewed gambling," [cxi] that may have hampered these cities in their competition with the more speculative New York traders. But regardless of the actual reason for New York's eventual domination of the global stock exchange competition, the fact is that New York did win this competition, which set in motion a number of very beneficial follow-on effects that enhanced New York's position even further. For example, New York became a magnet for trading activity to occur in New York derivatives, rather than in either the derivatives or their related underlying securities that may have originated or traded primarily elsewhere, thus making New York both *the* place to trade and, for that reason, *the* place to observe the latest prices. Most importantly, at least partly because of these advantages, New York also became *the* place to issue new securities.

> While Boston and Philadelphia securities markets kept their focus on local customers, New York's orientation became increasingly national. New York eventually became the place where issues could be sold to many investors, the place where funds of the multitudes with modest savings could be tapped. Both Philadelphia and Boston had their turn as wholesale markets, but they never developed significant retail markets where shares could be bought and sold. When the deep pockets in Boston and Philadelphia were emptied, all that was left were the savings of millions of small investors from across the country which were tied to Wall Street. At that point, New York became the center for issuers to raise funds as well as the premier trading market. [cxii]

In true network effect fashion (liquidity begets liquidity, as the saying goes), this snowballing interest in and focus on New York speculative trading thus had the effect of also centralizing capital formation in New York, a win that occurred in spite of the fact that New York was not the first mover in this contest. [cxiii] But it won because its penchant for speculation gave it the trading volume wherewithal to beat the other cities to the prize. And winning the nod as the nation's new issue market naturally flowed back into the attraction of its speculation-boosted trading market, enabling New York to win dominance in the secondary trading and primary issuance of the most attractive securities of the nineteenth century, such as railroads, even those that were "chartered and operating in other states." [cxiv]

Moreover, because of the need to borrow money to finance leveraged trading, New York's win at trading and new issue centralization also extended in further knock-on network effects to the concentration of money and banking in New York, as speculation on Wall Street drew money in from around the country.

> To finance the voluminous New York stock trading, a market developed for "call loans." Banks lent money repayable on demand, with securities as collateral. Demand for call money arose "almost wholly out of speculative transactions in securities." . . . Since extensive high-interest call loans helped New York banks to pay rates generally higher than those of other cities, funds flowed to the city. The source of these funds was twofold: 1) correspondent banks in rural areas, and 2) New York merchants who prospered from trade with the West. Speculation in the stock market and call loans fed upon each other: the stock market provided banks with borrowing customers holding liquid collateral and willing to pay high interest rates,

while the banks encouraged those customers to keep speculating by providing them with funds. Ultimately, a close relationship was forged between New York's chartered banks and the stock market. The growth of speculative activity in securities then directly affected the increasing importance of New York's banks. [cxv]

These concentration effects undoubtedly played a major role underwriting two centuries of American economic leadership on the world stage, an impossible to miss performance that is still yielding surprise benefits. Economist Eswar Prasad, for example, notes that the U.S. economy became the largest in the world by the 1870s, dominated global trade by the early 1900s, and these advantages eventually enabled the U.S. dollar to become the world's dominant currency, [cxvi] an advantage that gave the country an "exorbitant privilege" it still enjoys, much to the chagrin and jealousy of other nations that "have chafed" at the trade advantages this position confers on the United States that enable it to live beyond its means. [cxvii]

The super-centralization described by Werner and Smith was not only good for New York and the United States. It created, perhaps for the first time, a truly global capital market that, because of its concentration of global trading interest in one place was far more capable of raising capital and funding new enterprises than the more dispersed structures that preexisted it were. This may very well have created the basis for a rapid increase in business enterprises and technologies as railroad networks and other monopolizations led naturally to the industrial trusts of the robber barons, all of which corresponded with the increases in technology, productivity and living standards of what is sometimes called the "Second Industrial Revolution." [cxviii]

But what about the London Stock Exchange? And what about the actual Industrial Revolution? Although we do not have as clear a picture of how the LSE's membership organization began, there are enough glimpses of it in Werner's *Wall Street* and other sources to surmise that something very powerful and very new may have occurred there first, but along the same lines as what occurred roughly a century later in New York. If so, then London may in fact have been the real birthplace of modern stock exchanges. And the Industrial Revolution may not have begun just because it was time for some new manufacturing methods and machines to emerge, as is sometimes implied. Something very different occurred in early eighteenth century Britain, leading to what everyone now acknowledges was not just a garden-variety improvement in methods, but a *revolution*. But what set it off? Historians are not at all clear on the matter, as noted in chapter 2 in our discussion of Deirdre McCloskey's theory. Given how big a deal the Industrial Revolution was, it is strange that even now no one is sure what triggered it.

Perhaps looking back with the template of what happened in New York a century later as a guide, it is possible to piece together what happened in London and Britain, too. If London brokers and "stock-jobbers" felt as free as New Yorkers would a century later to service the speculating and gambling interest in securities trading of late-seventeenth century and early-eighteenth century London, then the same kinds of activities that supercharged capital formation in New York might have occurred just before the Industrial Revolution was getting under way, and this stock exchange formation may in fact have been the essential precursor and trigger of that revolution, too.

It appears at the very least that the speculation side of the equation was in place for that scenario to have played out, although it is a bit less clear that the deliberate monopolization of securities trading was occurring in London the way it would a century later in New York. All of the tools used in New York to facilitate speculation, such as time bargains, puts, calls, etc., were used in London in the 1690s, which also had a stock market boom and bust similar to New York's in the 1790s. As we learn from Anne L. Murphy in *The Origins of English Financial Markets*, the appearance of these characteristics was also relatively sudden.

> There were no more than fifteen English joint-stock companies in 1685 . . . There were no professional market-makers, the term stock-jobber was not in common use and there were few individuals who fulfilled the role of financial broker. Between 1685 and 1695 that situation was completely altered. Around a hundred new English joint-stock companies were established, a stock market grew up and proved surprisingly capable of supporting the exchange of large amounts of stock, as well as an active derivatives market, and a new class of stock-jobbers and brokers emerged. Thanks to investors like the fictional Mr. Hazzard, who believed there was 'more to be got by Stock in a Week, or sometimes in a Day than by any other Business that he ever was acquainted with in a Year', the new stock market boomed. And even those who did not invest found their lives being touched by the advent of the financial market. Indeed, while many were disturbed by the actions of speculators, clearly they could not be ignored. [cxix]

As to deliberate monopolization, Murphy produces no smoking guns like the oath-swearing documents and organizing meetings Werner finds in the early New York trading community. She does, however, find evidence that the functions of and distinctions among various securities professionals were being sorted out in the 1690s, just as the differences between auctioneers, brokers and dealers were sorted out in the Buttonwood era. She also notes that the distinctions amongst professionals were recognized by non-professionals, such as their clients, and that one of the purposes of "sworn broker" registration was the maintenance of those distinctions. [cxx] But if true stock exchange organizing was going on in London with the exclusionary intensity of 1790 New York, it appears that either there is little evidence of it left to discover, or that Murphy was less attuned to look for it the way Walter Werner was. Nonetheless, because the London market did eventually develop into a membership organization similar to the others, my intuition, as before, is that anticompetitive monopolizing was going on in London, too.

In any case, Murphy produces abundant evidence that the speculative and gambling components were all there: the booms, busts, manipulation, fraud, etc., were fully flowering in London -- and enabling capital formation -- a century before they did the same in New York. One of the most important implications of Werner's *inherence thesis*, as discussed in the previous chapter, is that the stock exchanges and the public corporations they helped finance developed simultaneously. It is not the case, as other historians have incorrectly believed, that public corporations developed first and then later the trading in their securities moved to exchanges. This incorrect view is one of the principal myths busted by Werner and Smith in *Wall Street*. The myth essentially puts exchanges in a parasitic position free riding on the corporations that presumably got going on their own. This is not how it happened, according to Werner and Smith, and the misconception is what caused conventional historians to miss entirely the importance of trading markets to capital formation. If Werner and Smith were right about New York, then it was probably also true of London, and indeed Murphy produces ample evidence of it, as in the quote above about the massive jump in the number of joint-stock companies that paralleled the interest in trading markets. If Werner and Smith and Murphy are right about this timing, that would open the way for considering that the sudden formation of the London stock market was the primary cause of the Industrial Revolution, just as the NYSE was the primary cause of the new industries created by the robber barons a century later in the United States.

While machines and coal and new manufacturing processes got the headlines for the Industrial Revolution, these improvements were more effects than causes, and may themselves have come into existence only because an essential precursor to the revolution occurred first in the form of the London Stock Exchange, originally known as "Exchange Alley." If so, then this dodgy sounding neighborhood in London was actually the paradigmatic monopoly undergirding all three subsequent centuries of new industry creation and consequent progress.

The timing would look something like this. London's market was fully formed in about 1720 and was in the process of formation at least by 1700 (Werner), and perhaps as early as around 1690 (Murphy). The Industrial Revolution started forty to seventy years later in 1760 and continued until 1820 or 1840, during which it was an almost exclusively British phenomenon. Exchange Alley would thus have had four to seven decades before 1760 to ignite a sufficient quantity and quality improvement in technologies and capitalist enterprises that historians would eventually call it, "The Industrial Revolution." [cxxi]

After its debut in England, the revolution spread to other places and eventually especially to the United States in pulses that are sometimes called the Second Industrial Revolution. The New York market had beginnings around 1790, but was not fully formed until about 1820, in other words a century later than the London market, both in terms of when it was in the early formation stages and in terms of when it was fully formed. [cxxii] The U.S. version of the revolution began about when the robber barons were getting going with their trusts and monopolies in around 1860, which would also be about a century behind Britain and a century after the Industrial Revolution began in 1760.

So in both countries where the freedoms of the English speaking peoples took root, we had a dominant global stock exchange monopoly formed in the first couple of decades of the eighteenth or nineteenth centuries, as the case may be, followed about forty years later by the onset of an industrial revolution centered in that country. And each of those exchanges had begun to form about thirty years before historians would consider them fully formed, giving each of them plenty of time by any measure to ignite their respective industrial revolutions.

It is harder to know how and why those revolutions eventually petered out or moved elsewhere, but surely in the case of the original Industrial Revolution it could not have helped the British case that New York took the title of dominant global stock exchange from London sometime in the middle of the nineteenth century, probably not much after 1840, after which Werner said, as noted above,

> there was no turning back. At that point, the New York securities market had realized its ultimate native genius: its capacity for unrestrained speculation. [cxxiii]

As to the ability of the United States to lead the continuation of the Industrial Revolution, it certainly has not helped that the robber barons were vilified, the antitrust laws were passed, and political leaders in the model of the Roosevelts took charge. It wasn't until the final decades of the nineteenth century as the robber barons were most active that wealth trickled down significantly to the working classes, and not until the twentieth century that higher living standards "became a tangible, unmistakable reality for everyone," as described by, among others, Thomas Piketty in *Capital in the Twenty-First Century*. [cxxiv]

Regardless of how one counts up or divides the wealth generated by the industrial revolutions, the unmistakable reality is that those revolutions were the original source of almost all the wealth in the world today. And the fact that they began in particular places before spreading is the primary reason for inequality, as a number of economists have noted.

> The large differences in mean incomes between countries are the product of the Industrial Revolution, which is akin to a Big Bang that pushed some countries forward onto the path to higher incomes while others stayed at the point where they had been for millennia. Real concern with intercountry inequality--or perhaps the realization that it is an important topic--begins only then. [cxxv]

It would have been impossible to ignite simultaneous industrial revolutions in the whole world equally, much less to assure within-country equality as they progressed. But if the poor nations and people of the world would like to figure out how they can reach prosperity, too, they could try adopting the kinds of freedoms that led the English-speaking peoples first, and then the rest of the West to stock exchanges. The wealth gap might close more quickly than they expect, in spite of the West's first-mover advantage. For some reason, the English-speaking peoples and the West, led by America, are abandoning their birthright of freedom and have decided to extinguish the stock exchanges that made them rich.

It may be no coincidence that the two countries that virtually invented the productivity category in their industrial revolutions are both perplexed now about why productivity is falling to surprisingly low levels, which it is doing in both England [cxxvi] and America. [cxxvii] My guess is the economists are looking too narrowly with their regressions. The answer could be as simple as that both countries have gone whole hog with this Nanny State thing, another category they seem to have virtually invented. Particularly as it applies to capital markets, the Nanny State has been strangling capital formation with reforms for many decades now, and it has finally nearly killed the patient.

The practical reality that ignited the industrial revolutions was, as we have seen, that citizens were free to speculate at will unrestrained by government, and to monopolize at will unrestrained by government. But now the Nanny State has eliminated those freedoms and is busy reforming the markets such that the intermediaries who used to design and run them have been elbowed aside by regulators who are eliminating any profitability from intermediation or investment banking. This is the effect of the NMS reforms in the United States, and it is the effect of the Libor reforms and similar reforms of currency and commodity fixes that the world's regulators are redesigning so bankers won't make any money anymore. [cxxviii] They may well succeed at that mission, unfortunately. This is unfortunate because, while the regulators know (or believe they know) all about fairness, efficiency, transparency, etc., they are clueless about how to create economic growth and jobs.

Also note that in their zeal to further their careers by punishing those rich intermediaries, the prosecutors and politicians in the UK, just as in the United States, are upping the ante by criminalizing normal market-making behaviors that had successfully standardized transaction processes such that ordinary people could understand them and feel comfortable participating in them.

> Manipulating financial benchmarks, including a key currencies benchmark, is set to become a criminal offense that could carry a prison sentence of up to seven years, Chancellor George Osborne said on Monday. Mr. Osborne confirmed that legislation originally introduced to regulate the Libor interest-rate benchmark will be extended to cover several other instruments, including the 4 p.m. London foreign-exchange benchmark rate and some key gold and silver fixes. The ICE Brent index and the Sterling Overnight Index Average, known as Sonia, is also included along with the ISDAFix, which is used to price swaps transactions. The move marks a tighter regime for banks and individuals working with these benchmarks, aimed at safeguarding public trust and stamping out any potential efforts at manipulation after a series of scandals. Already, institutions can face fines for misconduct and, in some cases, individuals can face criminal investigation for fraud. The government plans to implement the new rules from April 1. It had originally laid out the cleanup in June. "The integrity of the City matters to the economy of Britain," Mr. Osborne said in a statement. [cxxix]

Although thus ratcheting up the penalties is done in the supposed interest of instilling investor confidence, it will have the opposite effect. The only possible result on that front will be convincing investors, most of which never heard of these esoteric "manipulation" practices before, that professional bankers and traders are crooks and that financial transactions should be avoided at all times.

That would contrast sharply with the comfort the public previously had with these now standard transaction mechanisms. Like single price auctions and stock market opens and closes, fixings were events in which many buyers and many sellers would transact simultaneously and all at the same price, or at least for a while after the last benchmark was set. How could that be dangerous? And even if the dealers and brokers did have incentives via the "manipulation" built into the process to bring participants into them, so what? Why would that not be a good thing, rather than a bad thing? If regulators succeed in squeezing the incentive out of the process by eliminating whatever vigorish the dealers received from bringing their clients to the fixings, that would only result in less people participating, thereby reducing the safety-in-numbers effect that was the principal value of fixings as public transaction mechanisms. [cxxx] If that occurs, then more people will be thrown into continuous trading, the realm of HFT, the existence of which has so far only sapped investor confidence in spite of its low trading costs.

There is no evidence now and never has been that more market structure reforms or penalties will improve either confidence or markets. In fact, the more extensive and draconian the nannies are about their tasks, the more investors will be convinced that markets should be avoided, as the swarm of cops only proves that thieves are everywhere. Regulators should consider the possibility that their presence is the primary reason for the lack of confidence in capital markets. And while they are at it, they should have a read of Walter Werner's *Wall Street* and consider the virtual certainty that stock exchanges would never have existed in the first place if regulators had been involved as they were forming.

10. Counterfactual Fun

The last three centuries, from 1700 on, were entirely unique and unprecedented, producing advances in living standards and population that before they occurred would have been considered somewhere between highly unlikely and impossible. While the rise of England and then the United States as the leading nations of the world, and the Industrial Revolution, first in England and then elsewhere, but especially in America, are well known, there is no agreement on what started it, or on why or how it migrated as it did. The answer, as described in the previous chapter, may lie in the fact that the stock exchange structure that first appeared in London and New York around 1690 and 1790, respectively, had strange powers and abilities to capitalize and give life to new enterprises, a structure that was different in kind and degree from anything that had come before or existed anywhere else. They were both globally dominant stock exchanges, of which, by definition, there can only be one at a time. If they were capable of igniting an Industrial Revolution, then they were also capable of steering the locus of its activities. London had a century-long head start and made the most of it, which we call the Industrial Revolution. Then New York came up with a better version of the stock exchange, and the revolution moved from Britain to the United States. In this chapter I will further explore this hypothesis and, if proved, its implications.

Readers will no doubt recognize that much of my analysis and many of my conclusions rely on what debaters often refer to as "counterfactuals." One of the most common examples today, invoked both by those who use this technique and by those who criticize them for using it, is the "another Great Depression" reason, the presumed avoidance of which supposedly justified the adoption of emergency measures to rescue their economies by the United States and many other major governments during and after 2008. This is a counterfactual because we can never really know what would have happened if we had not adopted Quantitative Easing, etc., to see if letting the Great Recession run without QE, etc., would have turned it into another Great Depression. Another way of saying this is that it is impossible to rerun history to test out or "prove" theories. Although this inherent limitation on the efficacy of counterfactual arguments is acknowledged on all sides of the debate over QE, the we-avoided-another-Great-Depression argument is still the most common and powerful argument offered by all the Big Government types for advocating QE and similar policies. But two can play this game.

As I have said, if the United States had never established the freedom to pursue self-interest, i.e., to pursue inequality, we would never have developed stock markets, and if we had never developed stock markets, we would never have become a significant or powerful nation. Tagging along on those counterfactuals, I have just added another: if stock exchanges had not developed, either in London or the United States, the Industrial Revolution would not have occurred, either in Britain or anywhere. What I will do now is restate those and a few other points that

I have also already mentioned, but do so this time specifically as counterfactuals, and see where that takes us. And please forgive the repetition necessary to do this.

While counterfactuals, by definition, can never be proved, these come pretty close to it, or at least to being demonstrable beyond a reasonable doubt, thanks to the pioneering research done by Walter Werner and Steven T. Smith for *Wall Street*. While counterfactuals that support Big Government, like we-avoided-another-Great-Depression-with-QE, rely entirely on evidence that no one can ever agree on because we can't re-run history, my counterfactuals rely on historical facts that everyone agrees on, but would not have made the connections I have made from them until new potential facts entered the equation, such as those suggested by Werner and Smith. Since, as I have discovered, most people interested in market structure have never heard of Werner and Smith or *Wall Street*, this is new information. And unlike the counterfactuals that support Big Government, which rely on the fact that we can never know how history would have run under the hypothetical counterfactual, in this case the opposite is true. I can point to agreed facts that show this is how history in fact did run. Since the result without intervention was magnificent, as everyone agrees, my counterfactual is more challenging to Big Government, because it throws the gauntlet back at the would-be intervener and asks: Under what intervention, exactly, do you think the result would have been better?

If people still want to disagree, they would either have to disagree with agreed facts or with Werner and Smith's analysis or conclusions. To make the case for my counterfactuals, I will start with agreed historical facts on which there does not appear to be any disagreement and then fold in Werner and Smith's research, which establishes some new potential facts that are not yet agreed on, but only because most people are not aware of them or have not thought much about them. If the potential facts presented by Werner and Smith are accepted as a true description of what actually happened, that would either throw a huge "cognitive dissonance" or its equivalent into our understanding of history, or it would require us to reassess many accepted facts by adopting my counterfactuals as facts.

As anyone can easily confirm in a few minutes following Internet links, everyone agrees that the Industrial Revolution was a very big deal. While there is considerably less agreement on the specific definition of it, or on what was cause and what was effect, everyone seems to agree on the fact that many firsts in modern human history were at least associated with it. Among these is an explosion of economic growth, productivity and per capita output, as well as an explosion of population growth.

As anyone can also confirm in a few minutes on the Internet -- or over and over again in a few hours -- there is little agreement on exactly where this huge improvement came from, that is, on what ignited it. While there are many theories, often conflicting, the lack of any specific cause that can be pointed to by everyone for the onset of this revolution is strange and glaring, given how important it was. The Industrial Revolution is acknowledged to be the most important development in modern human history. How could it possibly be that we don't know or agree on what caused it?

Everyone seems to agree that it began in Britain around 1760 and continued until sometime between 1820 and 1840, and that it was primarily a British phenomenon, at least for this period. There is some disagreement about the onset and locations of what is usually referred to as the "Second Industrial Revolution," but such uncertainties do not cloud the virtual unanimity on the timing and location of the first one, which is the only one that can unquestionably claim the title of "The Industrial Revolution."

There is also agreement that, under whatever label, the economic growth, productivity, per capita output, and demographic growth that was associated with the Industrial Revolution ceased being a solely or even mainly British phenomenon by the end of the nineteenth century as these growth waves spread to other countries, but especially to the United States, which perhaps as early as the 1870s became the world's largest economy and by the early twentieth century had the largest share of global trade. Although there is agreement on these facts, as far as they go, there is little agreement on what caused the spread of the Industrial Revolution or its aftereffects to these other places, and especially most powerfully to the United States, beyond a simple assumption of what might be called economic imitation or a kind of beneficial contagion.

Switching now to facts mentioned by Werner and Smith in *Wall Street*, we look first at those that are not in dispute or outside the consensus of agreed history. The precursor trading crowds that eventually became the London Stock Exchange appear to have begun to form around 1690, and were fully formed in terms of exchange functionality by 1720. The New York Stock and Exchange Board, the precursor to the New York Stock Exchange, began to form around 1790, was fully formed by about 1820, and took the title of being the world's dominant stock exchange from London sometime in the middle of the nineteenth century, an advantageous position that it not only never relinquished, but also increased dramatically over the next century and a half.

At the very least, the apparent coincidence of similar "industrial revolutions" or great advances in economic growth beginning just a few decades after the formation for the first time of globally dominant stock exchanges, as well as the migration of the revolutionary focus to the area that had the biggest stock exchange -- and away from the area that no longer had the biggest -- is suggestive of something that would explain the mysteries, both of the ignition of the Industrial Revolution in the first place, and of its migration. In any case, judging by the lack of consensus on what caused them, it can fairly be said that it is an implicitly agreed fact that these questions -- what ignited the Industrial Revolution and what caused its spread or migration -- are indeed mysteries. So juxtaposing the agreed dates of stock exchange history and Industrial Revolution history to the agreed consensus on what we don't know about the Industrial Revolution appears to reveal a coincidence worth exploring, one that just might explain the mysteries.

Another important point that falls out of the history Werner and Smith recount, which also is part of the consensus, as it comes in their telling from some mostly standard sources, nor is it contradicted by their extraordinarily comprehensive coverage of all the historical precedents for the NYSE, is that the stock exchange concept and its structure, as evidenced in London and New York, was a new and different kind of beast on the commercial and financial landscape. Both were very large and significant monopolizations, implicitly in London's case, but explicitly and forcefully in the case of the NYSE. Thus the stock exchange structure that emerged in London and New York was different in both kind and degree from any previous social or commercial institution that could help corporations find capital. While lawyers, notaries and accountants may have provided ad hoc assistance to their clients on capital questions, for example, they were not organized with anything remotely resembling the force that could be applied to capital allocation the way the membership organizations of the stock exchanges were. And while stock exchanges existed in Amsterdam, Paris and other cities, they were not remotely as organized or powerful in their potential to monopolize the speculation servicing industry the way the London and New York stock exchanges were. If all that is so, then it can fairly be said that capital allocation, as an industry, did not exist prior to the time the London and New York stock exchanges came into existence.

Which takes us now to the most important point made by Werner and Smith in *Wall Street* that is not only not part of the consensus, but that busts a myth commonly held by other historians covering the same material. Werner, who, after an earlier stint at the SEC in the 1960s, taught corporation law for two decades at the Columbia University School of Law until he died in 1986, sees a continuum from the earliest days to today in the parallel development of trading markets and of public corporations raising funds through securities issuance. Werner's key point is that securities issuance was facilitated or made easier by the existence of those trading markets. From the beginning, according to Werner, public corporations (as opposed to private or "close" corporations) and securities trading markets had a symbiotic relationship in which trading markets, and especially speculative trading markets, fed the interest in buying new securities of corporations. Corporations thus benefited from the existence of trading markets, which enabled them to raise funds. And participants in those trading markets benefited from the creation by corporations of those securities, in which they always have had a keen interest in speculating, trading, and investing.

The consensus, in contrast, sees trading markets as arising somewhat after the existence of public corporations issuing securities, especially in the early days of both. This sequence of arrival is an implication of the "Erosion Doctrine" of Berle and Means discussed in *Wall Street*. [cxxxi] The difference between Werner's view and the consensus may be nearly moot in today's markets, since both securities trading markets and active corporate securities issuance have existed side by side for a long time now. Thus it may seem like only a technical quibble to argue over which came first. But the difference was very material to Werner and prominently highlighted in the book. The relevant point here is that, if securities markets developed simultaneously with corporations, as Werner argues, or before them, as his history implies and I believe, then the sudden appearance of stock exchanges as a powerful new force enabling corporations to raise capital would suggest that there might, indeed, have been a clear triggering event for the Industrial Revolution, an event so powerful that it could rise up above all other contenders and eventually be accepted by the consensus of historians as *the* cause of the Industrial Revolution.

Related to this view of Werner's that stock exchanges and corporations raising capital developed together is another myth-busting view of Werner's, namely that it was the speculating activities of stock exchanges, in particular, as opposed to their ordinary investing or trading activities, that was the key to corporations being able to raise capital and thus made it possible to get the most out of the parallel development of stock exchanges and corporations raising capital. Speculative trading engendered more interest in ever more risky corporate ventures, which was an important factor underlying the formation of early American industries, and was also an important reason why the exchanges and their trading activities expanded.

The consensus doesn't see it that way, which, according to Werner, may explain why the consensus also missed the simultaneity of the development of trading markets and corporations raising funds through securities issuance. The bias against speculation, according to Werner, which he associates with a regulatory view that was common, caused blindness when it came to the dual development picture. Further, it caused the consensus to miss out on understanding why the New York market came to dominate securities trading and issuance, which is its superior capacity for "unrestrained speculation." If Werner is correct, then his explanation may answer the questions of both why the dominant market for securities trading and the main locus of the Industrial Revolution switched from Britain to the United States, probably in the second half of the nineteenth or certainly by the early twentieth century. I will also say that, whether or not Werner is correct as to *why* New York won this contest, i.e., its "native genius" for speculation, the incontrovertible fact, acknowledged by everyone, is that New York did in fact win the title of dominant stock exchange. So even if there is some other explanation for why this occurred, the fact that it occurred would still imply strongly that the reason the continuation of or second phase of the Industrial Revolution came to be a primarily American, and not a British, phenomenon, had to do with the switch in dominance from one stock exchange to the other.

One other possible explanation for these changes that Werner takes up, and one that would be additive to the "unrestrained speculation" explanation, is the one that emerges from the busting of another myth or incorrect assumption that historians have had about the earliest days of NYSE formation. Werner makes a convincing case that the Buttonwood Agreement of May 17, 1792, rather than being the result of a dispute between brokers and auctioneers, as the consensus believes, actually demonstrated cooperation between them. The traditional broker vs. auctioneer dispute explanation was more comfortable for historians to adopt, apparently, perhaps because it suggested a less legally embarrassing and thus easier to imagine reason for the Buttonwood Agreement than a price fixing cartel, namely an internal corporate rivalry. The consensus seemed to relax its discomfort with that anticompetitive cartel when it settled on the corporate rivalry explanation. But the real reason, Werner shows, is more conspiratorial and anticompetitive than that, and more in keeping with the price-fixing cartel that is the literal essence of the Buttonwood Agreement.

And Werner brings up much evidence of the truly anticompetitive intent of not only the Buttonwood Agreement, but of much else besides, around and before and after the agreement was signed. In particular, the prospective or intended oath that would have been entered into at a coffee house meeting on September 21, 1791 announced in that "broadside" eight months before Buttonwood, indicates even more clearly than Buttonwood the exclusionary or shunning intent of the membership agreement the cartel was headed toward (although the agreement was probably not signed, and it is not certain the meeting it announced even took place). And the proud signatures of the Buttonwood Agreement, which looks like a smaller version of the Declaration of Independence, demonstrate confidence in the enterprise, as well as resolve to hold their conspiracy together, which by all accounts was needed at that time. The state of New York had just banned public auctions in April, a month before Buttonwood was signed and, as mentioned, had also barred use of the courts to enforce speculative contracts in the aftermath of the spring crash. The state, in other words, was clearly on the warpath, riding on the self-righteous fury of citizens after the boom had turned to bust, and might well have shut the exchange down if the Buttonwood brokers had not been so resolute.

If Werner is correct, then not only does this explanation provide the real reason that markets formed in the first place, but it also provides another metric by which to judge which exchanges are strong and which are weak, namely the strength of their anticompetitive oaths to enforce cooperation with each other and to enhance the value of their conspiracy over time. Although *Wall Street* spends much less time describing the similar understandings of the markets in London, Boston or Philadelphia, there is enough to indicate that similar anticompetitive intent probably prevailed in those other markets, too. The details are less important than the obvious fact that New York won the prize of dominant global stock exchange, not only taking it away from London, which had a 100-year head start or first mover advantage, but preventing either Boston or Philadelphia from winning it, too. Therefore, since all these exchanges, and certainly New York by Werner's account, were spending the bulk of their organizing energies in creating strong anticompetitive conspiracies, it is reasonable to assume that it is on this field of competition -- i.e., at being an anticompetitive conspiracy -- that the contest was won.

So we are now up to three possible explanations for why New York took the prize of dominant stock exchange: its greater ability to support the parallel development of trading markets and corporations' ability to raise capital, its greater natural interest in speculation, and its probably stronger anticompetitive conspiracy. And there is a fourth factor that would act like an afterburner to these three. The D.I.Y. monopoly example set by the NYSE, whether it was deliberately followed by some of the companies the exchange listed, or merely established by precedent what was legally permissible in terms of self-monopolization in the new America, may have enabled the robber baron revolution to be far more powerful as a force of capitalism than the Old World monopolies could make of the Industrial Revolution. In other words, not only was the exchange in New York, because of its explicit monopolization, an uptick on the original monopoly exchange model that formed in London, but the enterprises it fostered by example and precedent were superior to those previous monopolies granted by patent, license or other protected privilege of the King or Parliament. Of course it is possible that it was less by example and more by luck that New York was where these new and more powerful enterprises listed their shares; it may have been merely time for the Old World to give way to the New, rather than something specifically brought about by the NYSE. But even if so, it would still have been a significant advantage for New York to have these new self-made monopolies list on its market, as compared to the Old World government-created monopolies that listed in London. Any way you look at it, we have four significant possible reasons why the New York Stock Exchange was in a much better position than the London Stock Exchange to lead the continuation of the Industrial Revolution.

While each of these is plausible in isolation, and all together are extremely plausible, whether it is because of these or other reasons that New York won the prize, the fact is that it did win it, and at just about the right time to fit in to our counterfactual as the cause of the Industrial Revolution shifting from England to the United States. And if we want to explain why the Industrial Revolution began in the first place, then we really only need the first of the quartet to be true, namely that corporations developed along with stock exchanges (or after them), rather than before them, as the consensus believes.

So we conclude our little exercise in counterfactual fun by saying that, if you want to falsify my secondary hypothesis (that the Industrial Revolution began in England and shifted to the United States because of the development of stock exchanges) you would have to tangle either with one of the well-established and accepted facts of history, or with Walter Werner's non-consensus view that stock exchanges developed parallel to corporations seeking funding. And if you want to challenge my primary hypothesis, that the United States would never have become the dominant world power that it did become if antitrust laws had been around to prevent the formation of the New York Stock Exchange, you would have to hypothesize yourself about how a great outcome that happened without intervention would have been at least as great or better with intervention.

Both of my counterfactuals thus reverse the we-prevented-another-Great-Depression-with-QE type of counterfactual by putting the burden on the challenger to create the better scenario. While the QE counterfactual posits that disaster would have occurred without intervention, which is something that no one can prove isn't true, my counterfactual relies on the agreed fact that a great result did occur without intervention and challenges the would-be intervener to paint a scenario with intervention that would have been as good or better. This would be difficult given the fact that the bar for improvement is already set very high by the acknowledged success of the United States in many dimensions, but especially economically. So in this case the counterfactual works against Big Government and not for it.

The opposite of Big Government, of course, is freedom, as provided for in the traditions of the English speaking peoples. But while one must presume that the unalienable rights and other markers of our freedoms had something to do with generating the conditions in which stock exchanges first emerged, I cannot point to specific interpretations or legal traditions that made those fertile conditions possible. I can say, however, that there appear to be only two necessary legal conditions. First, people had to be free to engage in whatever speculations their hearts desired, without the Nanny State protecting them from the consequences of their actions. Second, there could be no competition policy or antitrust or other restrictions on monopoly formation.

Both of these are "negative" rights, ones that do not guarantee that we will be given something, but that guarantee that our freedoms to do as we please will not be taken away. Although these two negative rights, to be free to speculate and to form monopolies, appear to have been in place, I cannot point to any legal or social traditions that made this so. I can only say, mostly by pointing to Werner's history, that it must have been so. Further, while I assume that other conditions of critical mass and social interest, etc., must have been present against that free-to-speculate-and-monopolize backdrop to actually cause stock exchanges to spring up, I don't know what they are. I can only say that, based on the narrative in *Wall Street*, it does appear that, for the first time in history, ambitious wealth-seeking men came together in London and New York to form globally dominant stock exchanges.

Among the amazing things that followed on the emergence of those stock exchanges, with timing just too coincidental to have been unrelated, were the Industrial Revolution in England and the robber baron boom in the United States, in each case about 40 years after their respective exchanges were fully formed. If the connections hinted by these coincidences hold, then one could also throw in a few other interesting counterfactuals to consider, which would also seem likely to be demonstrated by the same basic source and logic. Summing up:

The Industrial Revolution would not have happened.

There would have been no British Empire worth remembering.

The United States would not be a wealthy or powerful nation.

The Great Enrichment of mankind from 1700 on would not have occurred.

One could go on in this vein, concluding, for example, that the bulk of living standards, capital and wealth in the world today would not be here if those stock exchanges had not emerged. In other words, the entire world would still be as impoverished as the poorest countries in Africa.

11. Murder, By Definition

I was on an airplane in 1990 reading a regulatory release when I learned that our single price auction company, eventually called AZX, [cxxxii] would meet the SEC's new definition of a stock exchange. Since what I was reading at the time was not directly related to our business, I was surprised to see the words "single price auction" tacked on at the end of a long regulatory definition as we were taxiing toward takeoff. [cxxxiii] This was worrisome, because our company was the only entity in the business that was known as a single price auction. Although I didn't realize it fully at the time, the new definition would permanently kill our auction's ability to operate at any time that our customers would want to use us, thus effectively killing our business. [cxxxiv]

But over time I also realized that the new definition had a much more momentous effect than just killing AZX. It killed all traditional stock exchanges, too.

When the original Securities Exchange Act of 1934 was written, which created the SEC, there had never been any question what the definition of a stock exchange was. In fact it was so obvious that the legal definition actually used several circular phrases or terms, saying in effect a stock exchange was something that performed the functions commonly performed by a stock exchange, as that term was generally understood. [cxxxv] Since it was obvious that stock exchanges were membership organizations that had broker-dealers as members, there had never been any question what the difference between an exchange and a member of an exchange was, nor any question about which regulatory bucket each fell into. Hence, the circular language and terms worked just fine.

But as the SEC gradually discovered the tools with which it would dismantle the NYSE -- the "club" -- and the privileges of membership on which it was based, it increasingly began to rely on creative authorizations for new and unusual competitors, such as the crossing networks, which got "no action" letters to operate as broker-dealers without having to worry about the SEC taking action forcing them to register as exchanges. For its part, AZX got a "low volume exemption" from exchange registration, giving it equivalent comfort to the crosses' no-action letters, so long as it remained very small and operated only off-hours. These creative authorizations took their place alongside other policies that sought to unwind the original iron-clad right of the NYSE to prevent members from violating its rules about where, when and how they would trade its listed stocks.

To get a feel for the regulatory dynamics of the SEC versus the NYSE, think again of a club. A club might have rules prohibiting, for example, drunk and disorderly behavior, pursuant to which it would retain the right in its absolute discretion to not accept as members those who were prone to such behavior, and to expel any members who broke its rules by engaging in them. But if you want to bust the club just for being a club, you might outlaw it by redefining "member" and "club" such that there is no longer any recognizable difference between them. You could do this by saying both are defined by their propensity to "host gatherings or parties in regularly constructed facilities such as 'rooms' or 'halls' or 'clubhouses.'" And only standard membership criteria would be allowed, such as access to a credit card. No other criteria would be allowed, such as a member's drinking habits or behavior when drunk. And there would be no more of this "in-its-absolute-discretion" nonsense. Under the new definitions and rules, the SEC would be the judge of whether membership criteria were properly applied.

In its zeal to break up the NYSE monopoly (which in practice included the other "primary" markets, namely Amex (the American Stock Exchange) and NASDAQ), the SEC did everything it could to authorize its competitors, including the two original "crosses" or electronic dark pools for anonymously matching blocks pioneered by Instinet and Jefferies' POSIT, the similar in practice AZX auction, "third market" dealers [cxxxvi] like Weeden and Madoff, and "19c3" dealers. [cxxxvii] The NYSE (and its fellow primary markets) tried hard to stop all of these, while the SEC tried hard to authorize them, often cheered on by famous academics and other champions of efficiency or the little guy. [cxxxviii] Thus the "we're-from-the-government-and-we're-here-to-help" approach seemed genuine. These mostly young, idealistic lawyers at the SEC (one had planned to be a "poverty lawyer" until he found he could do more good at the SEC) were sincerely doing good work, they thought, protecting investors and promoting efficiency and fairness while giving the little competitor some help against the big, bad, old, Luddite monopoly. They were basically in favor of anything that was electronic, entrepreneurial, new -- and opposed by the NYSE or NASDAQ. In their eyes we were the good guys, just like they were. None of us NYSE competitors were in any sense drunk or disorderly, but from the perspective of the orderly and profitable world the exchange had historically enforced, we might as well have been.

Unfortunately, however, AZX had a special problem with regard to this otherwise friendly and accommodative regulatory stance taken by the SEC. AZX could set its own price via a market-wide auction in which everyone traded at the same time and price and was thus, theoretically at least, not dependent on the main markets at NYSE, Amex and NASDAQ, unlike the crosses that relied on those regular markets to set their prices. Although those original crosses at Instinet and POSIT that AZX was most similar to also traded in batch at a single time and price, they were theoretically limited in how large they could get because of their need to use the regular markets to get their prices from, which might become unreliable in their setting of those prices in the degree to which the crosses became successful and thus attracted orders from them. Secondly, any continuous trading system, including third market dealers or the Instinet "real time" system, does not trade in batch with everyone getting the same price at the same time, but rather is a constant stream of mostly bilateral trades with only one buyer and one seller in each, thereby limiting its ability to be the focus of a market-wide consensus on price. This was of course a limitation also shared by the main markets, NYSE, Amex and NASDAQ, which were mostly continuous. Because AZX was the one system that bypassed all those limitations, AZX had the theoretical potential to compete with the traditional markets in a more complete way than the crosses or third market dealers did. In theory, small as AZX was, and remote as the possibility was in reality, it could replace them all.

Thus it made the SEC more than usually nervous about authorizing AZX to trade during the regular hours of the NYSE and NASDAQ, a move that, as it was explained to me, could cause all kinds of complaints to rain down on the Commission from its congressional overseers, who would have heard from the exchanges' lobbyists if the SEC authorized AZX to compete with them during *their* hours. So even though AZX was newer and much smaller than the crosses, which themselves only added up to one percent of the market, total, it was nonetheless understandable that the SEC would worry more about the political heat it would suffer if the Commission did authorize AZX. In any case, the SEC apparently did worry, and confined AZX, uniquely among all competitors in the marketplace, to off-hours operation. (Instinet's Crossing Network also operated off hours, usually a couple hours or more after the close of regular markets, but that was by choice of Instinet, not a regulatory requirement.) Apart from this loose, oral explanation, no other reason why AZX could not be allowed to operate during regular hours was ever given. [cxxxix]

In the old days, of course, the NYSE club would have simply expelled renegade broker-dealers from membership, or denied them access to membership in the first place, if they even so much as thought about offering competing crosses or auctions, or doing third market trades in NYSE-listed stocks. And it would have passed rules prohibiting its members from using or trading with any such competitors that did manage to spring up outside of its purview. So the SEC could with some legitimacy consider the crosses and AZX and third market dealers as comrades in its fight against the anticompetitive NYSE club. In any case it was my impression then and still is today, that the staff and even a few commissioners were doing everything they could to honestly help us understand their limits and find the most practical ways for us to comply with their rules so we could be authorized to compete. Indeed, I thought the evident candor of the explanation of the political problems that might attend authorizing AZX to be evidence of the staff's sincerity in their desire to help us in whatever ways they could.

Nonetheless, as I came to understand later, the big picture was that the SEC's primary mission was its campaign to take down the NYSE monopoly. And in the end it could not help but turn AZX into collateral damage in that anti-NYSE campaign.

But the bigger lesson I learned from the experience was that the power to define is the power to destroy. As the SEC gradually redefined the term, "stock exchange," it effectively withdrew the right of stock exchanges to exist. Under the new definition, the stock exchange category, once implicitly defined by the likes of the London Stock Exchange, the New York Stock Exchange, the Philadelphia Stock Exchange, and the Boston Stock Exchange, was dead. In particular, the membership organization structure, the powerful privileges of membership of which were the defining feature of these exchanges, was no longer allowed. This effectively killed the stock exchange, as that term was generally understood. (Remember, the original 1934 Securities Exchange Act definition of stock exchange included the key words, "or for otherwise performing with respect to securities the functions commonly performed by a stock exchange, as that term is generally understood.")

The underlying crime these exchanges committed that led to their demise was the ultimate horror, according to modern government: they created inequality, and they did it by discriminating. While it would take a couple of centuries before modern network scientists would recognize the discriminatory force of nature underlying network formation and call it "preferential attachment," aka "rich-get-richer," the NYSE's founders were instinctively discriminating as they organized their exchange, as the members preferentially attached their fortunes and wealth-seeking to each other, and they did get richer, really richer. Discriminating between members and nonmembers was the primal unfairness in the modern commercial and social world, according to modern antitrust regulators, as its intent and effect were to make members richer than nonmembers. Thus the destruction of the stock exchange can be seen as the paradigmatic example of the legal process by which America's freedoms are being destroyed, as our right to pursue inequality is being defined out of existence.

The freedoms to speculate and monopolize at will were, as we have seen, our two most important founding freedoms in a practical sense. They are the ones that led to the formation of the stock exchanges that enriched us. And they are the ones that are being smothered by the SEC's changing definitions now. Not only does this mean that no new stock exchanges like the old NYSE can be born, it means that the other market that had taken on the new company creation role for the NYSE via IPOs, namely, the NASDAQ dealer market, has been killed, too. What remains are the electronic HFT clones of the NMS that the SEC calls stock exchanges, which have been forced into that model in order to create competition for the NYSE and NASDAQ. Those old exchanges have also been forced by that same competition to adopt that same model and now, ridiculously, compete with each other, as each of the old markets runs several of the new clones. The clones, which number over a dozen, produce lots of trading, but no capital. While IPOs continue to dribble in, there is little connection anymore between secondary trading profits and IPOs, so the old symbiotic relationship between trading markets and new company creation described by Walter Werner no longer exists. The practical consequence is that the kind of market that can create new industries and jobs is not here now and is not coming back, at least not as long as the SEC is around.

As we try to figure out what happened to us, it is useful to keep in mind that the difference between competition, fragmentation and disintegration is very often in the eye of the beholder. While regulators like to portray their expertise as valuable because of their ability to discern the difference between beneficial competition and harmful fragmentation, what is really going on is disintegration, which is always harmful.

It is easy enough to see the difference when you note that the organized single monopoly market of NYSE/NASDAQ/Amex, [cxl] which used to produce more capital than any other market in the world, by far, is now divided, as noted, into a dozen or more "exchanges" as well as scores of exchange-light trading venues, all of which in combination produce very little capital. While the SEC's electronic National Market System of multiple competing exchanges nominally ties them together via rules such as "Reg NMS" that require all orders to get immediately to the best price so they can get "best execution," via re-routing among competing markets if necessary, the result is often confusing and sometimes chaotic or just plain dysfunctional, as it was in the Flash Crash of May 6, 2010.

In terms of disintegration, of which the Flash Crash was the prime example, the operating principle of regulation is that the monopoly stock exchange is no longer allowed to control its members such that in aggregate they produce a coordinated, sensible result in all trading circumstances. So the glitches and chaotic black swans we see more and more frequently today can be thought of as the result of a deliberate policy to revoke the former control the monopoly had, resulting in the forcible disorganization of the markets the regulators once proudly called the "organized markets." Again, Yeats' image is useful: "Things fall apart; the centre cannot hold; Mere anarchy is loosed upon the world." [cxli]

Regulators are creating this counterproductive anarchy by preventing the use of the most productive human faculty there is, namely the ability to discriminate. This is the practical effect of the murder by definition of the stock exchange. And lest we let policymakers off the hook on some notion of inevitable "competition" or "technology" or "evolution" being behind the impending final doom of the 225-year-old market, [cxlii] keep in mind that this is for all practical purposes a policy-based murder of the NYSE by the SEC. As the Big Board goes to its final resting place, wherever that may be, let us remember how it began.

Think back to the 1790s monopolization of the precursor to the NYSE. The main thing going on then was the separation of what would become the members from the nonmembers as the members swore oaths to support each other and to effectively shun non-members. Nonmembers could be customers, of course. But as to acting in the capacity of members with the privileges of direct access to trading and information, the difference was as absolute as the members and their oaths could make it. What these members were doing was discriminating between those who were in the club and those who were not.

Now think further about what this means, but seeing it through the lens of our modern anti-discrimination ethos. These members were conspiring to discriminate in favor of themselves by conspiring to discriminate against others. Their conspiracies were intended to have major consequences in terms of the resulting economic and social inequality of both members and nonmembers. And this discrimination was intended to create not just inequality in terms of results, but also inequality in terms of opportunity and mobility. Can you imagine anything more egregious in terms of modern politically correct thinking?

Now picture how the pattern matching of these members looking for strong and faithful compatriots to form their club with would work to include those who looked like each other and hung out together, and to exclude those who did not meet these criteria. It would certainly result, either inadvertently or on purpose, in discrimination against others on grounds of religion, race, sex and many similar currently prohibited grounds. In addition, prejudice in service of that discriminatory intent, as well as stereotyping and profiling, would often be evident.

But now to the meat of the matter: natural law and your right to the pursuit of happiness protects your right to discriminate in your associations, both in favor of some and against others, and even to be prejudiced, not to mention racist, sexist, homophobic, etc., as long as you do not violate the similar unalienable rights of others to life, liberty, property or the pursuit of happiness. You have the right to try to create property for yourself by conspiring with others to do so, and to keep it if you can get it. Your rights to property and the pursuit of happiness keep your rights to discriminate and be prejudiced from being taken away from you. These are among those "negative" rights referred to before. They do not give you something; they prevent something from being taken away from you. They are violated if something is missing that was yours, as if you had a negative balance in your unalienable rights ledger. Thinking again of stock exchanges as clubs, the negative right you have is the right to conspire with others to form a club that discriminates in favor of members and against nonmembers.

A "positive" right, in contrast, is satisfied when something that wasn't yours before is added to your possessions or rights, such as affirmative claims to housing or education or health care. In the context of thinking of stock exchanges as clubs, those who argue for competition policies to prevent your conspiring to form a club are in effect trying to bestow a positive right on themselves to not be excluded from your club. And they are violating your negative right to the pursuit of happiness to do so. These two rights, of course, the one negative and the other positive, would always be in direct conflict and mutually exclusive. You can't have in the same society both the right to form clubs and the right to not be excluded from clubs.

The bottom line is that you have the natural law right to form a club that includes some and excludes others. And no one has a right to join someone else's club. Moreover, natural law gives you the right to discriminate on any basis you like to determine whom to include and whom to exclude, including any and all of today's politically incorrect reasons for doing so. While theorists and historians may argue over such principles, there is little question that the history of stock exchanges demonstrates that these were in fact the interpretations of law and rights in practice at the times the London Stock Exchange and the New York Stock Exchange formed.

There is also little question, unfortunately, that this is not how things are interpreted today. Under antitrust principles, as well as under the political correctness principles that guide the larger society of which antitrust is a part, you no longer have the right to form clubs. In the big picture this means that your unalienable rights to property, inequality, the pursuit of happiness and discrimination have all disappeared, defined out of existence and killed off by the effective right of government to redistribute your property to others. We have thus entirely replaced the negative rights on which our original freedoms were based with positive rights.

The unalienables America started with were few, and all of them fell into the category of negative rights, i.e., rights that prevented things from being taken away from you, such as your life, your liberty or your property. Positive rights, in contrast, are countless, and all of them involve the supposed right of one class or group of people to have someone else's property redistributed to them. Not only are positive rights not unalienable or natural, they all involve the specific granting of them by government, and are thus inherently changeable in the future.

This change from negative rights to positive rights -- from unalienables to alienables -- is directly related to why our economy is no longer generating jobs, as we'll discuss next.

12. Speculation and Jobs

If the market for IPOs is to create new industries, it must be highly speculative. It is not the one talked about in all the regular reports one reads these days about the rebirth of IPOs, whether they are talking about Alibaba, [cxliii] or Facebook, or post-bailout GM, or a surprising upswing in German IPOs, because "the eurozone's largest online fashion retailer" is doing an IPO "with bankers estimating a value of up to 5 billion." [cxliv] These triumphal stories cover over what in another context would be called a "dead cat bounce." They only look good compared to the absolutely rotten IPO market that has been with us since 1997 when the SEC and the Justice Department's Antitrust Division imposed reforms on NASDAQ's dealer market that killed the IPO industry in the United States. And I include the mention of the German IPO to hint that, while the problem may be worse in the United States than elsewhere, it is not necessarily confined to the United States, as the rest of the West appears to be following our lead. This chapter explores in greater detail the subject introduced in chapter 3, where we learned that IPOs fell off a cliff so dramatically after 1996 that the experience inspired David Weild's white papers, beginning with *Why Are IPOs in the ICU?* which led to the JOBS Act and the Tick Pilot. As Walter Werner said of the early nineteenth century market, and as NASDAQ embodied as recently as the mid-1990s, you need a lot of speculative trading in secondary markets to excite real interest in the most speculative IPOs, which themselves must include a lot of long shots if in aggregate they are to create new industries and jobs. [cxlv] We do not have such an IPO market today.

You need lots of the most speculative IPOs because that is the way you get included in the mix the ones that are potentially new industries launched before their founders have to sell out to other big companies or give up their founding majority shares to VCs or as part of the IPO deal. Even if most of those speculative long shots fail, the ones that emerge from the formation process with their founders in charge are the ones that just might become new industries.

Being able to launch these long shots was the real genius of the NASDAQ "dealer market" before being busted on antitrust grounds in late 1996 (by the Justice Department) and early 1997 (by the SEC). [cxlvi] If even some companies have to become as established as the above behemoths are before doing an IPO, chances are you won't have hidden gems in the mix whose founders can shepherd them all the way to full monopoly and new industry status. Investment bankers will be too busy doing the big deals, which are obvious and easy in terms of banking opportunities, and will thus have little time or interest in doing the difficult work of finding small new companies, generating research on them, or helping them find investors.

The reason the bigger, safer deals are crowding out the little more speculative IPOs is not that the market has "evolved" to bigger deals, as is often claimed. It is that the investment-banking business model that made the hard work and risk of the smaller more speculative deals worthwhile was destroyed by the reforms. In addition to the headline electronic trading reforms such as the Order Handling Rules that hit in early 1997 (and created HFT), these additional reforms, aided by the further impetus to reform that the collapses of the dot-com and sub-prime bubbles provided in 2001 and 2008, respectively, set off a parade of similar customer protection and fair-competition initiatives, i.e., antitrust. And these reforms are still coming; indeed they are proliferating seemingly without end. There are a dozen big new rules in the hopper at the SEC as well as the "holistic review of market structure," which promises many more rules to come.

Not to be outdone, every other regulator and his uncle is trying desperately to get in on the SEC's act with their own ever-more draconian rules and prosecutions. Multibillion dollar fines hitting the big banks are being assessed by global regulators, who are also redesigning rules and policies to address the "rigging" of the markets for stocks, commodities, fixed income and currencies, especially if "dark pools" or "fixings" are involved, which could hardly sound more sinister. The Nanny State is in charge now, and the dealer market is literally or figuratively in jail. None of these trends show any sign of abating, or of pendulums swinging back in the other direction, as state and federal attorneys general and even the FBI add full criminal prosecutions and penalties to traditional bureaucratic or civil powers. [cxlvii]

Not surprisingly, investment bankers in equities feel like personae non grata as their methods and firms and in some cases their most successful people in the IPO business have been attacked with increasing ferocity for a decade and half. [cxlviii] Also unsurprisingly, bankers and banking have as a result shrunk into their protective politically correct shells and focused on safe things like HFT and big IPOs, as almost all the old practices that were associated with speculative IPOs were banned and abandoned. Among the many once common practices that were outlawed: price-fixing, spread fixing, spinning, laddering, mixing investment banking and research, failing to supervise conflicts of interest, Manning violations, front-running, spoofing, layering, insider trading, etc. [cxlix] The general thrust of these reforms is to outlaw the environment that made investment banking profitable and, where possible, to outlaw the specific actions that enabled profitability.

While regulators have their reasons for banning each of these, the point I want to make here is that in aggregate these now illegal practices were integral to raising capital for early stage companies. [cl] It may have been possible to do it otherwise, but *this is how we did it*. In other words, absent more research into how it could have been done differently or better, we have to assume that this whole bag of practices that characterized the pre-1997 IPO market *is why it was successful and thus why we have an American high-tech advantage today*. Although the capital formation engine might have survived without one or two of these practices, killing them all has had the effect, and seemingly the intent, of killing investment banking itself, at least as to its capacity to launch early stage companies.

Ironically, the intended beneficiary of the reform initiatives that killed investment banking and IPOs, the little retail investor who is supposedly no longer harmed by those conflicts of interest and unfair advantages, was not actually helped much if at all. While trading costs are down, that is a benefit the retail investor was not asking for and, by all accounts, does not even believe he has gotten, as retail investors reportedly despise the HFT market the SEC created with its reforms. In fact, the HFT market the SEC created now tops the list of reasons given by retail investors for why they lack confidence in the market. Moreover, the reforms prevented that same retail investor from speculating in those early stage companies that were never launched, which could be even more disappointing to him than the emergence of HFT, as these opportunities might have been why the market interested him in the first place. Adding insult to injury, the lack of those un-launched companies, some of which would almost certainly have succeeded as businesses, prevented the retail investor from basking along with everyone else in the economic growth those companies would have created -- along with millions of jobs.

When a Microsoft and an Intel, both of which were long shots when they launched their IPOs, worked together as Wintel, they created new categories they dominated as businesses, like computer operating systems, computer software applications and semiconductors, which became budding new industries. As these developments occurred, several other good things happened in addition to large numbers of high-paying jobs being created at those original companies. Many other companies were created or expanded that could, as Bill Gates put it once, "draft behind" the standards established by the leaders. Not only did this create large numbers of jobs at the companies of all sizes that locked in to the standard, it better organized the plethora of related technologies that otherwise exhibited all the fragmentation natural to new businesses, as monopolization pulled them all together and coordinated their activities. John D. Rockefeller may have been saying much the same thing, and perhaps even more succinctly, when he named his oil company, "Standard" Oil. Although originally aimed at persuading customers that his kerosene would not have the impurities that other refiners were known for, which often resulted in small explosions and fires, the follow-on effect of Standard's monopoly was to standardize the whole industrial sector of rail and pipeline transportation networks and other activities that surrounded the original product.

This coordination benefit arises in direct proportion to the control exercised by the monopolies, such as Microsoft and Standard Oil, which in turn is often a function of the personal control exercised by their founders, such as Gates and Rockefeller. While Rockefeller had his own means of remaining in control, which did not initially involve listing his company on the exchange, in modern times staying in control has been a function of how early in their development companies are able to IPO. The younger they are and the more speculative they are, the better the chance that the founders will emerge from the IPO in charge of the company and its future.

Getting back to my statement above that a successful IPO market must be a highly speculative one, what does that mean? The first thing it means is that companies must be able to go public at an early stage of their development, because the fresher the company is, the harder it is to tell if it will go out of business. Obviously, the more an IPO market includes significant numbers of companies that may go out of business, the more speculative it is. The second thing being highly speculative means is that even among the companies that don't go out of business, it is much harder with younger companies to tell which ones the real standout performers will be, not just the doubles or triples or even ten-baggers, but the hundred-baggers and thousand-baggers. Is it realistic to imagine that some companies can do that well? Yes, according to famed venture capitalist and PayPal co-founder Peter Thiel. It not only happens in the power law world of high tech investing, finding such standouts is what venture capital investing is all about. [cli]

While one normally thinks of such returns as the exclusive province of the angels and VCs, the genius of the pre-1997 NASDAQ dealer market was that it let little investors in on some of that action, too, by enabling many more companies to go public at earlier stages than the IPO market we have today does. This was obviously very good for those little investors. But it was also good for venture capitalists, because they were able to turn over their capital sooner as a result of the earlier "IPO exit." Because the earlier stage IPOs allowed VCs to turn over their capital far faster than they can now, they were able to do a much better job of being venture capitalists in the pre-1997 world than they can now. Thus, while the safer IPO market of today is often portrayed by the SEC and other Nanny State supporters as better than the Wild West market of the 1990s, the reality is that the losers today are all the constituents that matter: the investing public, the venture capitalists, the companies in need of capital, and the American economy's jobs-creating potential. The only winner is the Nanny State.

As the 2009 Weild and Kim paper discussed in chapter 3 said, at our peak in the mid 1990s we were doing over 500 IPOs a year, eighty percent of them raising less than $50 million, as opposed to only twenty percent raising that little in 2009, and from a much smaller pool of total IPOs. And twenty years before that (1989) it was common to do IPOs that raised only $10 million. [clii] Many of these companies failed, as would be expected in a highly speculative market. But some succeeded, a few spectacularly so. The high proportion of risky bets in IPOs was the key ingredient that gave birth to the American high tech companies we still celebrate today, some of which actually were thousand-baggers. Even Microsoft, which since its antitrust bust in 1998 has been called "dead money," is still a five-hundred-bagger. [cliii] This was clearly a market that included a fair number of speculative long shots where visionary entrepreneurs who wanted to hang on to control as long as possible to see if they could pull off their dreams on their own were given a chance to do so. Unfortunately, that process ended with the antitrust bust of NASDAQ by both the Justice Department and the SEC in coordinated actions in late 1996 and early 1997, the main effects of which were to create electronic high frequency trading and to kill that vibrant IPO market.

Now we do far fewer IPOs, and those we do manage to get out the door are not the early stage speculative long shots anymore. But just think what the market for IPOs would look like today if it had kept growing at its pre-bust pace. We would almost certainly be doing over 800 IPOs a year today, [cliv] including 600+ very speculative early stage small companies. Instead, the total number of IPOs is around 300, [clv] and with most of the market's IPO attention span taken up by less speculative ones at later stages of development, like Facebook and Alibaba, the number of true early stage long shots, like we used to have many hundreds of, is probably under 25 now. In other words, instead of the 640 micro cap IPOs we should have (800 x 80% (the proportion that Weild's studies said used to be under $50 million)), we actually have only about 25 now, and they are eclipsed by the hullabaloo devoted to the Alibabas of the world. That is just not enough spaghetti at the wall to have any real hope that something will stick as a new industry. Consequently, potentially promising founders of those new industries are selling out to other companies, who naturally take over the prospects and dreams of the founders that might have got going on their own back in the 1990s via NASDAQ's IPO machine.

Some may be encouraged by news that Alibaba is an active investor in new startups, clvi as Facebook has been. But there is a downside to that story. These companies' mega-IPOs not only took investor attention away from the smaller companies in the years in which they went public, by being active investors in startup companies themselves, these giants are in many cases obviating the need and desire for an IPO in the first place. They are thus preventing the kind of successes that created this country's high tech advantage. This is a situation welcomed with approval and almost relief by such observers as Shark Tank's Kevin O'Leary, who applauds the new companies' change in direction to look for "strategics" (i.e., big companies who believe their business models are compatible with the targets they are acquiring) to invest in them rather than to do IPOs on their own. clvii

But the safer environment works against the interests of entrepreneurs who would like to take the big risk of staying independent without selling out to a strategic. While the acquirer may promise "autonomy," a board seat on the parent, etc., under the new ownership's wing in order to get the target to agree to be acquired, the reality is we will never know how those acquired companies would have done had they stayed independent. But the high prices paid for the targeted startups, the board seats and autonomy, etc., are clear indications of the startups' founders' desire to stay independent, such as in the case of Facebook's $19 billion acquisition of WhatsApp. clviii Such deals sound very exciting of course, and the financial press is all over them. And what remains of the investment banking community is mesmerized by the chance to get in on the mega-deal action that everyone is talking about, including all their customers. But something is missing from this picture that is almost never mentioned.

To get a sense of what we are missing, consider the following: We now know how the new category of "search" is shaping up as a new industry because Google IPO'd, and how the new category of "social network" is shaping up as a new industry because Facebook IPO'd, just as before them, Microsoft, Intel, Apple and others defined new categories after their IPOs. It is possible that whatever the WhatsApp category would have become known as would have done the same. But now we will never know. In spite of the promised autonomy, board seat, etc., we will never know what Jan Koum would have made of an independent opportunity with WhatsApp, since that prospect has now been subsumed into Mark Zuckerberg's social network category and industry. The point here is not to bemoan this one situation, but to note that in its heyday, NASDAQ launched hundreds of independent companies via IPOs that created the Microsofts, Intels and Apples that now constitute America's high-tech advantage. Now, those opportunities are gone, fading into a storied past. Few new such opportunities are happening in the reformed market designed by the trustbusters.

And not only was the rug pulled out from under the entrepreneurial small company, but the willing, risk-taking speculative investor was left in the cold, too. The SEC may think it is doing these investors a favor protecting them from themselves, but most investors would probably rather be treated as adults than children and make their own choices about risk and return. Have the nannies really done anyone any good if by trimming hundreds of long shots from the market they have removed the main reason some investors wanted to be involved in the first place? And what if among those hundreds were a few natural monopolies that could have ridden the power law to being new industries providing millions of jobs? What good could those regulators possibly imagine they are doing by preventing all of these willing, eyes-open risk takers -- on both sides of the market -- from taking risks?

There is nothing wrong with big companies buying little companies or with strategics providing exits for entrepreneurs or their venture capital backers. It is what is missing that is the problem. The problem is that entrepreneurs no longer have the option of remaining an independent small business with the founder(s) in charge by doing an IPO. The removal of that option was the result of deliberate policy promulgated by regulators, a policy that amounted to American capitalism shooting itself in the foot. Sure, to a degree Silicon Valley can take care of its own now, without help from NASDAQ's IPOs. But why should it have to? Compared to what we could have done for the same startups in the pre-1997 days before the trustbusters at SEC and Justice destroyed the NASDAQ dealer market's IPO potential, there is much less chance today to see those new high tech companies get IPO funding at early enough stages that the founders will stay in charge.

Peter Thiel estimates that technology IPOs have dropped from about 300 per year in the late 1990s to 30 per year now, a 90 percent decline that he blames for the decline in new company formation, innovation and productivity in the modern American economy. [clix] Noting that Amazon went public at a $350 million valuation, [clx] he doesn't think those in the pipeline today, even assisted by the JOBS Act's streamlined shelf registration, can go public until they are "north of $10 billion" in valuation. Bottom line, far from being signs of health in our IPO market, the Alibabas, Facebooks and other giants -- whatever their own prospects -- are more appropriately considered signs of its constipation.

The new entrepreneurs and founders of technologies are unlikely to know how or why their opportunities were extinguished, but what is not happening for them by way of early stage IPOs is not happening because their government has effectively set itself up in the business of redistributing the property of the old exchanges to little investors, or at least that is what the SEC pretends to be doing. At the one end, regulators confiscate the property of the exchanges as their *negative right* to structure themselves as monopolies is extinguished. At the other end, the regulators redistribute the exchanges' loss as reforms guaranteeing investors' *positive rights* to "best execution," "efficiency," "fairness," "transparency," "investor protection," "decimal pricing" and a slew of other nebulous benefits. In so doing, the SEC has created jobs for itself in the form of the people needed to administer the massive number of new rules and bureaucratic expansion necessary to design and oversee the HFT market and an IPO market that is finally fully arms length and supposedly devoid of the dangers of all those dreaded conflicts of interest.

That is why the U.S. economy is stalling with piddling growth and few good jobs. Such benefits depend on the new companies and especially the new industries that are not being created. It is also why children can no longer expect to live better lives than their parents did. In the old days, living standards used to double every generation. No longer. That this metric, once the most reliable of the increasing economic numbers, is faltering is an implicit indictment of the U.S.'s economic leadership. Although it doesn't say by itself exactly what is wrong, it says unequivocally that something is wrong.

That something is clearly antitrust. It is not tax policy or Fed policy or any of the other more easily understandable policy levers that regularly hit the headlines and nightly news shows. While everyone fixates on the potential of the acknowledged interventions, such as deficit spending, austerity or Quantitative Easing, the policy tool the interventionists are most sure of, call it "efficiency" through antitrust, is actually the one that is poised to kill their economies regardless of what their other interventions accomplish. And, irony of ironies, it is not even thought of as an intervention, but is deemed to be a free market policy, as Bork explained in *The Antitrust Paradox*. The best evidence of its damaging effect, as discussed above and in chapter 3, is that the collapse of IPOs underlying the economic decline began its recent plunge almost immediately after the onset of one of the most significant elements of the SEC's crusade to dismantle the traditional structure of capital markets, namely the antitrust reforms of 1996 and 1997 that destroyed the NASDAQ dealer market. But there have been other signs. Going back to the launch of the National Market System in 1975, the weakness in the economy has been more than coincidentally connected to all of these related SEC reforms.

Economists have noted that the American economy seems to have hit an inflection point right around 1975, or somewhere in the 1970s anyway, after which the American dream of widely shared prosperity began to fade.

> More broadly, postwar economic growth in the United States was widely shared until the 1970s. Since then, economic growth has been slower, and it has no longer been shared by people at the bottom of the distribution. Postwar history is divided into two periods: one with relatively rapid, widely shared growth, and one with slower growth together with a growing gap between the poor and everyone else. [clxi]

This turn is ominous, as it seems to have occurred even as the momentum of global prosperity from American economic leadership was spreading benefits to the rest of the world, as it still is. Given that this turn or inflection point appears to have happened in the United States, but elsewhere, too, [clxii] it is worth a short review of what we have said in this book about the source of both American and global economic success and why the regulatory turn in America might be so consequential to global growth. The United States, after all, is not only the leading global economy, but it is also the world leader in regulatory theory and practice.

As we have seen, the markets began as price fixing cartels, conspiracies that went from fixing commissions and other insider advantages as far back as the 1690s in London and the 1790s in New York to running "fixes" in modern times for gold, Libor, currencies, etc., all of which added up to fantastic wealth for professionals in the City and on Wall Street. Regulators, none too pleased with the structures the markets came up with on their own, have taken it upon themselves to eliminate those conflicted structures and the wealth they created, and replace them with new structures designed by the regulators. Although the old structures were centuries in the making, while the regulators have only been at it for the eighty years since the SEC began in 1934, the regulators are winning. This is most unfortunate, because there is no evidence that regulators know how to design markets or economies.

The reality is that it was precisely through the selfish "fixing" or "rigging" conspiracies of unmolested markets that the uniquely modern miracle of growth finally appeared on the world stage. After millennia of seemingly permanent and universal poverty, such conspiracies lifted first the English-speaking peoples but then others to previously unimaginable prosperity in two successive industrial revolutions and global empires based, practically speaking, on two freedoms: number one, the freedom to speculate at will; and number two, the freedom to monopolize the business of serving as intermediaries for speculators.

The emergence of dominant stock exchange monopolies, the ultimate rigged enterprise, at the end of the seventeenth and eighteenth centuries in London and New York, respectively, set the pattern for forming enterprises around new technologies that carries forward to this day in a global enriching that is gradually spreading to everyone. Whereas Old World monopolies were licensed to the King's cronies as patents or other royal privileges to operate without competition, the paradigm established by the original stock exchanges, and especially by the one in New York, which was explicit about it and proud of it, was one of Do It Yourself monopolizations: no king, patent, license or other government process required or allowed. And the cornucopia of wealth that poured forth from such D.I.Y. monopolies, from the stock exchanges through Standard Oil to Microsoft and beyond, is still enriching us, in spite of trustbusters' efforts to kill them. Of course the rich benefited most. But the poor benefited, too. My favorite statistic in this regard is that the portion of people in the world living on less than a dollar a day dropped from 41 percent in 1981 to 14 percent in 2008. [clxiii]

Unfortunately, now that regulators are fully globally dominant as they attack the rigging paradigm at the heart of capital markets, it is almost certain that the enriching will cease. The beginnings of the global decline are already evident in the United States, and appeared right about when the SEC launched the National Market System in 1975.

> The golden apple of material progress contains a worm that is just about apparent in Figure 1 [not shown here]: average progress is slowing down, so that the gap between parents and their children is not what it used to be. If we look closely at the GDP figure, and compare its slope before and after 1970, we can see the decline, even if we ignore the last few years of the Great Recession. The decline is clearer in figures: in the decade from 1950 to 1959, GDP per capita grew at 2.3 percent a year; in the 1960s it grew at 3.0 percent; in the 1970s, at 2.1 percent; in the 1980s, at 2.0 percent; in the 1990s, at 1.9

percent; and in the first decade of the twenty-first century, at only 0.7 percent a year. Even if we exclude 2008 and 2009 from the last figure, we get only 1.6 percent. The difference between 3.0 and 1.6 percent might not seem very dramatic, but the power of compound growth means that, over a generation of twenty-five years, it is the difference between living standards more than doubling and living standards growing by less than 50 percent. [clxiv]

Not only did the inflection point in the economy coincide with the NMS launch on Mayday, 1975, give or take a few years, the continuing and accelerating declines in such metrics as new company formation, stock exchange listings and labor market fluidity appears in one study to be "much greater than those of other developed countries" [clxv] and in another as "specific to, or more pronounced in, the United States." [clxvi] Such U.S.-specific weakness has been unfolding roughly in parallel with SEC efforts to squeeze the revenues of Wall Street, the highlights of which would include: ending of fixed commissions in 1975, which paved the way for discount brokerage and online brokerage; ending of exchange control of trading information via mandatory tape and quotation transparency in the 1970s and 1980s; ending of the dealer market and spread-fixing and consequent full electronic trading of NASDAQ stocks with the Order Handling Rules in 1997 and other anti-dealer rules like the Manning Rule and Regulation ATS in the 1990s; ending of pricing in eighths and quarters via decimalization in 2001; and the full electronic trading of NYSE stocks via Regulation NMS in 2007, which brought HFT to NYSE stocks and the Flash Crash of May 6, 2010.

Even the wiggles within the general decline are consistent with the view that it was antitrust and NMS that are destroying IPOs and with them growth and jobs in America. Both the rapid economic growth during the latter half of the 1990s and the upswing in productivity then are consistent with the idea that the renewed conspiracy of quarter point spreads that NASDAQ and its dealers were busted for in 1996-1997 was able to briefly restore the promise of America again before the decline resumed with the antitrust bust. Productivity was 2.8 percent from 1948 to 1973. Then it dropped to 1.4 percent from 1973 to 1995, perhaps as capital formation discouragement set in after NMS was launched in 1975, along with the elimination of fixed commissions, which heralded the beginning of discount brokerage and online brokerage. Productivity rebounded to 2.6 percent from 1995 to 2010, perhaps on momentum from the IPO boom up through 1996, which was in my view largely based on the practices that the reforms banned. It then dropped to 0.7 percent from 2010 to 2013 as IPOs remained in the doldrums and the Flash Crash [clxvii] and other reform induced glitches proliferated after Reg NMS was rolled out in 2007. These productivity numbers are from an opinion piece in the Wall Street Journal by Alan Blinder [clxviii] lamenting the "mystery" of productivity and encouraging the Fed to spend more time trying to figure out what drives it. That would be a good idea, in my opinion.

The drastic anti-capital formation reforms we have seen so far are by no means the end of it. In fact they are only the beginning. Similar reforms are accumulating and accelerating as many other global regulators are piling on in the same spirit and to the same ends as the SEC's NMS crusades are aiming for. And all of these new and old joiners to the market structure party were given impetus and urgency from the reactions around the world to the credit crisis that precipitated the Great Recession of 2007-2009. There is the end of gold, currency, Libor and other fixes in 2012 - 2014, which will be followed by multiple banking authorities redesigning replacement structures. At the SEC, there is the Market Access Rule, the Large Trader Rule, the Consolidated Audit Trail (CAT) Rule, the SCI Rule (for Systems, Compliance and Integrity), etc., as the Volcker Rule and Dodd Frank push the SEC, the CFTC and many other agencies to go even faster in the same direction the SEC has been going since 1975, namely toward electronic trading, transparency, central clearing, best execution and, if possible, to consolidated limit order books (CLOBs) designed by and probably, in the end, run by regulators.

And there are many combinations of agencies into special new agencies for special purposes, such as FSOC (the Financial Stability Oversight Council), consisting of the Treasury, the SEC, the CFTC, the Federal Reserve and half a dozen others [clxix] to keep an eye on structures and firms that might threaten the markets with instability or "systemic" risk. In addition, there are many ad hoc and formal international alliances of global regulators for the purpose of redesigning equity markets, currency markets, commodity markets, fixed income markets, credit markets, centralized clearing as related to all of them, electronic trading as related to all of them, best execution and "fair" pricing (i.e., not "rigged" or "manipulated" pricing) as related to all of them, etc. And all of these mostly antitrust-based market structure initiatives will also be saturated at all times by full Nanny State investor protection.

The result can only be disastrous. With investor protection and antitrust driving regulators, the structure that emerges is by design going to be the opposite of the structure the markets were built on. Whereas the original markets sought to maximize intermediary income, which, by accident or design came in the end mostly from capital formation, the new, regulator-designed markets will seek to eliminate intermediary income. Even what little is left of capital formation is not likely to survive the assault. Just as the United States, the largest economy and most visible success at demonstrating the benefits of free-market capitalism, led the world in growth, it is now leading the world in decline as its antitrust, NMS and similar policies are adopted around the world. As fines mount and jail threatens, scores of global regulators, taking their cue from the SEC's presumption of moral superiority, feast on their reform powers in a bacchanal of regulatory overreach that cannot but fully destroy the source of all of the world's past and future wealth. Referring only to the currency fix scandals, the Financial Times said the following:

> The fines took the total to $56.5 bn, making it the most expensive year for banks on record since 2007 . . . The global probe has triggered a cascade of further civil, criminal and antitrust investigations by 20 authorities worldwide against more than 15 banks over allegations of collusion and manipulation in the forex market. [clxx]

In effect this is a reverse conspiracy, because it is now the regulators who collude and conspire with each other to reverse the original structures. Thus we are destroying structures that worked magnificently based on the rights of individuals to conspire with each other in their own interest. Those structures are being replaced in the face of multiple governments' assertion that those rights of individuals no longer exist. Instead it is now government that will do the conspiring in *its* own interest.

And we are no longer talking only about one government versus its people, but rather about a global conspiracy of *all* governments against *all* the world's peoples. There is no escape. Freedom and prosperity are under assault everywhere. The smothering government the English managed to escape from is everywhere now, and suppressing the prospects of mankind in all corners of the known commercial world. Most ironically and sadly, it is the English-speaking peoples that are leading the charge back to tyranny, and particularly the Americans who were until recently the modern keepers of freedom's flame. But now America, as both the leader of the world economically and as the primary inventor of the technical tools of the modern socialist state, such as antitrust and the National Market System, is also indirectly killing IPOs in the other OECD countries that imitate its policies:

> While the IPO decline is most extreme in the U.S., the world supply of IPOs has also suffered a material decline with the proliferation of electronic markets. Work by the OECD shows that the global number of IPOs has declined from over 2000 per year in the early 1990s to less than 750 IPOs in 2012. Two thirds of this decline comes from outside the U.S. [clxxi]

Thus the United States, as the world's largest economy, may not only be leading the world down economically through its own flagging innovation and growth, it may also be successfully indoctrinating other countries in the methods by which they can kill their own prospects more directly by adopting the same anti-growth capital markets policies.

13. What Do We Want? Redistribution! When Do We Want It? Now!

If antitrust is such a problem, can we conceivably go back to the drawing board and get Congress to rewrite the law or repeal it? Not likely. Antitrust is the quintessential redistribution program in America today. Camouflaged in theoretical and legal gobbledygook, the antitrust enterprise surges ever forward on conflicting views of inequality or inefficiency -- whatever -- which leaves it even more confused than when Bork wrote *Paradox* in 1978, and thus even more politically untouchable.

More troubling still, however, is not the confusion, but its opposite, namely the confidence that modern antitrust enforcement is on the right track economically, that focusing on lowering consumer prices by mandating price competition in each industry, separately, is all it should do, as if the big picture outlined in chapter 4 did not matter. As a result, and significantly with the help of conservatives like Bork, the field has effectively incorporated and officially adopted the traditional view that, in short, monopolies are evil.

Although Bork would never have called them that, nor would any of the theorists whose work Bork reprised in *Paradox*, there is no question that the common man's view of monopolies is approximately just that: they are evil. Although sophisticated legal scholars like Bork express their antipathy in more antiseptic and neutral terminology about allocative or productive efficiency and dead-weight losses, it still amounts to antipathy, and, for all practical purposes, might as well be pure hatred of the greed and evil of monopolization.

And so antitrust, too, for all practical purposes officially buys into the redistributionist view that monopolies should be stopped in order to give the common man a break, thus blocking the transformative monopoly enterprises that were the primary source of America's employment miracle. Giving the common man a break is blocking the much more important task of giving the common man a job.

14. Capitalism Sans Capital: An Embarrassment of Glitches

If there is still a conspiracy on Wall Street today it is the anti-HFT regulatory cartel, consisting of the SEC, other regulators, Congress, whistleblowers like Michael Lewis, and all the brokers selling anti-HFT algorithms and strategies. All of these have strong commercial and professional interests in selling investors on the false notion that trading is dangerous for them now as a result of HFT. But not only is that claim false, the exact opposite is true. The competition of HFT is probably the world's best example of "perfect competition" that exists today, because as a result of the intense nanosecond-by-nanosecond fight amongst HFTs to trade profitably, almost all intermediation costs have disappeared. Trading costs for simple average investors using "market" orders (ones that take what is available on the regular "lit" market immediately), experience costs that are highly visible and easy to understand and unbelievably low. They get roughly what they see on the screen in terms of spread, as low as a half-cent per share one way on active stocks (which comes from splitting the one-penny spread, on average), and they pay explicit commissions averaging as low as $8 per trade. While they can't know or assess in advance exactly what they will get, because no human process can move as fast as trading does now under HFT, it doesn't matter any more than you need to know exactly which oxygen molecules you are about to inhale when you breathe. You can trust the process to give you low costs, and you don't need to do anything special to get them.

If the SEC wanted to, it could do a victory lap and let investors in on the secret. The remaining profits of intermediaries are now tiny fractions of what they used to be under block trading, eighth or quarter ticks, and fixed commissions, a difference that has enabled trading cost declines of over 90 percent since the SEC began its NMS reforms, as HFTs, the only intermediaries left, now make only somewhere between one tenth and one twentieth of a cent per share, or about $1.25 billion per year in aggregate. [clxxii] This compares to previous profits from equity trading which, in spite of the obvious incentive to underplay the numbers for political reasons, had ranged from twenty billion to a hundred billion dollars per year, according to various estimates I have heard over the years. [clxxiii] Yes, the SEC certainly could do a victory lap.

But a victory lap would not serve the Commission's interest in expanding its own empire, which depends on investors not knowing that things are as good as they are. If investors knew that trading is now so cheap and easy to access that even the simplest average investor has nothing to fear from HFTs or anyone else, their lack of confidence could no longer be used as an excuse to write new rules, conduct holistic reviews of market structure, appoint panels of experts, participate in congressional hearings, etc., that are the stuff of SEC expansion. So the SEC promotes, and Congress helps it promote, an ever-expanding fleet of rules like the Consolidated Audit Trail, or CAT, as well as expansions of personnel and computer hardware and software oversight capabilities, such as MIDAS, [clxxiv] that will in aggregate cost billions and be massively disruptive to data collection and market structure, but will supposedly help the SEC monitor the markets and thereby bring trading costs down even further. And the regulated entities go out of their way to obsequiously compliment the Commission on its efforts and contribute their own suggestions, often exhorting others to join in on their public-spirited proposals to help the SEC improve things. But these efforts are far more likely to improve the SEC's control of market structure than to actually improve market structure itself. After all, if the $1.25 billion annual cost is already trivial now, as the one tenth of a cent per share earned by HFTs is, how much value can possibly come from "incremental improvement" that would shave it down a little further? [clxxv] That is good for the SEC, but not for investors.

Rather than creating confidence among investors, these market structure improvement initiatives, both individually and certainly in aggregate, will have the opposite effect. Their very existence implies *the SEC believes there is a boogeyman out there*, and, no matter how cheap and easy trading is, the boogeyman will get you! The SEC deliberately promulgates this impression. In short, the SEC isn't doing that victory lap because the SEC's existence and future growth depend on keeping investors frightened of HFTs and *un*-confident about market structure. So investors will remain frightened and lack confidence as long as the SEC exists. And it looks like the SEC will exist forever, no matter how poorly it performs. In fact, the worse it performs, the longer it will exist.

Since the increments of potential unfairness are already almost infinitesimally fine, and are bound to get even finer as competition progresses, there is infinite potential to increase what the reformers call "fairness" or "price-improvement." This means the SEC has infinite potential to expand its own enterprise to mandate change, squeezing out the remaining intermediation costs until there is nothing left, or at least pretend to be doing so, since there is already virtually nothing left to squeeze. Furthermore, rather than pleasing investors with the cost reduction, the SEC's electronic market is only making them mad, which in vicious circle fashion leads to more reforms that make them madder -- which leads to more reforms. The public revulsion to the market the SEC has created is something the SEC strongly encourages, because its entire regulatory strategy for expansion depends on the continuation of the revulsion and the consequent lack of confidence that the SEC can then use as justification for its own expansion.

Although the quixotic goal of cost reduction by its very asymptotic nature will remain elusive forever, thereby ensuring that regulators can likewise expand their enterprise forever, the value of intermediation to capital formation has already dropped far below critical mass. And what little remains is reaped only by HFTs, who have never had and probably never will have anything to do with capital formation. Thus, while the SEC is on a never-ending path to expansion, it does so only by harming the interests of both public investors and companies in search of capital, which amount to the sum total of the constituencies the SEC is supposed to be serving directly. And while the SEC does not have direct responsibility for economic growth or jobs, as the Federal Reserve does, an indirect victim of the SEC's market structure manipulations is the U.S. economy, which, as we have seen, has been increasingly unproductive of jobs roughly since 1975, a problem that is almost certainly the cause of the "decades-long trend that has widened the gap between the nation's richest citizens and everyone else" that worries President Obama, as described in the article referenced in the first footnote of this book and repeated here. [clxxvi]

Fed Chair Yellen, who *is* responsible for those things, identifies business ownership as a key pathway for economic mobility, which has been stagnant for decades, a condition that she, like President Obama, blames at least partly for the rise in inequality "and stagnant living standards for the majority." [clxxvii] "Research shows that business ownership is associated with higher levels of economic mobility," said Ms Yellen. "However, it appears that it has become harder to start and build businesses." [clxxviii] Pulling the rug out from under IPOs, as the SEC's market structure reforms have increasingly done since 1975, but with a particularly pernicious effect since the Order Handling Rules and related antitrust strictures of 1996-1997, as David Weild's studies demonstrated, is almost certainly the main reason for the drop-off in new business formation. Clearly, antitrust is killing the American economy and its jobs-generating potential, and the SEC is leading the charge. This is not helping anyone, but has a notably negative effect on the lower classes. Chair Yellen at least can make the connection the SEC misses: the lack of new businesses is a cause of inequality. The next time Congress grills her for helping the rich and hurting the poor with her low interest rate policies, she might simply suggest they look into another agency that actually *is* causing inequality.

Since the appropriately nicknamed "Mayday" 1975, the SEC has been shrinking the supply of stocks mostly owned by already rich people, which is causing them to rise and make those rich people even richer, at the same time that it is blocking the creation of new companies and jobs for working people. And it is doing these things pursuant to policies that are deliberate and long standing and, in its view, are all about fairness, i.e., helping the little guy. Those policies are clearly having the opposite effect. But like all regulatory agencies, the SEC is traditionally granted deference by Congress and the courts due to its supposed subject matter expertise. It is, in other words, supposed to know what it is doing. That is, to put it mildly, a stretch.

So this is as good a time as any to revisit the fundamental premise of antitrust. What is wrong with monopolies maximizing their own income and property value? In the case of the stock market monopoly, it has always been assumed by the SEC and academics that the friction of intermediation was a source of investor dissatisfaction and a bar to investor confidence. And since it was assumed that investor confidence was essential to raising capital, it was also assumed that getting rid of those intermediaries and their friction by forcing trading onto electronic screens would improve the ability to raise capital. But now that we have lost those old capital raisers due to these reforms, and little capital is being raised -- and fewer new businesses are forming -- let's ask the question again. If intermediaries were involved in raising capital, why did we not assume exactly the opposite of what we did assume? Why wouldn't it be good for raising capital, not bad, if those intermediaries made as much money as possible? If they structured their industry to make as much as they could from their monopoly, and the public kept buying their product, wouldn't that mean that the amount of capital raised would be maximized?

Even if capital formation was an afterthought to their monopolization, it certainly would have occurred to the monopolists running the exchange that they could maximize their income both by such means as maximizing commissions and tick sizes and restricting membership, but also by maximizing the number and quality of companies that would go public and list on the exchange. This may be the best example ever of a product improvement that came about because of monopolization. It created a whole new industry: the stock exchange built around a massive core of capital formation, a monopolization success that naturally led the way to all of the other capital formation via trusts and monopolies that the exchange's cartel was at least a legal precedent for and may have been the business model for. So again: even if, and maybe especially if, capital raising was an accidental externality that came about as a result of exchange monopoly formation, wouldn't that mean that we should allow such monopolization for that reason alone?

Why would we not assume that the better measure of confidence would be how much the public would pay, rather than how little, for the whole Wall Street package: trading, speculating, investing, stocks, bonds, IPOs, intermediation, etc? And who would be in a better position than the intermediaries that create these products and services to test out both what the most attractive mixes of them are and what the public will pay for them? After all, no one has to own stocks, or trade stocks, or speculate. If the intermediaries make the wrong calls on product or price, including the cost of intermediation, the public will do something else with their money.

To generalize this argument, why would it not be a good thing, not a bad thing, if all the monopolists who manage to latch on to a network effect and ride the power law to a widget monopoly would do the same thing as the stock market monopolists would: try to improve their products and get as much out of us as they can for them? As noted in chapter 6, there were 318 trusts operating in the United States when Teddy Roosevelt took office, accounting for 40 percent of economic activity. Why did we not assume that that was a very good thing to have that many serious enterprises dedicated to figuring out how to please the American consumer so they could get us to pay as much as possible for their wares? I know the argument is that monopolies have captive markets, and are thus in a position to gouge consumers. But that is seldom, if ever, true. In the first place, sometimes price signals are the best way to allocate suddenly scarce resources (umbrellas in rain storms, gasoline during OPEC embargoes, etc.), rather than through rationing, lotteries, or long lines. So raising prices is not always bad. And even gouging is a term of service that would be reacted to, and remembered as part of the general reputation of that monopoly, which could hurt its position in the long run if it was thought to have been unfair to the consumer or otherwise disrespectful. No prudent monopolist in charge of a lucrative monopoly would want to risk that, because it would only help a competitor who wanted to take his monopoly away from him. In TR's time there would have been 317 other monopolies you could spend your money on if you didn't like the product or terms of one of them, not to mention spending it somewhere else in the 60 percent of the economy that was not covered by a trust. Why don't we consider *that* to be competition? And why would we not consider the hierarchy of the amounts paid to monopolies to be a pretty accurate map of the things consumers really want and what their relative values to the economy are?

During our first century as a country, the NYSE achieved a justifiable reputation as the Big Board, clearly commanding its own category and giving birth to many other monopolies that confirmed America as the global center of capital formation. That is a reputation we are rapidly losing today, largely because the SEC has taken it upon itself to eliminate the intermediation component of the Wall Street product mix. That could not be more shortsighted, in large measure because the intermediaries were the effective owners and proprietors of that product mix, and it is not at all clear that if you eliminate them and their incentives, there will be anything else left. In any case, IPOs are clearly on the ropes. And the proliferation of glitches in the electronic National Market System is a sign that America is on the way out as the global leader in anything related to capital markets.

Solving our capital formation problems will not be possible through the Tick Pilot or any other combination of SEC rules or reforms or reviews of market structure. The SEC is the problem. Even if anything successful popped up out of the pilot, or if it came from crowd funding or Shark Tank or any of the other interesting sideshows surrounding today's capital formation wasteland, the SEC would have to kill it, because the SEC is now, by nature, opposed to capital formation. Not literally or explicitly, of course, but that is the inevitable effect of the SEC's preoccupation with imposing the antiseptic, arms length, no conflict of interest, no unfair advantage rules it is bound to enforce. So the only way to see capital formation return is to get rid of the SEC. That task would be very difficult but not unimaginable, and is becoming ever easier with the regular embarrassments of glitches resulting in commissioners and staff being called onto the carpet in front of congressional committees every few months when another one of their NMS creations goes bonkers.

People at the SEC have long prided themselves on being self-sacrificing public servants working hard on the investor's behalf, which should improve investor confidence, in their universal opinion. At one time, this might have been true, or at least it would have been hard to blame those at the SEC if it were not, because, in their naïveté, they wouldn't have known any better. I have known many hard-working, self-sacrificing professionals at the SEC over the years for which such sentiments would have been reflexive and understandable.

But the situation is different now. Certainly the Flash Crash, the Facebook IPO, the Knight debacle and the four-hour shutdown of NASDAQ trading and many more glitches have demonstrated that there is something terribly wrong with what the SEC has created. And with all the ongoing concern on the part of the public over HFT, as well as the dearth of IPOs that, at Congress's direction via the JOBS Act, has forced the SEC to conduct the Tick Pilot, and all of this punctuated by regular congressional hearings into market problems, as well as the recently-announced investigations of various state attorneys general, the FBI and the Justice Department into whatever it is that is going wrong with Wall Street, it would be impossible for honest people even at the SEC not to have noticed that there is something very suspicious about at least the results of their activities, if not their own motives and competence.

If they would consider, as we have, the evidence submitted in *Wall Street* by their former SEC colleague, Walter Werner, which demonstrates beyond any reasonable doubt that the main mission of the SEC since inception, restraining speculation, is fundamentally misguided, and that its other mission, restraining monopolization via antitrust, is at the very least fraught with problems and perhaps equally misguided, it would be impossible for an open-minded SEC staffer or commissioner to miss the fact that the problem is them.

And as far as their alleged self-sacrifice is concerned, it is a phony sham. Designing and regulating the National Market System has created good, secure jobs and lucrative careers for the SEC's bureaucrats at the expense of the American economy and all those unemployed Americans whose jobs have never been created due to the SEC's supposedly self-sacrificing activities. While the ranks of the industry were decimated, [clxxix] the ranks of regulators have been on a never-ending expansion track.

The industry was eviscerated in absolute numbers, and what is left of its historical trading core has no connection whatever to capital formation now. Not only is HFT, which has nothing to do with capital formation, the dominant trading function, but by wringing out the conflicts between investment banking, trading and research, the reforms destroyed the most productive parts of Wall Street that were tightly connected to the trading process from their beginnings in the 1790s to today, as Werner and Smith described in *Wall Street*. Or they were, that is, until the 1997 reforms, which finally severed that connection completely. What remains are HFTs and a narrow regulation-focused sub-profession called "market structure experts," whose main mission is to participate in all of the SEC processes, none of which have anything to do with raising capital.

Meanwhile, SEC jobs are secure, well paid and, like all government jobs, have excellent benefits. Best of all from their perspective, they are on the cutting edge of market structure developments in the industry, all of which are forced by regulation. For that reason, SEC jobs are also ideal launching pads for HFT jobs or as market structure experts on the stub of Wall Street for any bureaucrat that does want to leave the comfort of the SEC for better pay by walking through that always-revolving door. Let's face it, the SEC is a cushy gig, and any implication that there is any self-sacrifice going on by these "public servants" is nonsense. The greed is not on Wall Street. The greed is at the SEC. Investors, far from feeling comforted and confident as a result of the SEC's activities, should instead be angry and demand they all resign.

To unwind the antitrust monstrosity the easiest and most appropriate place to start is by getting rid of the SEC. Since nothing the Commission does has any beneficial effect, and all of it is harmful, any move to freeze funding, or to force a moratorium on new rules or other regulatory activities would be useful and welcome. I have no doubt that, absent the SEC and antitrust, capital allocation could make a comeback. If freed from the trivial concerns of the Nanny State, some combination of the existing players and new ones would certainly give it a try.

Pursuing inequality is not dead, at least conceptually, and could still work its *invisible hand* wonders if given half a chance.

I assume the democratic debates over redistribution will continue unabated on all topics and indeed will expand, from big ones like tax policy and such affirmative social rights as those to health care, housing and education, to little ones like investors' rights to compete with HFTs on a level playing field in the stock market. As observant human beings, we will all be drawn to these debates regardless of whether we recognize their futility or that they amount to nothing more than all of us debaters behaving nonlogically under the pretense of behaving logically, as Pareto said. But while we may not be able to restrain ourselves from participating in these inevitable exercises in socialism, we should not fool ourselves into thinking there is any realistic hope of getting back to freedom through such normal political or regulatory processes.

We should not fool ourselves, for example, into thinking repealing Obamacare would do any good in terms of getting us back to the principles America was founded on. As Newt Gingrich once said in a fit of honesty for which he was nearly drummed out of the Republican Party, "I don't think right wing social engineering is any more desirable than left wing social engineering." [clxxx] But in spite of the Liberty Bell ring to Gingrich's always inspiring rhetoric, closer examination reveals that he was just pushing a Red Team, upward redistribution view to counter Obama's Blue Team, downward redistribution policy. The "national conversation" Gingrich called for would focus on "a better Medicare system with more choices for seniors," a popular upward-redistribution program, as a counter to Obama's downward redistribution program of Obamacare. As I said in *Nature's God*, there is little chance Obamacare will be repealed. Three years later, and four years after Gingrich's comment, I still think the chances are nil that Obamacare can be repealed, in spite of the Republican gains in 2014. But it would not matter in terms of freedom if Obamacare were repealed, because replacing it with a less downward redistributionist and more upward redistributionist Republican program would still amount to socialized medicine. And that kind of right wing social engineering is still all that any of the Republicans are talking about. [clxxxi]

It is true that healthcare is an area that sorely needs freedom to solve the big problems: new drugs to fight drug-resistant bacteria, capitalizing on decoding the human genome to actually get something useful out of it, and the ever-present problem of universal coverage. These are all challenges that I believe could be solved just by getting rid of antitrust and letting a natural health care monopoly form, where instead of the patent-by-patent approach with its corruption prone overspending that we see today that is producing only increasingly feckless stabs at solving these problems, we could see a natural monopoly solve them all in one fell swoop. But health care is one of those areas where the redistribution directions of the arguments are too clear, where the Right and Left troops are too clearly lined up against each other to imagine success in a strategy of directly attacking the socialist illogic of the current democratic debate or national conversation. Rather, I would leave that and all other similarly locked in socialist processes aside for the moment in order to attack the one that is most vulnerable.

What the SEC does is little understood and less appreciated by most people. An attack on the SEC, therefore, just might be successful and work to halt government expansion in its tracks. If it did, which would mark the beginning of the end of antitrust, it might be possible someday to see healthcare, education, space exploration, cybercrime and many other big problems solved naturally with D.I.Y. monopolies. So don't bother with Obamacare or any of the other hot button issues for now. The one realistic hope is that Americans will find the path back to freedom *without debate over any specific issues*, but just by saying "no" to that perennial government expansion vehicle known as SEC budget requests.

For reference, the SEC is currently asking for $1.722 billion for 2016 so it can hire hundreds of additional people. [clxxxii]

15. Reality, Unfortunately

With the number of superrich people in the United States continuing to outstrip the rest of the world by far, [clxxxiii] while the middle class and poor are increasingly left behind, [clxxxiv] the underlying reality is that the democratic debates over inequality, and all the escalating tensions they engender, will continue and grow. We now turn to what that means to our society and to peace and security in the world, focusing in this chapter on our society, and in the next chapter on the global situation. The background trajectory is toward horrible results, on the order of or worse than the horrors of the twentieth century.

There are only two practical ways to avoid this horrible result, as most people would see it, neither of which is actually very practical or likely to work, including my own proposal above. The standard view is that democratic debate will lead to a resolution, either by taking us to acceptable amounts of downward redistribution to alleviate inequality or by taking us on an upward redistribution path by, say, repealing Obamacare or going "back to the Constitution." My solution, which is the opposite of democratic debate, has its own challenges, as the reader can easily imagine. But one of its challenges that might not be obvious is its apparent similarity to standard political calls from the Right to go back to the Constitution. So let me start by describing how the democratic debate sets up and why my proposal, whatever its challenges, is not like a standard approach from the Right.

On the one side of the debate, call it the Right or Red Team, is my proposal to get rid of antitrust, starting with the SEC. One could also include on this side any number of even more unrealistic means of returning to the principles of America's founding, such as those calls to go back to the Constitution. The Constitution is still the gold standard of Red Team identification with founders' intent, even though it is now interpreted primarily as an instrument of tyranny that denies the key rights to discriminate that early Americans unquestionably had. Not only did we have the private right to discriminate on any basis we saw fit as our Wall Street monopoly formed, but an implication of that history is that our government did not have the right to discriminate in favor of any groups, as it does now on behalf of, say, working women or homosexuals. The government does such things today both by enacting affirmative rights to, for example, equal pay for equal work and marriage equality, and by outlawing private acts of discrimination against such groups in, for example, employment and housing. The Red Team is thus in all likelihood chasing a false hope that the Constitution might help us return to the America of our founders, since the Supreme Court, the political culture and political correctness generally all prove that the America our Constitution supports today is in most respects the opposite of the America of our founders.

In any case, regardless of their underlying merits on an intellectual level, on a practical political level such proposals and strategies from the Right are generally not meant to be serious in terms of getting something done, but are primarily intended to be confrontational in order to demonstrate team loyalty and fervor by their opposition to the Blue Team's platform, as discussed at the end of the previous chapter with respect to Obamacare and at length in my previous book, *Nature's God.* [clxxxv] In all cases except my own proposal, the Red Team adopts these stances in the democratic debates to better shape its arguments for upward redistribution as a defense against the Blue Team's arguments for downward redistribution. In contrast, my proposal would dismantle a particularly harmful piece of modern tyranny, namely the SEC, but would have nothing to do with redistribution in any direction, or with democratic debate.

On the Left or Blue Team is the democratic debate aimed at downward redistribution to alleviate tensions over inequality championed by Thomas Piketty and Nobel Prize winner Joseph Stiglitz (*The Price of Inequality*), but in practice participated in by most politicians and debaters of any stripe. While the Red Team also has a dog in the redistribution fight, as just noted, it is the Blue Team that far more fervently embraces democratic debate, because they believe it serves their interests in downward redistribution, largely because of the always glowing picture of inequality that everyone can point to, whatever their political persuasion. Although Piketty acknowledges that the chances of success for his strategy of democratic debate leading to, say, satisfactory progressivity in taxes are low ("Admittedly, a global tax on capital would require a very high and no doubt unrealistic level of international cooperation"), [clxxxvi] I believe they are actually far lower than he acknowledges, in fact nil. But because most people regardless of their politics can't help themselves from believing in and participating in the debates, their likely choice will be to go with the debates anyway. It is precisely due to the frustrations and political conflicts that will inevitably accompany such debates that the horrors will descend.

The reason is that this is not just an ordinary Right versus Left debate over the direction of redistribution. This is about the means and efficacy of the debating process itself. And in this debate, virtually one hundred percent of the debaters line up on Piketty's side, whether they have roots in the Red Team traditions of the founders or in the Blue Team traditions of FDR's New Deal or the French Revolution that Piketty champions. In this debate, the traditions of the founders have been long forgotten, subsumed by a tacit agreement that everyone, regardless of their views on current policy, should and must participate in democratic debate, which itself assumes that the founders' traditions are irrelevant to the matters under discussion. In other words, the *"negative"* unalienable rights in the Declaration of Independence that prevented things from being taken away from us, have already been cast aside in favor of *"positive"* rights that give things to us, and thus the debates are only about who gets what and who pays.

This means that almost everyone has bought into the view of rights that will foment the maximum amount of tension and violence. Even if some redistribution occurs on the Piketty model, as was proposed recently in Columbia, where a Piketty-inspired wealth tax was floated, [clxxxvii] that would still leave all the tensions and arguments unresolved. Both in the specific locale where the redistribution occurred, and in the wider world that can observe it, the resolution will have resolved nothing, and in fact is bound to engender further tension and anger. Because some inequality will remain in all cases, which neither Piketty nor Stiglitz nor anyone else disputes, the tensions and anger will remain and grow no matter how much redistribution occurs. There is no such thing as a socially acceptable amount of inequality that would be agreed on by everyone or a so-called "social compact" that will permanently satisfy everyone with a particular wealth or income distribution. Even if inequality is tempered in the short run as wealth is redistributed downward, enough of it will remain in any and every case that the tensions and conflict over it will persist. Any split between rich and poor, whether seemingly brought about through redistribution or the lack of it, or through natural or unnatural forces of any description, will eventually give way to more argument as both those dissatisfied with the current arrangement speak up, and as the natural tendency toward inequality continues, whether that tendency is thought of in terms of Piketty's laws of capitalism, Pareto's 80-20 rule, or the rich-get-richer of modern network science.

Piketty and others from the Left do not want to admit this possibility, nor do those on the Right. They are all at pains to emphasize the effects of tax rates and other inequality modifiers as the significant or sometimes sole causes of any given levels of inequality. Their reluctance to admit the inevitable uselessness of their countermeasures to arrive at permanently satisfactory levels of inequality is understandable, because to do otherwise would be to admit that they, too, are useless, and that perhaps you shouldn't waste your time reading their books or send your money to their political fundraisers. So rather than admit that inequality will remain at socially unacceptable levels no matter what, those on the Left at least focus on vilifying the rich, instead, which they have found is a proven formula for selling books, as authors from Piketty to Stiglitz to Michael Lewis have discovered.

As mentioned earlier, Piketty never says why inequality is bad or harmful to the people who are not rich, other than that it incites jealousy and violent revolution from time to time. His nominal justification for this vilification of the rich is that they do not deserve their wealth. He leads off his book with a quote from article 1 of the Declaration of the Rights of Man and the Citizen from 1789 as the French Revolution was getting under way: "Social distinction can be based only on common utility." But although he purports to have written the book in order to make this judgment, he never arrives at any hard and fast or even loose rules by which "common utility" should be judged. Instead, he merely says that such issues can be worked out through democratic debate. But the anger at undeserved wealth, which is bound to linger and fester and grow as inequality inevitably swells from time to time, puts an impossible burden on democratic debate to solve the perceived problem.

To better understand why democratic debate won't work, we need to delve a little deeper into the implied view of rights held by those who believe in it. The unalienable rights to life, liberty and property were called unalienable because you can't alienate them from yourself even if you try. Short of no longer existing (dying), human beings do not have the ability to reorient their own minds so that they would be OK with giving up their lives, their liberty or their property. The unalienables essentially defined what could not legitimately be taken away from you by others or government, not what you were owed by others or the government or were entitled to. As such these were negative rights, as we have discussed before, not positive rights, or what are more frequently today called affirmative rights or entitlements.

106

Believers in democratic debate, in contrast, focus almost solely on positive or affirmative rights. And the positive or affirmative rights they focus on are distinctly not unalienable. That is why they will always cause conflict at any level and kind of inequality, and why affirmative action is always an emotional issue on all sides. Such rights and claims don't exist unless and until government through its political processes determines what they are and establishes your claim to them. But once government is in the business of giving out affirmative rights, there is no possible end to it. Once you learn the language of fighting for your fair share by vilifying the rich -- how they actively "take" or "appropriate" or "claim" what you believe you are entitled to -- that language and the anger it implies are never forgotten. And always in the background is the threat of violence and revolution if the rich do not give up their property willingly through the political process of democratic debate. Some academics are guiltier than others of promoting such anger and potential violence. For an academic, for example, Piketty seems unusually prone to un-academic wording that appears to be deliberately chosen to promote anger at the rich.

> In more inegalitarian societies, the top decile *claimed* as much as 50 percent of national income (with about 20 percent going to the top centile). This was true in France and Britain during the Ancien Régime as well as the Belle Époque and is true in the United States today. Is it possible to imagine societies in which the concentration of income is much greater? Probably not. If, for example, the top decile *appropriates* 90 percent of each year's output (and the top centile *took* 50 percent *just for itself*, as in the case of wealth), a revolution will likely occur, unless some peculiarly effective repressive apparatus exists to keep it from happening. When it comes to ownership of capital, such a high degree of concentration is already a source of powerful political tensions, which are often difficult to reconcile with universal suffrage. [clxxxviii] [Emphasis added]

Thus Piketty implies that democracy itself ("universal suffrage") requires redistribution and affirmative rights. Further, he implies throughout the book that democratic debate can determine how much and which kinds of redistributions would be acceptable without leading to violence and revolution, presumably because the rich will realize from his descriptions that they have already *taken* or *appropriated* more than their fair share. But this will never happen with affirmative rights. Not only can any of them be taken away at any time through the same political process that created them, i.e., democratic debate, they are always subject to constant adjustment as their relative amounts are increased or decreased in relation to each other and as new ones are added. By their very nature affirmative rights must be fought over politically and thus are always the subject of endless disputes and anger, not just over how much and what types of property to pry from the wealthy, but over how to divvy it up, as in current Scotland after the failed independence referendum:

> Some residents even say they would rather Gigha was still in the hands of a laird, or rural landowner. "You go to a laird and he says yes or no; you go to a trust and they say 'let's have a meeting'," complains Matthew Steele, who

works at a fish farm that was not included in the buyout. "It's the lunatics taking over the asylum, the blind leading the blind. That's what this place has become: one big cliché." For some residents a downside of community control is the fact that it means neighbors can fall out over everything from rent levels to investment strategy. "This place was more enjoyable under a laird -- there was less back-stabbing," says Mr. Steele. Retired farmer Kenny Robison recalls one resident who said after the buyout that "we all used to hate the landowner, but who are we going to hate now?" clxxxix

Unlike the original unalienables, in which everyone has a common interest and claim, *as individuals*, affirmative rights have winners and losers, *as groups*, such as the claims of health care workers versus the claims of teachers, or the claims of elderly retirees versus the claims of the working poor or unemployed youth or students with education debt, or the claims of those with government jobs versus the claims of those who work for private companies, or the claims of those with pre-K children versus those with claims to higher education subsidies, etc. There are literally thousands of such actual or potential affirmative rights and entitlements, as well as countless nuances that emphasize the claims of one or another within subsets of each of the main ones.

If you then add in the disputes over whether the taxpayers' or landowners' rights to property are being abridged to fund these affirmative rights, i.e., whether their unalienable rights are being violated, you wind up where we are today with the unending disputes over inequality. And these disputes are inevitably unending, since everyone who has property taken from him to fund someone else's benefit will always believe the confiscated amount was too much. And everyone on the receiving end of the transfer will always believe the amount was too little. Once the unalienable right to property goes, and it is gone now, there can be no end to the anger and potential for violence elicited by conflicting claims over affirmative rights.

But it gets worse, much worse. So far we have been talking only about property: land or money. But the same unending conflict that erupts over inequality of incomes and wealth becomes much worse when money is only the backdrop for much more emotional disputes over relative positions in society, such as those over civil rights. This is where group rights come into serious and potentially violent contention, pitting conflicting claims of different ethnicities, religions, nationalities, cultures, sexes, sexual preferences, etc., against each other. If the unalienable right of individuals to property is no longer assumed, then groups will assume their rights are being attacked by other groups, and not just in terms of wealth, but also in terms of status and positions in society. This is understandable, since, as with money, whatever you get by way of affirmative rights means that someone else didn't get an affirmative right he thought he deserved, or had his unalienable right to property or to his position in society taken away to fund your right. Either way, that means war, figuratively or literally.

It starts when measures of a group's participation in the benefits of society come up short of expectations or hopes, such as when women or blacks do not appear to share the incomes or jobs or educations that their proportions in the relevant populations imply they should enjoy. If individual rights to property were

108

all that mattered, such suspicions could be resolved merely by making sure there was nothing government was doing to take away anyone's property. But if that unalienable right is ignored in favor of a focus on group rights, and the lack of proportional representation is deemed prima facie evidence of the ill intent of other groups to let you receive what you believe is your due, then all hell will break loose. Discrimination will be charged. Affirmative action will be proposed. Re-education will be administered. Diversity programs will be instituted. Inclusion will be mandated.

Amidst the political mayhem that inevitably follows such charges it is easy to forget that economic inequality is the main underlying driver of these raw disputes, albeit in hidden ways that can often go unspoken. But that fact comes back into focus when one notices that the one group that is always deemed to be in violation of these group rights claims is the rich. This group is ever in arrears because it is assumed to be unjustly wealthy, and therefore the wealth it has could and should by rights have been owned by or spread around to the non-rich groups. While many of the aggrieved groups may hate each other (or at least argue constantly over their relative claims to the presumed pool of entitlements), the one thing they can generally agree on is that they should all with one voice hate the rich. Hatred of the rich is, therefore, a sign that a society is coming apart at the seams. It means that its respect for property and the natural order it creates has been replaced by sectarian warfare over other peoples' property, as the diversity and inclusion warlords marshal their forces.

Here in America, the danger of tensions and anger over inequality, including violent anger, is growing apace. Even to be able to say out loud that inequality is not the fault of rich people, rich venture capitalist Thomas Perkins had to acknowledge that inequality *is* a problem. Perkins started a firestorm when he wrote a letter to the editor of the Wall Street Journal warning that today's demonization of the rich, which so far has led to only isolated instances of violence and property damage, could nonetheless develop in time into something far worse. The firestorm started because he compared that hidden danger in today's America to similarly hidden dangers in the Germany of the early 1930s when the horrors of Kristallnacht and the Holocaust were still years away and beyond imagination.

> I would call attention to the parallels of fascist Nazi Germany to its war on its "one percent," namely its Jews, to the progressive war on the American one percent, namely the "rich." ... This is a very dangerous drift in our American thinking. Kristallnacht was unthinkable in the 1930s; is its descendant "progressive" radicalism unthinkable now? [cxc]

Although he was demonstrably not anti-Semitic, Perkins felt forced to apologize and explain his remarks in the most commented-on flurry of letters and news show commentary ever ignited by a WSJ letter to the editor. He clearly did not want to offend anyone, and apologized over and over for use of the word "Kristallnacht" in his analogy. But Perkins was adamant that he did not apologize for his message, nor for the basic thrust of his analogy, saying in an interview with Emily Chang of Bloomberg West, "now that you've thoroughly killed the messenger, at least listen to the message." [cxci]

The message is that the demonization of the rich in America today bears some resemblance to the early stages of the gathering persecution of Jews in Nazi Germany. As he rephrased it more sensitively to Chang in their interview: "There's sharks in that water. Don't go there." He explained how his late good friend and partner, Eugene Kleiner, who was Jewish and had fled Hitler from Austria, had always warned that we "should never imagine that the unimaginable can't become real." As Perkins summarized Kleiner's warning:

> Anytime the majority starts to demonize a minority, it's wrong, it's dangerous, and nothing good ever comes of it. [cxcii]

In spite of his explanations and apologies, attacks on Perkins proliferated not just in the Chang interview, but in hundreds of discussions led by the media at the Wall Street-focused cable channels, Bloomberg and CNBC, as well as at almost all other media venues, all of which, and every invited guest of which, made some version of the following charges against Perkins. It was stated or implied that he was either anti-Semitic or at least insensitive to the feelings of Holocaust survivors. Second, he was alleged to have "equated" some broken glass at luxury car dealerships in San Francisco, or rocks thrown at "Google buses," with the atrocities of Kristallnacht and the Holocaust. And third, because he is rich, he was accused of being out of touch with the real world and the inequality problem in America today.

The problem with these charges is that they either maliciously mischaracterize Perkins personally, or fail to understand what he said. He was neither anti-Semitic nor insensitive to Jews, as his memories of Kleiner referenced above, and his apology letter to the Anti-Defamation League demonstrate (which he read to Chang). And he did not *equate* the broken glass incidents to Kristallnacht, much less to the Holocaust, which the media panels invariably accused him of doing. Instead, he merely stated the incontrovertible fact that, in the early stages of Nazi persecution of Jews, Kristallnacht, too, was unimaginable, as was the Holocaust, points that his late partner Kleiner had made to him. He was only trying, as the Holocaust remembrance initiatives all around the world have endeavored to do with their "never again" focus, to point out that we are headed in the same dangerous direction.

The whole point of *never again* is to stop such trends early, before they get out of hand, by recognizing them. Perkins clearly believes, as he told Chang, that the Holocaust was and will remain in a class by itself in terms of human horror. But he also said, in keeping with Jewish thought ever since the Holocaust, that we should beware of any tendencies of majorities to persecute minorities. In the current "We Are The Ninety-Nine Percent" atmosphere, America is exhibiting that dangerous trend in spades. That Perkins himself was so incorrectly and disingenuously attacked is proof of that. America is clearly exhibiting at least the early stages of the same social disease that overwhelmed Nazi Germany and plunged that nation and the world into the violent convulsions of World War II that killed tens of millions, including the six million Jews in the Holocaust.

The most frightening thing about the Holocaust was not the horrors themselves, vicious and evil as they were, but that they were perpetrated in a modern, civilized society. Germany had developed all the cultural and government institutions, such as democracy, that supposedly protected citizens from such unimaginable cruelty. What went wrong? We may never know for sure or, as Perkins said to Chang, "the Holocaust was unbelievably horrible and [so horrible that] it can never be explained." On the other hand, there is a growing body of work by scientists into the social causes of genocide that is beginning to provide some insight into the phenomenon. While the Holocaust remains the worst example these authors can find, there are many other examples, and some significant patterns are beginning to emerge. Perhaps the most prominent pattern in this regard is the presence of jealousy and hatred of the rich as a motivator to genocide.

In *World On Fire: How Exporting Free Market Democracy Breeds Ethnic Hatred and Global Instability*, Amy Chua identifies this precursor to genocide and other sub-genocide abuses, such as ethnic cleansing. She cites incident after incident of jealousy-based attacks on a "market dominant minority," where attacks are motivated by revenge against the supposedly undeserved success of a visible minority in the midst of a less-successful majority. Chua is hesitant to generalize her case for application to the Holocaust, perhaps in deference to its extra-horrific status. But such a comparison would be apt. It was the Jews' relative economic success that particularly angered the Nazis, as illustrated in a propaganda film, *Der Ewige Jude*, produced by Nazi propaganda minister Joseph Goebbels at Hitler's request. [cxciii] But for all of her penetrating insights into the causes of genocide, Chua says little about cures, beyond the rather conventional suggestions of some to address inequality through "redistribution institutions." [cxciv] Thus she, too, would appear to accept the conventional wisdom of Piketty and others that inequality is a problem that needs to be addressed via redistribution.

Even more strangely, so does Tom Perkins. For all his defense of the one percent as not being the cause of inequality, he makes no effort to defend inequality itself and even seems comfortable with the application of redistribution remedies to address it. In the Chang interview, Perkins expresses agreement with his friends, former Vice President Al Gore and California Governor Jerry Brown, who tell him, "inequality is the number one problem in America." Perkins responds, "that's probably and possibly true, and I think that President Obama is going to make that point [in a speech] tomorrow night." Thus Perkins, too, believes that inequality is a problem that must be addressed somehow. And, like Chua, he does not appear to be overly annoyed at redistribution remedies for it, saying that he still considers Jerry Brown to be a friend even though he raised Perkins's taxes by thirty percent. And while Perkins does not claim to be a friend of President Obama, neither does he take issue with the President's focus on inequality or with redistribution remedies for it.

Unfortunately, the fight over inequality or redistribution is seldom civil. And it is increasingly verging on or spilling into violence, with the tacit support of government leaders. When the Supreme Court endorses income-based affirmative action to get around constitutional bans on racial discrimination, the effect is the apparent support and endorsement of race-based allocation of wealth or incomes at the highest levels of our government. It is hard to imagine a greater inducement to the feeling of entitlement the lower classes have now, or for self-righteous anger at the upper classes for any opposition to such entitlements. Against this official legal backdrop, the unemployed poor, and especially the unemployed black poor, feel fully justified in their anger at rich whites for their situation.

So why wouldn't they lash out on occasion in physical attacks? And against the same backdrop, why wouldn't whites be angered at official government sponsored discrimination against them in hiring and entrance to education institutions. Why wouldn't they seek to defend themselves against physical attacks on their persons or property by organizing "watch" duties in their neighborhoods or living in gated communities? "Trayvon Martin could have been me," says President Obama, making it clear whose side he is on. [cxcv] And New York is a "plantation," according to a speaker chosen by Mayor de Blasio to highlight his "tale of two cities" inauguration to a mayoralty that promises to address inequality. [cxcvi] Neither the Mayor nor the President has provided any similar moral guidance regarding the "knockout game" [cxcvii] played by young black men that has resulted in some deaths of innocent white men, nor when an elderly man died after being punched in a New York City park when a black man said he was going to "punch the first white man I see." [cxcviii]

Everyone in politics supports "affordable housing," a form of downward redistribution. Even wealthy former New York City mayor Michael Bloomberg had affordable housing policies, although not such aggressively redistributive ones as Mayor de Blasio now supports. So when crowds in Brooklyn hear from black filmmaker Spike Lee that gentrification is pushing them out of their homes, they seethe with anger. [cxcix] Similarly, when every official in California and all the experts on all the news shows rail against the unfairness of Google buses for tech workers, and demand that those rich tech companies give even more money to solve the housing shortage they have allegedly caused with their success and jobs, this form of gentrification inspires some to throw rocks at the buses and to break windows at the luxury dealerships where the rich buy their cars, as Tom Perkins noted in his ill-fated Kristallnacht analogy, which was triggered not just by the broken glass, but, as Perkins explained, by the fact that the police just stood around and watched it happen.

While we may be a long way from our own Kristallnacht, we are certainly heading in that direction. Moreover the only remedy that anyone is talking about is redistribution, forms of which are even embraced by many of the rich, like Tom Perkins. Unfortunately, this remedy cannot possibly work to solve the problem. The only thing that can work, as the founders of America discovered, is to protect the natural right of all people, as individuals, to pursue inequality, what they called "the pursuit of happiness." That right has been abandoned now in favor of group rights, and consequently its polar opposite political principle prevails, namely redistribution driven by vilification of the rich.

Those who see redistribution as a moral imperative and trust in the efficacy of democratic debate to reach consensus on how much it should be and what forms it should take, are generally blind to the potential for violent chaos to emerge from these very processes. Piketty and Stiglitz, for example, go on for hundreds of pages in their books describing the dimensions and sources of inequality, always apparently assuming that with enough experts like themselves informing the public about how much inequality is tolerable, and what types of inequality are "inefficient" as to their ability to support economic growth, we, as a society, will happily vote or otherwise arrive at consensus public policies that everyone will accept. So when Stiglitz recounts studies, including an earlier one by Piketty, purporting to show that seventy percent is the right marginal tax rate for incomes of the wealthy, [cc] we are to presume, I suppose, that because they and their respective legions of experts agree (which they don't, but just pretend!), now we all know how to vote.

What these experts miss is that when the consequences of their determinations are considered by the affected groups, the very political process they recommend to reach consensus is more likely to produce conflict, anger and, at the extreme, violence. In Hitler's Germany, it was the consensus of the ordinary German people in the Volksgemeinschaft (folk community) or "Volk," [cci] a group similar in its universal appeal and target audience to that of "the middle class" or "the ninety-nine percent" in today's America, that brought out the Brownshirts, that led to Kristallnacht and, ultimately, to the Holocaust. They also had their experts: experts on the science of race and eugenics, for example, that warned of letting their one percent, the Jews, take unfair portions of income and wealth from "true" Germans, or Aryans. Perkins is right to flag the building hatred of the one percent, which is inflamed by experts like Piketty and Stiglitz, as well as by most of our political leaders, as a sign that our society is headed in a very dangerous direction.

And it is when the income and wealth consequences of policy can be boiled down to easily identifiable group effects, like race, that riots and, ultimately, civil wars, break out. Here is where the violence gets vicious. Here is where a black man can say to bystanders, "watch what I'm going to do," [ccii] just before he murders two unsuspecting policemen, confident that *his* crowd of *his* people will approve. While this particular man, Ismaaiyl Brinsley, was no doubt overconfident in this regard, there is also no doubt that the political leaders and experts on the Left have consistently approved of the "right" of blacks to protest their treatment at the hands of police, and that these leaders have been none too careful about defining where the right to protest goes too far.

"Pluralism," "diversity," "equality" and "inclusion" are typical of the political labels often applied to the general set of policies meant to forcibly raise the presumably downtrodden and oppressed groups in our society to new levels of acceptance, position and potential wealth. Improvement is expected via various affirmative rights, affirmative actions and even mandatory quotas designed to counter past or current discrimination against these groups, which is presumed to be the cause of their downtrodden or oppressed status. Because discrimination is deemed to be evil per se, affirmative actions to counter discrimination are morally justified, even morally and "constitutionally" required, according to advocates of these policies, who include presidents of the United States, mayors of major cities and Supreme Court justices.

The potential for violence is evident in the conflicts between police and blacks over how their community is affected by policing practices. Against the backdrop of the presumed need to affirmatively help the mostly poorer blacks economically, there are the additional issues of presumed requirements to relax policing practices that police have found to work effectively, such as stop-and-frisk, and the presumed need to not uniformly apply surveillance or arrest methods, if their application to blacks would offend them by showing that blacks commit disproportionate amounts of crime. And most controversially, significant violence erupted as normal grand jury procedures failed to indict white police officers in the aftermath of the Michael Brown and Alex Garner incidents in Ferguson, Missouri and Staten Island, New York, respectively.

Anyone who has watched the "debates" between representatives of the two groups on TV has witnessed the impossibility of civil or reasoned discussion between them. When, for example, in an incident subsequent to the Brown and Garner incidents, protesters raged and rioted over a white policeman who shot and killed a black man who was pointing a gun at him, [cciii] the protesters, who included many whites wanting to show "solidarity" with the blacks, raged and rioted anyway, even though the cop probably feared for his life. Their defenders on TV embraced the dead man's rights and cause as their own, as if the First Amendment included over-the-top threats to cops to get their points across, like pointing guns at them. No one on that side of the debate could grasp the absurdity of their position.

Similarly, however, no one on the Right has grasped the probable correctness of the basic argument in Michelle Alexander's *The New Jim Crow: Mass Incarceration in the Age of Colorblindness*, which depicts powerfully the problems that blacks face due to the War on Drugs and other seemingly permanent hurdles to their acceptance by and success in America.

> Like Jim Crow, mass incarceration marginalizes large segments of the African American community, segregates them physically (in prisons, jails, and ghettos), and then authorizes discrimination against them in voting, employment, housing, education, public benefits, and jury service. The federal court system has effectively immunized the current system from challenges on the grounds of racial bias, much as earlier systems of control were protected and endorsed by the U.S. Supreme Court. The parallels do not end there, however. Mass incarceration, like Jim Crow, helps to define the meaning and significance of race in America. Indeed, the stigma of criminality functions in much the same way that the stigma of race once did. It justifies a legal, social, and economic boundary between "us" and "them." [cciv]

The pundits on the Right dismiss Alexander's argument as completely and unjustifiably, it seems to me, as the pundits on the Left dismiss those who defend the actions of police during the Michael Brown and Alex Garner protests. When conservative talk show host Bill O'Reilly repeatedly shuts down his guest Russell Simmons's attempts to reference Alexander's arguments with interruptions demanding his guest acknowledge that drugs are a "violent" crime, it is clear that no hearing of Alexander's views will ever by countenanced by the Right.

> They kept going about crime and drugs before O'Reilly said, "You are so desperately wrong it pains me to talk to you." Simmons shot back, "I feel the same way about you." [ccv]

Neither side can hear the other in either case. Piketty and Stiglitz should have a look and let us know what the difference between these inevitably incoherent arguments and "democratic debate" really is. What, exactly, is the "social compact" now when it comes to race relations in America?

In spite of the demonstrated potential for violence when inequality is framed as the consequence of racial discrimination, there is another dimension of this group versus group problem that has, I believe, far greater potential for violence and, in this case, global violence. I am speaking of the offspring of the gender wars that began with feminism, and now include both women and non-traditional sexuality of both sexes. These have the potential to line up on the inequality battlefield all of the easily identifiable and emotionally agitated groups, such as those separated by sex, race, religion, national origin, etc., and to ultimately incite nations or terrorists to unleash all manner of atrocities, including weapons of mass destruction. As dangerous as these risks in the long run are, they are hidden for the moment in America behind a universally accepted assumption of good redistributionist intentions, as the political consensus rapidly shifts to support marriage equality.

The calls for female equality in the workplace, equal pay for equal work, and for gay and LGBT rights fit this mold, and the supporters of at least some of these policies now include most politicians. But few of these supporters have thought through how far this line of thinking is bound to go. The rapidly growing fashion for increasingly variegated versions of gender dispersion that come from the LGBT community, for example, is just getting under way. As with Lego blocks, which can be combined in virtually infinite ways, gender choice is virtually infinite, too, if one accepts the many variations claimed by the hyper-diverse LGBT community. Unlike traditional sexual distinctions, which are observable and obvious to the eye, and not dependant on what the individual being observed thinks, these new distinctions are based more and more on the subjective perceptions and opinions of each individual and thus are not observable or obvious, which is why they can be nearly infinite. Politicians might want to think through what being born this way will ultimately mean when applied to all of these versions, which the Supreme Court will eventually be forced by its own inclusion and diversity logic to do.

How about the right to marry of a former man transgendered surgically into a woman who chooses to cross-dress as a man with a sexual preference for former females transgendered into men -- to marry the opposite of that combination? Or never mind opposite: since we're talking about same-sex marriage, why not same-*surgically-reengineered-sex-and-preference-choice* marriage? Such convoluted outcomes are the inevitable consequence of the belief that homosexuals and lesbians were born with their preferences and that it took only time and personal courage for them to come out of the closet and announce what they are.

Not only does this belief underlie the entire LGBT political platform that is breaking out in Supreme Court acceptance of gay marriage and other forms of nontraditional relationships, acceptance of this born-this-way belief even by traditional heterosexual families is leading to ever more strange attitudes, such as in parents' child-rearing, education and medical practices. For example, some heterosexual couples are now so confused about how to raise their children who might be gay or trans that they are engaging in extended parent-teacher conferences to avoid pushing their children in the wrong direction, as the right direction becomes ever more elusive. Some parents are even putting their children on drugs that delay the onset of puberty in order to give them more time to figure out what they really are.

In recent years, the most striking change for trans people is the possibility of switching gender at younger and younger ages. Some children have been encouraged to socially transition as early as preschool. And, according to some estimates, thousands of American adolescents are taking hormones that forestall puberty until they decide whether they want medical or surgical interventions to change their biological sex. [ccvi]

While it is easy enough to see that there are many confused parties in this morality play -- children, parents, teachers, judges, Supreme Court justices, etc. -- we tend to forget that the whole belief system rests on a supposedly scientific fact that is non-existent, namely that people are born either heterosexual or homosexual, presumably in some proportion that will reveal itself as more people come out of the closet. The social acceptance of this belief system is surprisingly resistant to contrary evidence, even when it is abundantly available to the LGBT community, such as, for example, when some of its members participate in studies looking into the matter of whether bisexuality exists. Many gays and lesbians challenge the idea of bisexuality -- and are highly prejudiced against bisexuals -- because their existence implies that someone is lying about his or her sexual orientation.

As out gay men and lesbians, after all, we're supposed to be sure -- we're supposed to be "born this way." It's a politically important position (one that's helping us achieve marriage equality and other rights), but it leaves little space for out gay men to muddy the waters with talk of Kinsey 4s and 5s [a system for measuring degrees of straight versus gay sexual attraction ranging from 1 (fully opposite sex attraction) to 6 (fully same sex attraction)]. [ccvii]

The Nazi persecution of Jews was supported infamously by the pseudoscience of eugenics. Darwin was often misunderstood to have believed that because his theory of natural selection brought about evolution of species, then governments and societies should adopt *un*-natural selection to design a better human race going forward. Darwin of course never said any such thing. He used examples of deliberate "*selection*" of traits for breeding purposes -- animal breeding, husbandry, etc. -- to demonstrate how "*natural selection*" could also work to bring about evolution in nature. These examples were useful, because many people believed that species had been fixed since creation, a belief that was disproved regularly by the breeding practices of farmers. Since these breeding practices were well understood by at least some of those same believers, bringing up such examples enabled Darwin to open the minds of his readers to the possibility of species change at all, which was helpful as background before going on to articulate the full concept of natural selection and evolution in nature, i.e., not on the farm. But such examples were never meant by Darwin to imply that societies should deliberately attempt to engineer a better human species or race via the artificial means of eugenics.

116

This must be brought up to understand how the persecution of Jews became so widely supported, including by some not just in Germany, but also in Great Britain, France and the United States. Eugenics theories were presented as logical and scientific -- and Darwinian -- to justify the presumed wisdom of anti-Semitism. The science's adherents believed they were merely being rational about issues of great import to their societies and indeed to the human race, and thus were able to believe, or at least pretend, that they were not anti-Semitic.

Similarly, equally unsupportable pseudoscience is used today to justify the various forms of downward redistribution that address inequality. In addition to the supposed truth-beyond-question that homosexuals are born gay, as if there were a gay gene somewhere, there is the belief that women should represent half of all occupations they enter, since they are half of the population. If they represent less than that, or if they only earn seventy-eight cents for every dollar a man earns, the pseudoscience says that is proof of discrimination. Likewise if they fail to rise into the C-suite as regularly or rapidly as men, or if they seem to lose interest in their careers sooner than men, corporations and their male employees must be discriminating against the women, the pseudoscience assumes, regardless of how many affirmative action policies and diversity and inclusion policies the corporations or universities or government have adopted to promote women, and even though women have now far outnumbered men for some years in higher education, the on-ramp to corporate opportunities. Still, anything less than fifty percent participation at all levels of corporate competition is proof positive of culpable discrimination, the pseudoscience assumes, and justifies more forceful affirmative action in the future to assist women in their quest to compete with men.

Men seem particularly challenged in the new environment, as many have noted, such as in the popular *The End of Men* article in The Atlantic and subsequent book by Hanna Rosin. [ccviii] Could the malaise of men be at least partly attributable to the changes engineered by the government's pseudo-scientists and their expert academic supporters, which seem by design to promote shame and guilt for being a traditional man? If that thought occurs to you, or if it seems that perhaps men's sense of themselves as breadwinners, heads of households, or even as manly men, feel as if they were taken away from them and that this may have something to do with why men seem lost as "the end of men" is upon them, well, if you have such thoughts, you have to keep them under your hat if you want to continue in your career. Honesty and standing up to the pseudo-scientists are not allowed. If you even hint at such a connection you will be required to undergo diversity training and re-education before you can resume your career, if you ever really can.

Although these issues are extremely complicated and it is difficult to discern the distribution effects of such policies, the relative rise of women and homosexuals in the commercial and social realms has perforce been accompanied by a relative decline of heterosexual men in the same realms. While this is progress from the perspective of the women and non-traditional sexualities and their supporters on the Left, traditional heterosexual men almost certainly do not view it that way, no matter how they hide their feelings in order to be politically correct so as to keep their careers and social lives on track. While it is not a direct transfer payment in which the right of traditional men to property is abridged by the right of women and homosexuals to their incomes and wealth, it has the same effect.

The sense of emotional and self-worth loss that men must feel as their traditional roles are confiscated in order to transfer them to working women or to gays and lesbians, i.e., to anyone who is not a heterosexual man, amounts to a forceful redistribution by their own government and society of something that was once theirs, and had been so as a result of centuries or millennia of natural evolution during which they had been successful. Whereas their society had formerly respected traditional men, now the official policy of society via its government is to disrespect those same traditional men. Whereas traditional men could once feel proud, now they are supposed to feel shame. This is what political correctness does, as it forces a person to keep quiet, to cower and grovel before his own thoughts in his own mind.

Parallel to the devaluation and decline of traditional men in the eyes of society, and maybe even more devastating in terms of self-worth loss, is the devalued feeling that women who stay at home in traditional roles supporting their men and raising their children are made to feel for not taking up the "lean in" feminist cause of careers and competition with men. Neither of these emotional confiscations affecting both traditional men and women is considered to be an issue worth noting in the politically correct atmosphere dictated by a presumed need for further affirmative uplifting of career women and homosexuals.

As with the traditional "stock exchange" that was a commonly understood term before the SEC redefined it, the existence of pervasive redistributive feminism and affirmative support for homosexuality causes a forced redefinition of both "man" and "woman" in terms of their roles in our society. It is not that either of them or people in general cannot handle changing environments. But when the change is one that is deliberately forced upon them as a result of government policy, it cannot be felt as anything other than a deliberate devaluation, a confiscation and redistribution that is in all likelihood as or more emotionally consequential as an economic confiscation and redistribution would feel. Further, since the traditional social roles were always embedded in economic roles, too, the social role redistributions are probably reinforced by economic redistributions happening parallel to, in the same direction as, and partly in consequence of the social role redistributions.

Like the definition of "stock exchange," the definitions of such basic words as "man," "woman" and "marriage" were in the past so clear and obvious that if they ever had to be put into law at all for some reason, the use of circular phrases like "as that term is generally understood" or even "self evident" would have caused no confusion or misunderstandings. This was clearly true in the stock exchange case, since, as was discussed earlier, when the definition of what didn't need to be defined was introduced with the creation of the SEC in 1934, it did use the circular "commonly performed" and "generally understood" to define "stock exchange." The circular language defining what was self-evidently a stock exchange never caused any confusion until the SEC introduced its own version of diversity to the equation, culminating in the redefinition I discovered on that airplane flight in 1990 discussed in chapter 11 that included the term "single price auction," but effectively excluded the membership organization structure that had always been the one and only key identifying characteristic of stock exchanges since their invention in the eighteenth century.

A similar situation, but of even much longer vintage, pertains to the definition of marriage, which for millennia was commonly understood to be between a man and a woman. But now, with marriage equality on the nation's front burner, a concept with which the bulk of the population is about as familiar as they are with extraterrestrials, a number of key implied definitions of terms that were so critical to our sense of self worth that we didn't even know they existed, are up for grabs. The lynchpin in the grab-bag is of course the definition of "marriage," which is now being forced to *include* what would have previously been commonly thought of as bizarre practices that had nothing to do with marriage, and to *exclude* the key identifying characteristic of being between a man and a woman that was always implied before. Thus not only is the national conversation about marriage equality causing a forcible redistribution of the respect and self worth once accorded to traditional men and women, but by forcing the implicit redefinitions of "man," "woman" and "marriage" at the highest echelons of power in America, it is also causing related redefinitions of terms such as "democracy" and even of technical ones, such as "states' rights." That the many states that have voted on the matter have all tried to stop the parade of affirmative support for the LGBT agenda, but are one by one being denied their democratic rights by federal courts and the Supreme Court, means that "democracy" itself is being redefined before our eyes, and that if states' rights ever did mean anything, they clearly don't now.

Obviously, all this forced redistribution of roles and rights and respect and advantage could be emotionally devastating as well as economically enervating to the overwhelming majority of the people in our society, and is clearly being done only in order to placate a visible and vociferous minority, and not as a matter of their unalienable rights as individuals, but with respect to their aggregate claims to affirmative rights as a group. But while this could have huge consequences, it is not a possibility that any of the pseudo-scientists are even considering. From an emotional standpoint as well as from an economic efficiency standpoint, it is clear that the engineers have not thought any of these possibilities through, or what their effects on incomes, growth and social stability might be. But as in the case of the government engineers that turned the greatest capital formation engine of all time into an electronic high-frequency-trading casino that raises no capital, the pseudo-scientists of social and sexual policy, too, are impervious to signs that the flat society they are trying to engineer is exhibiting massive unintended consequences.

Just as flash crashes and other glitches caused by our government's stock market engineers invariably result in even more power for those same engineers, ostensibly to fix the market so the mistakes the engineers caused won't happen again, the more our society falls apart socially and economically under the changing definitions, the more we are forced by government to rely on the same government processes that are causing the problems. And this, too, amounts to another hidden definition change, this time in the concept of "limited government" that was once so important to America's founders. America's government is no longer limited by any conceivably honest definition of "limited." It is now the monster the founders wanted to avoid, a monster that regularly violates the rights as well as the common sense of the citizens it rules.

Its refusal to engage in profiling in policing and homeland security matters, for example, regularly spends resources we don't have, given deficits and high taxes, as well as results in reduced security and safety, not to mention elevated inconvenience, for the bulk of the population. But there is no natural or unalienable right to not be profiled. Such an alleged right belongs squarely amongst the positive or affirmative rights that can only be ginned up and redistributed by government as resources are removed from some groups and given to others. As such they violate the very concept that America was founded on, namely that there were some truths that were so self-evident that they didn't need definition. Which means, in the end, that "America" itself is another of those terms undergoing renovation by government.

Eventually the analytical failings and intellectual dishonesty that led to these strange transformations will be revealed. But the point I want to make now is that true democratic debate is impossible when pseudoscience is around. In fact, so-called democratic debate becomes in that circumstance merely the vehicle for locking in the prerogatives of a government riding the pseudoscience toward full fascism. The big risk today is that we, like the Germans, may not see the error of our ways until we are on the other side of a cataclysm that kills millions.

16. Taking Inclusion Abroad

The feeling of déjà vu Americans had over the renewed War On Terrorism as air attacks on ISIS were launched in September 2014 was understandable. As we went back into Iraq, we were told that this time we would insist that the Iraqis adopt "inclusive" policies. Not only did our president, our secretary of state and all the other officials of our government that could get on camera utter that word hundreds of times prior to starting bombing again, but that was the same word that had accompanied every one of our failed previous attempts at peace agreements, peace processes and similar policies for the last several decades to force our way of life on the resistant mostly Muslim populations of the world. That word was used in this case mostly to apply to the obligation we put on the Shiite prime minister, representing the majority population in Iraq, to include meaningful accommodation of the interests of minority Sunni and Kurd populations, too. The previous prime minister had not done that, we were told, presumably because he had not obeyed our wishes on this point. So this time, we were told, our policy of inclusion would finally work, because this time the new prime minister would obey our wishes. While the leaders who would run the government got the most attention (as if it mattered on the inclusion front which token Sunni or token Kurd was picked to "share" power with the prime minister, who all acknowledged in fact had almost all the power), the inclusion word was also mentioned with respect to the policies they would be expected to follow, just to make sure that women and LGBT communities would not be ignored, either. [ccix] Whether the Iraqis follow our wishes on inclusion on any of these levels (and there are many reasons why they might not, no matter what they say), we couldn't help feeling we'd seen this movie before, and we had.

Leaving aside the pure hypocrisy of continuing to claim we are promoting democracy and freedom, when these quota-like policies are contrary to anything our founders would have countenanced (and in fact directly contradict their understanding of both democracy and freedom), just imagine what inclusive looks like in Iraq or Syria or Yemen. And in particular, look at it from the two perspectives that would matter most to the people in these and other mostly Muslim countries that have no choice but to deal with U.S. incursions into their world. First, from a strictly strategic perspective, our group versus group, quota-like inclusive policies are sharply dividing combatants in the civil wars between those who side with America and those who don't. But with our ever-vacillating wobbles between alliances of convenience to fight the most threatening-sounding enemy of the moment; our switching between all-in surges and date-certain exits; between red lines and diplomacy; between boots on the ground and no boots bombing; between Iraq first, then no Iraq but Afghanistan, then neither, and then Iraq again; firm support forever, to our people are tired of war now -- we exasperate our allies and cheer our enemies. It is clear we are in over our heads strictly from a strategic alliance perspective and do not have any idea where our real interests lie, which is not surprising because of problem number two, which is that we have no moral compass in spite of our supposed certainty about our "values." And this second problem with our inclusion policies is much worse than the first one.

That second problem is the following. Those who side against us, or against those we side with, have an existential fear that, if they lose, the society America imposes on them will be grossly unfamiliar, chaotic and immoral. And from their perspective, they are almost certainly right. Artificially promoting the rise of career women and sexual choice diversity through affirmative inclusion has been a tough nut for us to swallow. Just imagine how much harder such policies will be to accept by a less advanced society, particularly when forced upon them from the outside. The resulting civil wars not only pit Sunnis against Shiites or Kurds, they often pit Sunnis against Sunnis or Shiites against Shiites or Kurds against Kurds based on where they stand vis-à-vis America and its policies, such as diversity, inclusion, the education of girls, and homosexuality. While ISIS commits atrocities against all of the above, it has also managed to recruit 15,000 fighters from 80 countries, which means it can now legitimately boast of having fighters on its side who are from all of the countries normally associated with its enemies, including Britain, France and the United States, [ccx] as well as from all the ethnic and religious divisions of Islam. Ironically, our worst enemies are now doing better at the diversity and inclusion game than we are when it comes to assembling forces for their fight against the American values of diversity and inclusion.

As is the case for blacks in the U.S., economic inequality is the issue that most clearly divides Muslim individuals and communities from Western society generally, causing alienation, anger and a desire for revenge, whether they are Muslims living in the West, [ccxi] or Muslims living in poor countries that see the West as immigration targets. In all these cases, inequality both fosters occasional riots and makes jihad attractive. France discovered this in the deadly January 7 attacks on the satiric magazine Charlie Hebdo and a Jewish grocery by French Muslim citizens of Algerian and West African extraction that had been inspired at least and perhaps trained by Yemeni al Qaeda affiliate AQAP and also perhaps by ISIS. These conditions of non-assimilating and poor Muslim populations are ideal for ISIS and al Qaeda and Boko Haram and Al-Shabaab and Taliban and other terrorist organizations' recruiting and training purposes, including training that is increasingly fostering attacks in the Western homelands, such as recently in Canada, Australia and now, again, France.

World leaders recognized the renewed risk with solemn concern and resolve as they converged on Paris in solidarity after the January 7 attacks. While they agreed on the need to address terrorism by better explaining our presumptively attractive inclusion and assimilation policies, none noticed that these very values are almost certainly the main reason the West is under attack. The confusion of the Western powers was evident as their solidarity was mirrored in spontaneous violent riots across the Muslim world [ccxii] where Muslims were easily able to identify by that very defense of Western values and its sudden slogan, "Je suis Charlie," whom they for sure wanted to kill, as they held up signs saying "Je Suis Muslim" or "Je Suis Muhammad" or "Je Suis Kouachi," for the brothers who executed the Charlie Hebdo attack. [ccxiii]

ISIS is known for its sophistication with social media, [ccxiv] as is al Qaeda, [ccxv] which means that if we think they haven't yet figured out what inclusion means, we had better think again. They know exactly what it has meant to us, and can easily imagine exactly what it will mean for them, if it comes to that. So logically, they conclude: Why not go all out in this war? Why not fight to the death? Why not become suicide bombers? Why not engage in suicidal attacks on soft Western targets like Charlie Hebdo? In the eyes of Muslims who hate us, it is the very diversity policies we espouse most fervently that are at the top of the list of policies that inspire their most fervent hatred. We cannot conceivably hearts-and-minds our way around this hatred through better explanations of what inclusion and diversity mean. They already know what they mean. They see it every day on Twitter and Facebook and YouTube and in our newspapers and on television and the Internet.

They have seen these policies result in the affirmative discrimination by our government from its highest levels -- the President, the Attorney General, the Secretary of State, the Supreme Court, etc. -- in favor of women putting their careers ahead of their families, and promoting the rise of homosexuals and ever more variegated iterations of what it means to be transgender. To be clear: "diversity" and "inclusion," as these words drive policy in the United States today, do not mean simply allowing diversity of individuals to exist in our society by not discriminating against anyone. They mean government officially discriminating in favor of groups like career women and homosexuals by, for example, promoting equal pay for equal work or by redefining previously self-evident terms like "marriage." The Muslims who hate us know all about how this works and are not likely to be surprised when our Supreme Court approves gay marriage across America next summer.

Our Muslim enemies can easily see and anticipate all of this, and as a result are coalescing and gaining confidence as their threat to us rises with each new attack -- and as our threat to them rises for the same reason. They can see our inclusion policies highlighted ironically but very clearly on our own technological inventions like the Internet and social media. And what they see is not playing well. Studies show that Muslims, although they are no less tolerant than others of racial differences, "are much less tolerant of gay individuals." [ccxvi] So being able to "offer a life without homosexuality" has risen up as one of the reasons ISIS is so easily recruiting thousands upon thousands to their cause, [ccxvii] including many from Western countries such as the United States.

This is creating a never-ending threat to America that will only grow in the degree to which we organize coalitions against them, hit them with drones and airstrikes, and aggressively propagandize our new way of life as better than theirs. Even if inclusion is better, by our definition, it could still be our undoing, because there is no chance that the enemies that are gathering against our wealth, power and -- in their view -- immorality, will ever accept our view, at least not in the rapid time frames in which we expect them to convert. In fact, this is a problem that will only grow worse as we try harder to propagandize and indoctrinate these foreign cultures into our values. They already know what our values are and what those values would mean for them. So the more they hear about them from us, the more they will hate us for the very values we want to tell them about. In other words, our propaganda is bound to backfire on us, and the more we do of it, the worse will be its effect.

While we have the luxury of centuries of prosperity that has attracted such widespread diversity that we can work through assimilations of new roles for women or trans-gendered individuals through the leisurely legal and political processes we enjoy, less advanced Muslim nations that have only two or three major competing groups within them can only view our diversity as radical, bizarre, and even as an existential threat. That we demand they adopt these new and repulsive policies, from *their* perspective, on *our* time and not theirs, is proof positive for many of them that we deserve all the terror they can deliver upon us.

The War On Terrorism, whether waged under that name by Republicans or something softer sounding by Democrats, could not be better designed to produce enemies of America who will one day have the capacity to strike our homeland with one or more weapons of mass destruction. And yet we continue to ratchet it up under both Republican and Democratic administrations in spite of all its failures. The one thing we could do to reduce or eliminate this risk of a devastating attack on our homeland is to drop this counterproductive war that has cost thousands of lives and trillions of dollars that "might as well have been burned," since the number of terrorist groups has jumped from 28 to 49 from 2007 to 2013 while the number of annual terrorist incidents jumped from 100 to 950. [ccxviii]

But eliminating this counterproductive war is the one thing that no political party can contemplate when they see potential threats like ISIS springing up everywhere. It is just too politically attractive to appear as if we are defending ourselves by "taking the fight to the enemy," as the advocates of these policies like to think they are doing. In the midst of all that reflexive aggression and belligerence on both sides, do we really think we would be able to restrain ourselves from responding in kind if a WMD took out one of our cities? Do we really think we could control how all the parties and alliances would shift if such true terror entered the picture? What would Russia do? What would China do? What would North Korea, or Pakistan, or Iran, or Israel, do?

How bad could things get? Well, as Tom Perkins said, the Holocaust was the worst imaginable. That was not just eugenics in a metaphorical or analogous sense, as my applications of the term to the stock market and antitrust generally are. That was eugenics in its original genetic sense, and it created special horrors that probably cannot be topped, and hopefully won't be. But let's think for a minute about what eugenics is. It is basically a do-over, a taking over of design responsibility from whatever force had produced a social structure naturally, whether God or evolution, depending on your views on that subject. But either way, it is an attempt by government to re-form, as in to form again, a structure that had been created naturally, without government help. That is what it was for the Nazis in their attempt to recreate the human race without the wealthy Jews. That is what it is for the SEC in its attempt to recreate the stock market without the wealthy monopolists at the NYSE. And that is what it is for America where all of the affirmative actions and similar policies are attempting to re-do the social organization of society without the wealthy white males at the top. While it may well be that the special horrors created by the genetic do-over of the Holocaust cannot be topped in terms of human cruelty, the six million Jews killed in the Holocaust were by no means the end of the deaths even in that period, which contained at least fifty million deaths. [ccxix] So, in terms of the sheer number of deaths, it certainly could get worse. What forces could make it so?

Obviously the presence this time of WMD could make it so. Whether nuclear, chemical or biological, many countries now possess such weapons, including a few of our adversaries, and some have allegedly used them, even recently, such as Syria. Since the United States is the wealthiest country and the most visibly unequal in wealth distribution, as the news coverage of our obsession with inequality demonstrates daily, we are also for these very reasons the most evil nation and people in the eyes of many, both at home and abroad. That being the case, it is clear that, if WMD are to be used, there are many out there who would want to see them used on us first and foremost. I am not the only one to have suggested we could "lose a city." Republicans Newt Gingrich and Dick Cheney have said so repeatedly. But when they mention this possibility it is invariably in the context of a call for the United States to increase its military involvement in the world so that we can control terrorism by controlling all of the people in the world who would do us harm. As strategy, this is foolhardy. It is in fact the primary cause of the danger it is trying to prevent.

Far Right pundits often label Islamic terrorists "fascists" or "Islamo-Fascists," on the presumed notion that their barbarity puts them in the same inhuman category that the Nazis and Fascists of World War II were in, and because their stated desire to extend their new "caliphates" (such as those announced by ISIS and Boko Haram, which means "Western education is forbidden") causes fear in the West that they will someday rule the world with Sharia law. This is a misattribution of the characteristics of fascism, and a gross exaggeration of these groups' actual potential to harm the West. There is no realistic chance that any or all of them together could actually take over and control any Western country, much less the world. Their barbarity is meant to showcase their capacity to resist the West and its values, such as inclusion, and to state very clearly that they reject those values absolutely and categorically. While we think they should recognize our value of free speech, their barbaric acts are in effect their own free speech answer to that value. The beheadings and burnings alive, the slaughters of school children and kidnappings of schoolgirls, etc., are meant to show they still have the capacity to resist the West in spite of our military might, coalitions, and technology. Their barbaric acts demonstrate strength and resolve -- and are recruiting thousands of Western Muslims to the ranks of ISIS and other terrorist groups.

The sad reality from before 9/11 to today is that our own military and democratizing policies that we think are making us safer are in fact the primary reasons that we face our own existential threat, if not yet to our country, then at least to a city or two. Taking the fight to the enemy has produced lots of deaths, of our enemies and of our own. But that strategy is producing far more enemies than it is killing, as I warned it would shortly after 9/11 in *Countdown*, when I said "both the number and strength of our enemies will expand without limit unless we stand again for the principles our Founding Fathers enunciated two centuries ago." [ccxx] If you think about it in light of the distorted values we are attempting to enforce by the strategy, it is easy to see why. As our founders would have known, no country that attempts to take over the critical life functions of even its own people, much less of other people, can expect anything but to reap the whirlwind. As to who the fascists are, Tom Perkins got it right: It is the United States and the West that are in the early stages of that disease, not the Muslim terrorists.

To quickly summarize the threat we are creating with our own policy, recall that ISIS was partly created by a previous "success" of that policy, namely the killing by our forces of Abu Musab al-Zarqawi in 2006. Zarqawi had headed a precursor of ISIS known as Al Qaeda in Iraq (AQI), [ccxxi] which, awful as it seemed at the time, was not as bad as ISIS is now. No clairvoyance or strategy genius is required to see that merely following the current trend lines will produce an even more challenging threat to America in the future, as all the tentacles of terrorism continue to find ever more fertile recruiting roots in America and other Western countries, and as the potential to acquire more devastating weapons, such as from our known adversaries who have them, expands, as it surely will if we continue the War on Terror.

The real tragedy of our attempts to enforce an artificial diversity is that they don't even work. The path to genuine diversity is a natural one, requiring no government mandates at all. Already in 1600 the opportunity to be in and to transact in *The Island at the Center of the World,* [ccxxii] including the area around Wall Street, attracted the most diverse populations imaginable at that time as Dutch laws protected their natural right to be there -- and to trade and seek their fortunes -- which brought in more diversity than was present in any other city on earth.

Throughout its history, the diverse populations attracted to New York came not because of any trumped up right to inclusion or pluralism or diversity, but rather due to its opposite, which was the natural right of all people to pursue inequality by being free, which they understood as allowing them to be selective and discriminating in their associations and dealings as they pursued their dreams and opportunities. There was no right in early America to not be profiled, or to not be stop-and-frisked, or to not be excluded from an apartment building, or to not be excluded as an employee of a company, or to be paid a minimum wage. And yet the populations that emerged in New York both four centuries ago and two centuries ago were the most diverse in the world.

And they still are. Even though we have fallen away from freedom, and have introduced economic support and diversity measures today, it is still primarily New York's natural economic vibrancy that is its main attraction. Just as it attracted Munsees and Walloons in 1600, which modern readers may need to Google to refresh themselves on, the New York of today is attracting many unfamiliar identifications that also need to be Googled, such as the proliferating spinoffs from the GenderBread Man of the trans movement. [ccxxiii] But the beauty of New York is not its official diversity policy or economic support measures, but that its diverse economy gives all people a shot at becoming whatever they'd like to become. None of us can honestly claim to know which of the new categories will stick in the long run or which ones we won't need to Google a century from now to identify (or whether Google will still exist, for that matter).

The same diversity of opportunity was evident not just in New York before the American Revolution, but also in the New World generally. It was economic opportunity and the freedom to pursue it that attracted the diverse populations of the Old World to America. And it is by and large still true. The reason the United

States is the most diverse country and New York City is the most diverse city in the world is that they still dominate their categories in terms of economic opportunity, in spite of the problems described in this book. Anyone who thinks we are diverse because of our diversity policies is missing the real story. In fact, true diversity is hindered by the adoption of counterproductive policies like affordable housing that seek to create diversity artificially by, for example, making rich people and poor people live in the same buildings together.

Think about the natural dynamics of gentrification that attend the growing success of a city such as New York, due to Wall Street, or of San Francisco, due to Silicon Valley. The more the economic opportunities draw ambitious people in, the more rents will rise, inevitably forcing those who had been there before to be priced out of their old homes. But while this gentrification might inspire a Spike Lee rant in Brooklyn or some to throw rocks at Google buses in San Francisco, the fact is that the growing opportunity that created the gentrification and the affordable housing gap is a sign that the city in question is rising relative to other cities in terms of economic opportunity, and even those who are priced out of their old homes could benefit from the increased jobs in the area. In any case, the only way to allegedly close the gap or equalize rich and poor living arrangements is to remove the vibrancy of that rising city by, say, having portions of apartments set aside for low income people so they can live with high income people. But this never works and never satisfies anyone. In addition to the problem of how to allocate the subsidized apartments by lottery or other non-economic means among the hundreds of applicants for each subsidized apartment, the living opportunities are bound to become less attractive at least for the wealthier tenants. And they are often unattractive for the poor as well, who are sometimes forced to suffer the indignities of separate entrances to the buildings or are otherwise made to feel unwelcome in them. [ccxxiv]

In the end, redistribution through affordable housing policies can make housing so unattractive that the wealthy would rather move to London or Moscow or Hong Kong to pursue their dreams, thus draining the tax base from which the attempted redistribution was funded. So, not only is the redistribution going to hit a dead end eventually anyway, but the retarded growth in the meantime and the conflict and dissatisfaction attending the lotteries, which produce mostly losers, and the demonstrations, which produce mostly anger, can only cause perpetual misery along the way for both rich and poor. As usual, only government bureaucrats that administer these programs, as well as the politicians and other demagogues that promote them, benefit from their existence.

As I said at the beginning of this book, moving to better neighborhoods is what pursuing inequality, or "moving up," means, and it is what Americans have by unalienable right been able to do since roughly July 4, 1776. The world would be a safer place if any of our domestic politicians could recognize that once self-evident truth. As it is, housing is just another showcase policy demonstrating that America no longer considers the pursuit of happiness to be an unalienable right. By inserting government into housing distribution, we make our hypocrisy clear, and encourage our enemies to view our wealth more as a target to attack than a goal to pursue.

17. Finale In Sum

The title of this book is of course a provocative perversion of the most-memorable line in liberty literature. Its purpose is to force the consideration of three equally provocative propositions:

1.   The phrase, "the pursuit of happiness," in our Declaration of Independence, could not practically speaking mean anything other than the pursuit of inequality.

2.   That is how it was understood in practice, and what it effectively did mean, at the founding of America and for over a century afterwards.

3.   If that had not been how it was interpreted, America as we know it would not exist today.

To demonstrate these propositions, we did not need to get entangled in historical arguments of constitutional interpretation or retrospective psychoanalysis of founders' intent. But just for the record, James Madison "believed that the preservation of people's 'different and unequal faculties of acquiring property' was 'the first object of government.'" [ccxxv] Whether he consistently held this view, or whether he and the other founders successfully incorporated it into the Constitution turned out to be unimportant for our purposes.

What matters now is that had early Americans not understood their rights as including the ability to pursue inequality, and to keep it if they could get it, there would be no America as we know it today, for overwhelming wealth is the one essential feature of America that cannot be removed without making the rest of the story uninteresting. For example, we would not be having this increasingly rancorous argument over inequality, or tearing our hair out over the disappearing middle class, if America had not become wealthy and unequal enough to fight over these things.

No one, American or foreign, including Tocqueville, would ever have wondered if America is "exceptional" or deserves its place in the world or its dominant wealth, if America had not been on the fast track to great wealth when Tocqueville toured America in the early nineteenth century. Modern authors would not marvel that "the U.S. economy is estimated to have become the largest in the world in the 1870s," [ccxxvi] and Tocqueville, who wrote of Americans' "longing to rise," [ccxxvii] would have had no interested readers in his time or devoted followers today.

These things would not have happened, because the United States of America would never have become the wealthiest nation in the world, if the right to pursue inequality had not been enshrined, however imperfectly, in our beliefs, laws and culture. Wall Street would be just another street, with no revered or reviled history, no generator of booms and busts, no railroads or Internets, no Morgans or Madoffs.

While this counterfactual game is a little like those Hollywood movies such as *Back To The Future* and *The Terminator* that hinge on altering history by erasing certain people before they or their descendents could do good or ill, in this case we're simply talking about erasing wealth. The storied people may well still exist in our fantasy, but they would not be storied, since they would never have achieved great wealth, and would thus not have been important enough to grab a role on the stage of history, or be remembered today.

Some of this would be a mixed blessing, even a relief. While the Kennedy Camelot dream, which depended on the Wall Street wealth of patriarch Joseph Kennedy, would never have inspired millions, the assassinations of John and Bobby Kennedy would not have happened, either, nor would Chappaquiddick. The Crash of '29 would not have happened, nor the Depression. The SEC would not have been created to rein in the speculative excesses of the Roaring Twenties that led to the Crash and the Depression, nor would the SEC's first chairman, that same Joseph Kennedy, have been wealthy and noticed enough to have been appointed by Franklin Roosevelt to run it. For that matter, neither Franklin nor Theodore Roosevelt would have become prominent enough to become presidents. Hollywood would not have happened, either, whether as the world's leading film industry, or as the chronicler of wealth and power in America. There would have been no Edison inventing the technology behind film projection, no money to finance films, and no interesting stories to tell.

None of these things would have happened if Americans had not become the wealthiest people on earth, for the right to pursue inequality was the key factor that enabled the pursuit and accumulation of America's wealth, both individually and collectively. Contrary to the universal opinion of all politicians, left, right and center, and even of all the wealthy themselves who opine on the matter today, inequality is not only not the problem everyone sees it to be, it is the sine qua non of America qua America. Furthermore, a restoration of the right to pursue inequality is the one and only possible solution to all the conflict in the world, which always boils down to disputes over how to address the "inequality problem."

But, realistically, we should not get our hopes up.

While some might wish along with me that America's promise could be restored through a restoration of the freedom to pursue inequality, realistically the chances are not good. Others hope that some resolution of the inequality problem through redistribution or political compromise or democratic debate will result in a different and more peaceful path forward. But such hopes are inevitably based on the incorrect belief that the political debate over inequality can ever be resolved. This, as we have learned, is wishful thinking at best, and the debate itself is bound to lead to ever more bitter and violent conflict.

This book has spent less time describing the prospects of doing something about inequality than on the dynamics of the national and global civil war that we are headed toward if we stay focused on it. The problem is that no one can be found in the modern political spectrum who believes that the thesis of this book, as embodied in the above three propositions, is correct. Everyone, almost without exception, believes, at least in public, that inequality is a problem.

Cardinal Dolan, for example, extols the virtues of the "via media" in defending Pope Francis from the charges of being anti-capitalist or Marxist that have been leveled at him recently. Cardinal Dolan says both Marxism ("Marxism/communism/socialism") and unbridled free-market capitalism are the extremes. What is good, according to Cardinal Dolan on Meet the Press with David Gregory (3/9/13), is the debate that Pope Francis is initiating with his inequality comments to find the via media between the extremes. What neither Cardinal Dolan nor Pope Francis (nor Thomas Piketty, for that matter) appear to be aware of is that any form of this debate is a formula for unending societal conflict, since the precise location of the via media path is inevitably elusive, because any hypothetical location of it would be unacceptable to at least a great many people on both sides. In other words, there is no via media. Not only is there no via media, when it comes to inequality and redistribution questions there is no golden mean, either, or any Simpson-Bowles or any other compromise balancing the forces of redistribution that can last longer than a brief moment. At best these are all just new lines of scrimmage from which the battle will begin again, immediately, and with no meaningful cessation of hostilities in the interim.

There can be no argument against religious choices or choices of conscience to engage in acts of charity to alleviate poverty or inequality or anything similar, because such sentiments and actions are presumably entirely voluntary. But problems are bound to arise if a nation's government attempts to turn such impulses into policy, because this can only be done at the expense of the unalienable rights of its citizens, which -- in the United States of America, at least -- were believed to have derived from God.

This is true regardless of how one reads the teachings of Jesus. However downward redistributionist He may have been in His teachings to His followers or the world, generally, in the American political context it would be entirely out of character to let those teachings carry over to the political realm, even if followers, as a matter of personal conscience, engage in as much charity as they can on their own, and even if they advocate that others do the same. And this is true even if all followers advocate that political choices be made for the nation as a whole that are consistent with their personal beliefs in charity. It is even OK for the Pope to believe this and advocate it, both personally and for the Church. What is not OK is for America to adopt that view as a policy matter. To avoid unending strife between groups, it is imperative to stick with the founders' view that the freedom to pursue inequality is God-given and unalienable regardless of how much inequality there is.

It would take strength of moral character for Americans to reclaim the freedom we have lost, and it is not at all clear that we are up to the task. Two and a quarter centuries into our experiment with limited government we seem addicted to government interventions that may well be our undoing. The two most important addictions we have discussed in this book are antitrust and the War on Terror. Antitrust is rapidly draining our economic potential, and the War on Terror is creating extraordinary physical dangers to our homeland as well as huge costs in blood and treasure. That both of these existential threats are viewed, incorrectly, indeed absurdly, as defenses of freedom is a sign that we have misunderstood or corrupted the message of liberty our founders wanted us to remember. And even if we could muster the courage and character as individuals to challenge these addictions, there may be little that individuals can do anymore, as both *antitrust and the War on Terror are tyrannies in control of us* now.

If we can still recognize freedom at all in our drugged state, we may take heart from the confused stirrings of libertarian youth, or Tea Party incoherence, or government gridlock, or stubborn shutdowns over debt ceilings, not because these make any sense from a policy perspective, but precisely because they don't. These inchoate political rebellions show that we may still have the strength to just say "no" to tyranny, regardless of conventional wisdom and political correctness. And these are not the only signs that freedom may still have a pulse.

In the real world of conflicted medicine, individuals are demonstrating a newfound readiness to reject the hyper-interventionist medical habits their doctors lured them into that were good for doctors economically but bad for their patients' health and pocketbooks. This shows a willingness and ability to reject conventional wisdom when it comes to one of the most fundamental fields of intervention affecting every American personally. When evidence shows up demonstrating the downsides of intervention, such as those that occur when hurrying births with drugs or cesarean sections instead of waiting for a natural birth, [ccxxviii] or when engaging in such excessive screening for disease that the screening creates complications worse than the diseases, individuals do appear capable of cutting back on intervention. In fact, enough of them may be doing so to explain a surprising recent decline in medical costs. [ccxxix]

Encouraging as these signs of life for liberty may be, however, confronting conventional wisdom as individuals is a long way from the collective courage needed to break free of government's grip. But there is a way to turn individual courage into collective action that just might work. Although challenging either antitrust or the War on Terror through normal channels would be hopeless, antitrust has a weakness called the SEC. Individuals who recognize the SEC is harming America can simply reject any and all of its rationales for expansion or just silently shun its processes. Given the regular hearings into market problems the SEC is responsible for, the career risk to individuals of acknowledging the SEC's obvious and well-publicized failures is decreasing with each passing day. If enough people both inside and outside the SEC develop disaffection with its mission or results or both, the agency itself might implode politically and practically. If it did, that could break up the logjam that is choking the life out of the America our founders left us.

Endnotes

[i] *Obama: Income inequality "the defining challenge of our time,"* Rebecca Kaplan, CBS News, December 4, 2013. "President Obama pointed to a combination of growing income inequality and a lack of upward mobility as "the defining challenge of our time," arguing the government should take further steps to reverse a decades-long trend that has widened the gap between the nation's richest citizens and everyone else. "The basic bargain at the heart of our economy has frayed," Mr. Obama said. He repeated later in his speech that "the combined trends of increased inequality and decreasing mobility pose a fundamental threat to the American dream, our way of life, and what we stand for around the globe."

[ii] *De Blasio vows action on inequality to tackle New York's 'Tale of Two Cities,'* Ed Pilkington, The Guardian, January 1, 2014. "De Blasio, 52, struck an uncompromisingly progressive note in his [inauguration] speech, promising to implement his campaign promise to reunite a city torn apart by a Dickensian gap between rich and poor. "When I said we would take dead aim at the Tale of Two Cities, I meant it," De Blasio said. "And we will do it. We will succeed as one city. De Blasio equated what he called an "inequality crisis" in modern New York with the city's historic struggles from the financial collapse to the crime epidemic, the terrorist attacks on 9/11 and the devastation of Hurricane Sandy. He said the inequality crisis was "not the stuff of banner headlines in our daily newspapers. It's a quiet crisis, but one no less pernicious than those that have come before.""

[iii] *Fed's Yellen Says Extreme Inequality Could Be Un-American; Central Bank Chief Says Income Inequality Could Be Impeding Economic Mobility*, Pedro Nicolaci Da Costa, The Wall Street Journal, October 17, 2014. "Boston -- Federal Reserve Chairwoman Janet Yellen delivered a strong indictment of rising inequality of wealth and income in the U.S., saying it was creating a vicious circle that was impeding the economic mobility that used to be at the heart of American economic values. Delivering a number of rather startling statistics to back her case, Ms. Yellen, who was speaking at a conference on economic opportunity and inequality sponsored by the Boston Fed, argued the trend of worsening disparities was effectively curtailing the country's economic potential. "The extent and continuing increase in inequality in the United States greatly concern me," Ms. Yellen said in a keynote address. "I think it is appropriate to ask whether this trend is compatible with values rooted in our nation's history, among them the high value Americans have traditionally placed on equality of opportunity."

[iv] *In New Tack, I.M.F. Aims at Income Inequality*, Eduardo Porter, The New York Times, April 9, 2014. "A flatter distribution of income, the study concluded, contributes more to sustainable economic growth than the quality of a country's political institutions, its foreign debt and openness to trade, its foreign investment and whether its exchange rate is competitive."

[v] *'Enormous increase' in global inequality: OECD*, Kay Barnato, CNBC, October 1, 2014. "The sharp rise in income inequality across the world is one of the most

worrying developments of the past 200 years, the Organization for Economic Co-operation and Development (OECD), said on Thursday. In a flagship report tracking wellbeing in eight world regions over two centuries, the OECD noted that personal incomes had diverged in the last 30 years as GDP (gross domestic product) per head had risen. "It is hard not to notice the sharp increase in income inequality experienced by the vast majority of countries from the 1980s. There are few exceptions to this," said the OECD economists in the report."

[vi] *Boosting Shared Prosperity is Key to Tackling Inequality, says World Bank Group President*, Press Release, The World Bank News, October 1, 2014. ""For the first time in the history of the World Bank Group, we have set a goal that aims to reduce global inequality." - World Bank Group President Kim. World Bank Group President Jim Yong Kim today called for economic growth that creates more just societies, and he defined the institution's goal of boosting shared prosperity as the World Bank Group's way of tackling the global challenge of inequality."

[vii] "Today in many places we hear a call for greater security. But until exclusion and inequality in society and between peoples are reversed, it will be impossible to eliminate violence. The poor and the poorer peoples are accused of violence, yet without equal opportunities the different forms of aggression and conflict will find a fertile terrain for growth and eventually explode. When a society - whether local, national or global - is willing to leave a part of itself on the fringes, no political programmes or resources spent on law enforcement or surveillance systems can indefinitely guarantee tranquility. This is not the case simply because inequality provokes a violent reaction from those excluded from the system, but because the socioeconomic system is unjust at its root. ... Today's economic mechanisms promote inordinate consumption, yet it is evident that unbridled consumerism combined with inequality proves doubly damaging to the social fabric. Inequality eventually engenders a violence which recourse to arms cannot and never will be able to resolve. It serves only to offer false hopes to those clamouring for heightened security, even though nowadays we know that weapons and violence, rather than providing solutions, create new and more serious conflicts." *Evangelii Gaudium*, Pope Francis, November 24, 2013, excerpts from paragraphs 59 and 60.

[viii] *How Do We Know Hillary's Approach to Inequality Won't Work? Brazil, There's no alternative to targeting the rich*, Noam Scheiber, The New Republic, September 28, 2014. "To her credit, Hillary Clinton has seized on inequality as a theme of her proto-presidential campaign. She has despaired about the increasing "share of income and wealth going to those at the very top--not just the top 1 percent, but the top .1 percent or the .01 percent." She has warned that inequality is an issue that "affects our democracy.""

[ix] "So quite recently Mitt Romney announced that fighting poverty and income inequality was the theme of his new quest for the White House. Many of us laughed (I did) given the campaign he ran in 2012. But tonight on 60 Minutes both John Boehner and Mitch McConnell solemnly announced that income inequality is a major issue. They went on to point out that its gotten worse in the Obama years. This was an interview done only minutes after the State of the Union speech . . . McConnell: Look, things are getting better but the point is, who is benefitting from

this? This has been a top of the income recovery, ahh, the so called 1% that the President is always talking about have done quite well, but middle and lower income Americans are about $3000 dollars a year worse off than when he came to office. Pelley: Is income inequality a problem in this country? Is it a problem Republicans want to address? Boehner: (enthusiastically) It is. And frankly the President's policies have made income inequality worse." *Income inequality - the tide is shifting. Astonishing 60 minutes segment tonight*, calebfaux, Daily Kos, Jan. 25, 2015. Also: "The way to solve [the problem of inequality] in America is not to bring the top down, it's to bring the middle up. The middle class is the consumer class in America." Comment by Senator Marco Rubio a day after his new book, *American Dreams: Restoring Economic Opportunity for Everyone*, came out, CNBC Squawk Box, Jan. 14, 2015.

[x] Wikipedia presents a lively debate over the origins and meaning of the phrase, with the majority saying it derives from John Locke, who argued that "political society" existed for the sake of protecting "property," which he defined as a person's "life, liberty, and estate." Locke also wrote, "the highest perfection of intellectual nature lies in a careful and constant pursuit of true and solid happiness." And in *A Letter Concerning Toleration*, he wrote that the magistrate's power was limited to preserving a person's "civil interest," which he described as "life, liberty, health, and indolency of body; and the possession of outward things." Others would de-emphasize or remove the property or estates or possession-of-outward-things interpretations, such as Richard Cumberland, who "wrote that promoting the well-being of our fellow humans is essential to the "pursuit of our own happiness."" Although I favor the theory that the founders were inspired more by Locke than, say, Cumberland, I will not argue that case. Rather, my bigger point, which forms the core of this book, is that the nation behaved during its first century as if the right to pursue property and possessions were what the founders had in mind, thereby obviating, for my purposes anyway, any need to discuss alternative interpretations or argue over founders' intent.

[xi] The New York Stock Exchange considers the Buttonwood Agreement of May 17, 1792 to be its founding document, although there were earlier brokers meetings and documents going back to at least September, 1791 that may have been equally or more important to the formation of the cartel. [*Wall Street*, Walter Werner, Steven T. Smith, Columbia University Press, 1991, p. 26]. There were also some gaps in activity before the NYSE was formally founded in 1817 as The New York Stock and Exchange Board, although it was not fully established until regular active trading began in 1820. In addition to fixing commissions at a minimum of "one quarter per cent," the Buttonwood Agreement required its signing members to "give a preference to each other" when trading, which effectively barred the public or non-member professionals from accessing the exchange without coming through a member. This provision established the foundation for many other advantages of membership that enabled the members to make money, such as having exclusive access to trading privileges and to being able to see current information about prices. Because of such anticompetitive understandings among members that were undertaken under oath to enhance the value of their monopoly, this Wall Street

model could be considered the paradigm for many subsequent monopolies, which also included exclusionary and preferential arrangements similar to the "membership organization" structure on Wall Street. The shares of those subsequent monopolies, of course, were often underwritten in public offerings by exchange members and listed for trading on the exchange.

[xii] *Why decimalization is a bad idea*, Felix Salmon, Reuters, May 14, 2013. "The combination of decimalization and high-frequency trading has, in the words of former SEC commissioner Arthur Levitt, "transferred billions of dollars from the pockets of brokers into the pockets of investors;" for the first time ever, small investors get the *best* execution in the market, rather than the worst" [emphasis in original].

[xiii] Belief in American exceptionalism is universally embraced by those on the political right in the United States, but often disparaged by those on the left. But the same effective policy is also embraced from the left under the "one essential nation" doctrine, as described by former Secretary of State Madeline Albright during an interview on CNBC for the Clinton Global Initiative 9/23/14 where she credited her old boss, President Clinton, with inventing the term (although she says the press mostly attributed it to her). While the *exceptionalism* believers would emphasize individual freedom and the *one essential nation* believers would emphasize inclusion and diversity, both believe that America must lead the world to the type of democracy its advocates believe in and, practically speaking, both wind up in the same place, for example, on the need for America-led military coalitions of nations to stand up against terrorism or America-led political coalitions to stand up against Russian adventurism in Ukraine or nuclear weapons in Iran or North Korea, etc. This is a good example of how the differences between the Right and the Left and between Republicans and Democrats is only over nuance and engaged in during political arguments primarily to engender party loyalty, as I discussed in my book, *Nature's God.* p. 84-85. But under whatever labels and for whatever purpose the claim that America should lead the world is made, the main point here is that that claim would never have been made in the first place if American had not had the wealth to carry it off.

[xiv] *Inventing Freedom*, Daniel Hannan, HarperCollins e-books, 2013, Kindle location 124. Speaking of Alexis de Tocqueville's impressions in *Democracy in America*, Hannan writes, "English-speakers carried a unique political culture with them to the New World and developed it there in ways far removed from what happened in French and Spanish America. "The American," he wrote, "is the Englishman left to himself." Or, speaking of Paul Revere's ride, Hannan says, "In reality he shouted no such thing. It would have been extremely eccentric to yell "The British are coming!" at a population that had never thought of itself as anything other than British." Kindle location 731. Properly understood, according to both Hannan [*Inventing Freedom*, Kindle location 738] and Kevin Phillips, our Revolution was really just the middle one in a series of three conflicts that constituted the English Civil War in the 1640s, the 1770s and the 1860s: "In a grand sense, stepping around the enmity, gore, and destruction, the English-speaking peoples' three principal civil wars -- the English Revolution (or English Civil War), the American Revolution, and the

American Civil War -- can be acclaimed and exalted. Their cumulative transformation can be likened to a three-century historical ladder, up which the two leading nations climbed and in doing so sorted out their respective populations, ideologies, and economics in a way that ultimately produced two successive global hegemonies." *1775, A Good Year for Revolution*, Kevin Phillips, Viking, Penguin Group, New York, 2012, Kindle location 7929.

[xv] *A Royal Experiment*: The Private Life of King George III, Janice Hadlow, Henry Holt and Company, New York, 2014, Kindle location 310. "What struck foreign visitors most powerfully, however, was the degree to which the middle classes, and even some of the poor, shared in the general sense of improved wellbeing. In the opinion of one German writer in the 1770s, the 'luxury' enjoyed by the middle and lower classes 'had risen to such a pitch as never before seen in the world'. A few years later, a Russian traveler compared the general wellbeing he saw in London with the gulf between rich and poor he had witnessed in France. 'How different this from Paris! There vastness and filth, here simplicity and astonishing cleanliness; there wealth and poverty in continual contrast, here a general air of sufficiency; there palaces out of which crawls poverty, here tiny brick cottages with an air of dignity and tranquility, lord and artisan almost indistinguishable in their immaculate dress.' As he went on to remind his readers, squalor and poverty were of course still to be found in eighteenth-century England, but most foreign observers agreed that a larger proportion of the British now seemed to have escaped the worst deprivations that were the general experience of the European poor. Back in the 1720s, de Saussure had observed with surprise that the 'lower classes are usually well dressed, wearing good cloth and linen. You never see wooden shoes in England, and the poorest individuals never go with naked feet.' Indeed, in England, the wearing of 'wooden shoes' was indelibly associated with the desperate poverty held to be the inevitable product of life under Catholic absolute monarchies. The passionate cry of: 'No popery and no wooden shoes!', which so often resounded through the streets of eighteenth-century London, was an expression of the conviction held by even the poorest Britons that they enjoyed a standard of living of which their foreign counterparts could only dream."

[xvi] *Wall Street*, Walter Werner, Steven T. Smith, Columbia University Press, 1991, p. 11. ""Exchange Alley" in London, boasted a thriving securities market at the beginning of the eighteenth century. By 1720, England had all the essentials of securities markets as they exist today. First, there was a group of actively traded securities, representing both the government and private companies. Second, in accessible places like the coffee houses, there was continuous trading with publicity of prices and quotes. Third, there were professional brokers and dealers specializing in trading securities. Fourth, and perhaps most importantly, there was an investing public eager to buy and sell."

[xvii] 24 brokers signed the Buttonwood Agreement in 1792 that the New York Stock Exchange considers its founding document, although the exchange was not fully established until active trading began in about 1820. And "there were a number of such brokers operating [in London] during the early 1690s, perhaps as many as thirty," and one apparently typical broker "acted as broker for more than 150

individuals." Also one popular lottery, the Million Adventure lottery, "provided the opportunity for tens of thousands of investors to share in the excitement and potential of financial markets." "The Million adventure inspired dozens of private projectors to float their own lottery schemes and although financial historians have seldom considered lotteries to be part of the financial revolution, contemporaries were in no doubt about the similarities between the aims and actions of those who played the lotteries and those who invested in joint-stocks." *The Origins of English Financial Markets*: Investment and Speculation before the South Sea Bubble, Anne L. Murphy, Cambridge University Press, 2009, p. 20, p. 34. For comparison, around 1720 London's population was 700,000 and England's was 5.25 million. Macrohistory and World Timeline. In 1820 New York City's population was 123,706 and the United States total was 9,638,453. Wikipedia.

xviii *Capital in the Twenty-First Century,* Thomas Piketty, Belknap Press, Harvard University Press, Cambridge, Massachusetts, London, England, 2014. Kindle location 1353: "Indeed, according to Madison's calculations, both demographic and economic growth rates between year 0 and 1700 were below 0.1 percent (more precisely, 0.06 percent for population growth and 0.02 percent for per capita output). To be sure, the precision of such estimates is illusory. We actually possess very little information about the growth of the world's population between 0 and 1700 and even less about output per head. Nevertheless, no matter how much uncertainty there is about the exact figures (which are not very important in any case), there is no doubt whatsoever that the pace of growth was quite slow from antiquity to the Industrial Revolution, certainly no more than 0.1-0.2 percent per year. The reason is quite simple: higher growth rates would imply, implausibly, that the world's population at the beginning of the Common Era was miniscule, or else that the standard of living was very substantially below commonly accepted levels of subsistence."

xix *Capital in the Twenty-First Century,* Thomas Piketty, Belknap Press, Harvard University Press, Cambridge, Massachusetts, London, England, 2014. Kindle location 1348. A note to Table 2.1, World growth since the Industrial Revolution, states: "Between 1913 and 2012, the growth of world GDP was 3.0 percent per year on average. This growth rate can be broken down between 1.4 percent for world population and 1.6 percent for per capita GDP."

xx McCloskey uses the term in her forthcoming book, *Bourgeois Equality*, the third in a trilogy on "the bourgeois era," which she discussed in an opinion piece for the Financial Times on August 12, 2014, *Equality versus Lifting Up the Poor.*

xxi *Bourgeois Dignity: The Virtue of the Modern World*, Deirdre McCloskey, Gregory Clark, Matt Ridley, Jonathan Feinstein, Cato Unbound, Cato Institute, 2010, Kindle location 41.

xxii *Bourgeois Dignity: The Virtue of the Modern World*, Deirdre McCloskey, Gregory Clark, Matt Ridley, Jonathan Feinstein, Cato Unbound, Cato Institute, 2010, Kindle location 87. While all of the other economists disagreed with McCloskey (and with each other) on what caused the Industrial Revolution, none argued with her estimates of the economic betterment it brought about. McCloskey makes similar claims of the magnitude of economic betterment at various other points in the debate, as for example: "a factor at minimum of 16 (that 1500% I mentioned)" [Kindle location 354], "modern innovation of a factor of 16 or 30 or 100" [Kindle location 378], "the 2000 percent or more increase in human scope," [Kindle location 483], and "a factor of anywhere from 20 to 100" [Kindle location 513].

[xxiii] *Capital in the Twenty-First Century,* Thomas Piketty, Belknap Press, Harvard University Press, Cambridge, Massachusetts, London, England, 2014. Kindle location 1382. Table 2.2, The law of cumulated growth, shows that at 0.1 percent growth, a population will increase by a coefficient of 1.72 in a thousand years, while at 0.5 percent growth, a population will increase almost as much (by a coefficient of 1.65) in only a hundred years. Clearly, the 0.8 percent population growth rate from 1700 to 2012 [Kindle location 1348] would be more than enough compared to the 0.1 percent rate that pertained prior to 1700 to enable us to say that the bulk of people alive today would not exist if the old growth rate had continued.

[xxiv] Wikipedia puts the end of the Industrial Revolution at between 1820 and 1840. The *Communist Manifesto* was published in 1848.

[xxv] "Over the past several years, the IPO market in the United States has practically disappeared. Just 12 companies went public in the first half of 2009, and only eight of them were U.S. companies. Is the U.S. IPO market going through a cyclical downturn exacerbated by the recent credit crisis, or is today's market structure failing the IPO?" This question is followed by a chart showing the dramatic collapse of the small IPO, defined as transactions raising less than $50 million, from over 80% of the market through most of the 1990s up through 1996 down to about 20% from the end of 1999 on. The text under the chart reads: "A "perfect storm" of events pressures small IPOs as the number of transactions falls markedly. From 1991 to 1997 nearly 80% of IPOs were smaller than $50 million. By 2000 the number of sub-$50 million IPOs had declined to only 20% of the market. The market for underwritten IPOs, given its current structure, is closed to 80% of the companies that need it." Summarizing the problem in the text of the report: "The median IPO in the first half of 2009 was $135 million in size. This contrasts to 20 years ago when it was common for Wall Street to do $10 million IPOs and have them succeed." *Market Structure is causing the IPO crisis,* David Weild, Edward Kim, Grant Thornton, October 2009.

[xxvi] The Jumpstart Our Business Startups, or JOBS Act, was proposed by Eric Cantor on March 1, 2012 and signed into law by President Obama at a White House ceremony on April 5, 2012. It was largely a hodgepodge of previous bills meant to loosen up restrictions on issuing or buying securities in order to streamline capital formation. The part of it that matters to the securities industry is a little-noticed requirement that the SEC look into whether smaller tick sizes (the minimum increments for trading), and particularly the decimalization required by the SEC in 2000, might have hurt the investment banking industry's ability to support IPOs and capital formation. "The bill was supported by David Weild IV, former vice-chairman of NASDAQ, who also testified before Congress. Studies written by Weild, co-authored by Edward H. Kim and published by Grant Thornton, "identif[ied] changes to stock market structure that gave rise to a decline in the IPO market", and thus

"gave rise to the JOBS ACT", according to Devin Thorpe of *Forbes Magazine.* This has led some to refer to Weild as the "father of the JOBS act."" Wikipedia.

xxvii These would include, as Weild's studies demonstrate: the Gramm-Leach-Bliley Act (1999), Regulation Fair Disclosure (2000), Sarbanes Oxley (2002) and the reforms of conflicts of interest in the research market known as the Global Research Analyst Settlement (2003).

xxviii Letter to Chairman Joseph Dear, Investment Advisory Committee, United States Securities and Exchange Commission, from David Weild IV, Chairman & CEO, Edward H. Kim, Managing Director, IssuWorks, January 27, 2014.

xxix "Comprising professionals from across America's startup and small-capitalization company ecosystems, the Equity Capital Formation Task Force was formed in June 2013 to 1) examine the challenges that America's startups and small-cap companies face in raising equity capital in the current public market environment, and 2) develop recommendations for policy-makers that will help such companies gain greater access to the capital they need to grow their businesses and generate private sector job growth. The task force's efforts have been informed by discussions flowing from The Securities and Exchange Commission's Decimalization Roundtable (February 2013), which examined the impacts of decimalized pricing of securities on IPOs, trading, and liquidity for small and middle capitalization companies; and from the Capital Access Innovation Summit convened by the Treasury Department and the Small Business Administration in June 2013, which focused on the impact of the JOBS Act of 2012 on capital formation for emerging growth companies and what additional measures might benefit this process." From the "About" section of the Equity Capital Formation Task Force website 10/24/14.

xxx *Labor Market Fluidity and Economic Performance*, Steven J. Davis, John Haltiwanger, Jackson Hole, August 22, 2014. The paper paints a dire picture of the poor and worsening employment prospects in the United States, the dramatic deterioration of which predated the Great Recession. Although the authors do not highlight them, the dates when the problem showed up would appear to me to coincide with dates associated with stock market structure changes, such as the onset or ratcheting up of the SEC's National Market System electronic trading initiatives going back to its initiation in 1975, or that David Weild points out began in 1997 with the Order Handling Rules. The Jackson Hole paper lists the lack of new company formation and the consequent aging of the firms in the economy's employer base at the top of the list of probable reasons for the declining employment. The metrics demonstrating deterioration of fluidity in employment also "resonate with Schumpeterian theories of creative destruction that see reallocation as critical. From the perspective of creative destruction theories, the declining share of economic activity accounted for by younger businesses is especially worrisome. Even the high-tech sector, an important source of innovation and productivity growth, experienced a decline in startups and fast-growing young firms after 2000 (Decker et al., 2014b) [footnote 10]." Footnote 10: "The frequency of initial public offerings (IPOs) in the United States also plunged after 2000. According to Ritter (2013), the annual IPO rate for U.S. operating companies fell by more than two-thirds from the 1980-2000 period to the 2001-2012 period." The Davis/Haltiwanger paper also shows that the declining fluidity problem is "pervasive across states" and appears to be unique to, or at least significantly worse in, the United States than in other countries. "While a more extensive set of international comparisons might tell a different story, the evidence here suggests that secular declines in U.S. labor market flows largely reflect forces and developments that are specific to, or more pronounced in, the United States."

xxxi Wikipedia on "JOBS Act" 10/24/14.

xxxii David Weild interviewed 12/18/14 by Larry Tabb, TabbFORUM.com, viewed Jan. 16, 2015. Weild claims that the IPO market should be producing at least 900 IPOs now, "GDP-adjusted," [for comparison, it produced less than 300 in the supposedly good 2014 year] and that the difference between the 14,000 stocks we should have in our market by now if it had remained healthy [i.e., instead of being converted to HFT by the SEC's reforms] and the less-than 5,000 stocks we do have, means that the U.S. is missing 10 million or more jobs as a result.

xxxiii *Sexy and 17! New SEC Equity Market Structure Advisory Committee*, Sal Arnuk, Joe Salluzi, TabbFORUM.com, Jan. 14, 2015. "You may recall that recently word leaked that Nobel Prize winning economist [Joseph E.] Stiglitz was nixed from this panel for "faulting high-speed traders." Other notable market structure critics also were not chosen for this panel."

xxxiv "What those who are calling for reviews of market structure don't realize is that such discussions organized by the SEC are how we got into the mess we are in today. More discussion will only make matters worse. These problems are endemic to NMS and the SEC's oversight of it, and will not go away until NMS and the SEC go away." *Nature's God*, Steve Wunsch, 2012, Amazon CreateSpace, p. 119, Amazon Kindle Direct Publishing, Kindle location 3063.

xxxv In an interesting postscript, Stiglitz was asked by Adam Ross Sorkin if he thought the SEC was in the pocket of the high-frequency traders, hinting that that might have been why his participation on the SEC's expert panel was rejected, and Stiglitz agreed: "Yes, I think there is a real problem." Squawk Box, CNBC, Jan. 26, 2015.

xxxvi Locke said political society exists for the sake of protecting "property," which he defined as a person's "life, liberty, and estate." Locke also wrote, "the highest perfection of intellectual nature lies in a careful and constant pursuit of true and solid happiness." And in *A Letter Concerning Toleration*, he suggested government's legitimate power was limited to preserving a person's "civil interest," which he described as "life, liberty, health, and indolency of body; and the possession of outward things."

xxxvii *The Antitrust Paradox: A Policy at War with Itself*, Robert H. Bork, Basic Books, Inc. New York, 1978, p. 15.

xxxviii *The Antitrust Paradox: A Policy at War with Itself*, Robert H. Bork, Basic Books, Inc. New York, 1978, p. 7.

xxxix *Amazon Loves Government: How the online retailer leveraged federal power to crush the publishers*, Review and Outlook, The Wall Street Journal, Sept. 10, 2014. "The larger point is that the executive and judicial branches intervened to aid Amazon, a quasi-monopolist incumbent at a crucial competitive juncture amid the shift to digital from print, preventing a market resolution. Apple is appealing Judge Cote's ruling as a matter of antitrust law, and the outcome is by no means clear. What is clear is that Amazon ought to stop claiming to be a tribune of the market when its chief patron is government." What is interesting here is that the presumably knowledgeable Wall Street Journal editorial staff either are not aware of the per se prohibition against price fixing, or prefer to ignore it in order to make their own political point. As Judge Cote made clear in some statements months before handing down her decision, Apple and the publishers had clearly colluded to fix price, and that was all there was to it. But confusion reigns still, in spite of that supposed per se certainty, or perhaps because of it, as in all antitrust cases.

xl *The Antitrust Paradox: A Policy at War with Itself*, Robert H. Bork, Basic Books, Inc. New York, 1978, p. 111. " . . . it seems clear the income distribution effects of economic activity should be completely excluded from the determination of the antitrust legality of the activity. It may be sufficient to note that the shift in income distribution does not lessen total wealth, and a decision about it requires a choice between two groups of consumers that should be made by the legislature rather than by the judiciary." "It would be improper to include income redistribution as a factor *because* we disapprove of monopolistic restriction of output, for that would be to count the dead-weight loss against the merger twice. The dead-weight loss has already been subtracted, and we must now consider whether the remaining net efficiency gain is to be overcome by redistribution." [Emphasis in original]

xli I discuss the importance of Darwinian competition, as opposed to sports competition concepts such as fairness and "level playing fields," in a letter to the SEC that is included in *Auction Countdown*, Amazon Kindle, 2010, Kindle location 5107. "Darwinian competition, by contrast [to sports competition], discovers which new forms of competitors are better at surviving than old forms, particularly when conditions change, such as when a large meteor strikes the earth, or when new technologies emerge. Because their struggle for survival is between different forms of competitors, it is inherently unfair by the terms of sports competition. But, far from hindering the effectiveness of evolution, this unfairness is essential to producing ever more capable competitors and ever more complex forms of biological, social and economic organization. In a very real sense, Darwinian competition must be unfair to work properly."

xlii Industries are called "deregulated" in these "natural monopoly" contexts because the government does not actually oversee the service provided as a regulated public utility. "['Public utility'] regulation is assumed by nearly all who work or write in the field, as by the public in general, to be fundamentally inevitable, wise, and necessary. However, personal experience as a government lawyer involved in regulatory matters made me skeptical about the validity of the assumption and this study has convinced me that in fact public utility regulation is probably not a useful exertion of governmental powers; that its benefits cannot be shown to outweigh its costs; and that even in markets where efficiency dictates monopoly we might do better to allow natural economic forces to determine business conduct and performance subject only to the constraints of antitrust policy. I would stress, however, that no general challenge to government regulation of business is intended. One regulatory framework whose continued existence is explicitly presupposed by my analysis is, as just mentioned, the antitrust laws." *Natural Monopoly and its Regulation*, Richard A. Posner, 30th Anniversary Edition, Cato Institute, p. 3. Posner offers a defense of the theory of deregulation in this seminal work. See my book *Countdown* for a critique of the theory, Kindle location 399: "By deciding that our natural monopolies can be deregulated under antitrust, we have opened the way for a far more pervasive and intrusive takeover, supported by the propaganda that says deregulation is a laissez faire approach that will make multi-firm competition as coordinated and efficient as a single firm monopoly."

[xliii] "Also, the Study placed a great emphasis on alternative markets. I think we placed too much emphasis on encouraging competitive alternative markets, primarily directed at the power of the New York Stock Exchange. If I had to do it all over again, I would have written that part of the study a little differently. But Milton brought a Brandeisive emphasis to the Study in the name of fostering competition and innovation. I started from the premise that the natural tendency of markets was towards concentration because of the greater liquidity and lower transaction costs. I felt that we artificially encouraged the development of alternative markets. For example, we encouraged unlisted trading which basically fed off the New York Stock Exchange. They did so because New York had the advantage -- for better or worse -- of being the market where orders were primarily concentrated and where the transaction costs would be naturally lower than they would be in any alternative market because of the liquidity factor. So I think the Commission encouraged, under the name of innovation and competition, alternative markets to compete with New York. Now, there's nothing wrong with applying technology to the trading of securities, but I think to have a regulatory scheme that's in a way biased towards alternatives for their own sake as a counterbalance to New York is troubling. I think if the Commission is troubled by the concentration of power in New York, the way to deal with that is to have the exchange become more of a public institution. I'm not saying we're there yet. But I'm saying that they have become more of a public utility." "I think in the Study, with Chapters 8 and 9, we went too far. I know Milton does not agree with this, but I felt we encouraged the Commission to develop the third market and to try to revive the regional exchanges in competition to New York. Our objective should have been to make sure that the public gets good executions at the lowest possible transaction costs. Another thing that I think we missed out on is defining what is competition in the trading market. What kind of competition are we talking about? Are we talking about competition between markets or among markets, or are we talking about competition among public orders? It's a competition among public orders that's more important than developing competing institutions just to get at the hegemony of the New York Stock Exchange." Securities and Exchange Commission Historical Society, Interview with Ralph S. Saul, Conducted on November 29, 2001 by David Silver. Ralph Saul was the Associate Director of the Division of Trading and Exchanges at the SEC from 1958 to 1965. Saul and Milton Cohen were associate directors responsible for the Special Study Report, released in stages in 1963. The Study laid the groundwork for all of the market structure regulation in the half-century since its release.

[xliv] For an extended discussion of the causes and consequences of the Flash Crash of May 6, 2010, see my eight articles published in various places in the following months, all of which are collected in Appendix I of my 2011 book, *War On Wealth*, Kindle location 869.

[xlv] *The Dollar Trap: How the U.S. Dollar Tightened Its Grip On Global Finance*, Eswar S. Prasad, Princeton University Press, 2014, Kindle location 519. "The U.S. dollar has been the principal global currency for most of post-World War II history. In fact, the U.S. economy is estimated to have become the largest in the world in the 1870s. By the early 1900s it also accounted for the largest share of global trade."

[xlvi] The jealousy was general by then and Sherman appears to have been doing nothing more than piling on: "By the late 19th century, business began to form combinations, known as trusts, which claimed a larger and larger share of the market -- large enough to dictate prices, their detractors claimed. Members of both major parties were concerned with the growth of the power of trusts and monopolies, and, at the opening of the 51st Congress Sherman proposed what would become the Sherman Antitrust Act." "Until 1888, Sherman had shown little interest in the trust question but it was rising in the national consciousness and Sherman now entered the fray. In debate, Sherman praised the effects of corporations in developing industry and railroads and asserted the right for people to form corporations, so long as they were "not in any sense a monopoly."" Wikipedia: "Senator Sherman" 10/25/14.

[xlvii] *The Antitrust Paradox: A Policy at War with Itself*, Robert H. Bork, Basic Books, Inc. New York, 1978, p. 110.

[xlviii] *The Antitrust Paradox: A Policy at War with Itself*, Robert H. Bork, Basic Books, Inc. New York, 1978, page 26.

[xlix] "It takes a heap of Harberger triangles (another term for what economists call the "dead weight loss" due to restraint-of-trade monopolization) to fill an Okun gap (an economists' term for output gaps between actual GNP and ideal or theoretically potential GNP)."

[l] *Monopoly is a bureaucrat's friend, but a democrat's foe*, Financial Times, August 13, 2014. "As human freedoms go, the freedom to take your custom elsewhere is not a grand or noble one -- but neither is it one that we should abandon without a fight."

[li] *Everything for Sale: The Virtues and Limits of Markets*, Robert Kuttner, Alfred A. Knopf, Inc. The University of Chicago Press, 1996, p. 25.

[lii] For example, Fox News's archconservative pundit Bill O'Reilly proudly calls himself a "Teddy Roosevelt conservative" when trying to help his viewers quickly understand where to place him politically in his commentaries. The comment came in the discussion just following the day's highlighted "memo" on the 9/9/14 show.

[liii] "The Square Deal was President Theodore Roosevelt's domestic program formed upon three basic ideas: conservation of natural resources, control of corporations, and consumer protection. These three demands are often referred to as the "three C's" of Roosevelt's Square Deal. Thus, it aimed at helping middle class citizens and involved attacking plutocracy and bad trusts while at the same time protecting business from the most extreme demands of organized labor. A progressive Republican, Roosevelt believed in government action to mitigate social evils, and as

president denounced "the representatives of predatory wealth" as guilty of "all forms of iniquity from oppression of wage workers to defrauding the public."" Wikipedia: "Square Deal" 1/6/15.

liv Teddy was Franklin's fifth cousin, but was actually more closely related to Franklin's wife, Eleanor, who was his niece. Her father was Teddy's younger brother.

lv FDR's October 31, 1936 campaign speech in Madison Square Garden announced the Second New Deal. "Never before in all our history have these forces been so united against one candidate as they stand today. They are unanimous in their hate for me--and I welcome their hatred." Among other memorable quotes from that speech, Roosevelt attacked big money monopolies by saying, "Government by organized money is just as dangerous as Government by organized mob;" and "I should like to have it said of my first Administration that in it the forces of selfishness and of lust for power met their match. I should like to have it said of my second Administration that in it these forces met their master." Franklin D. Roosevelt Presidential Library and Museum.

lvi "If the international Finance-Jewry inside and outside of Europe should succeed in plunging the peoples of the earth once again into a world war, the result will not be the bolshevization of earth, and thus a Jewish victory, but the annihilation of the Jewish race in Europe." Adolf Hitler speaking to the Reichstag, January 30, 1939, United States Holocaust Memorial Museum.

lvii The TR tally of busting trusts, which different accounts put at between 40 and 44, was against the backdrop of 318 trusts that existed in the United States when he assumed office, accounting for about 40% of economic activity or GDP at the time. "For his aggressive use of the United States antitrust law he became known as the "trust-buster." He brought 40 antitrust suits, and broke up such major combinations as the largest railroad and Standard Oil, the largest oil company." Wikipedia 10/26/14: "Teddy Roosevelt."

lviii "Theodore Roosevelt, we should say this bluntly, liked war." George Will, comment in *The Roosevelts*, first episode, PBS documentary by Ken Burns, Sept. 16, 2014.

lix TR's immediate successor, William Howard Taft, for example, with TR's blessing and encouragement, launched 90 antitrust suits in one term of office, although TR still retains history's "trustbuster" label, probably because he was first and certainly the more militaristic and nationalistic about it. Taft's successor, Woodrow Wilson, carried on the tradition, heading the Progressive Party and beefing up antitrust: "In addition, he pushed through Congress the Clayton Antitrust Act making certain business practices illegal, such as price discrimination, agreements prohibiting retailers from handling other companies' products, and directorates and agreements to control other companies. The power of this legislation was greater than that of previous anti-trust laws since it dictated accountability of individual corporate officers and clarified guidelines." Wikipedia 10/26/14: "Woodrow Wilson."

lx A German convention at the time would combine into an acronym the first syllable of the first word, *na*tional, and the second syllable of the second word, so*zi*alismus, to produce NAZI in this case. The party's full name was the Nationalsozialistische Deutsche Arbeiterpartei, or the National Socialist German Workers Party.

[lxi] *The Second Coming*, William Butler Yeats, 1919: "Things fall apart; the centre cannot hold; Mere anarchy is loosed upon the world, The blood-dimmed tide is loosed, and everywhere The ceremony of innocence is drowned; The best lack all conviction, while the worst Are full of passionate intensity." "When Yeats wrote that in 1919, he may have foreseen that the twentieth century would experience the "blood-dimmed tide," as indeed it has. But he can hardly have had any conception of just how thoroughly things would fall apart as the center failed to hold in the last third of this century. He can hardly have foreseen that the passionate intensity, uncoupled from morality, would shred the fabric of Western culture. The rough beast of decadence, a long time in gestation, having reached its maturity in the last three decades, now sends us slouching towards our new home, not Bethlehem, but Gomorrah." *Slouching Towards Gomorrah*, Robert H. Bork, Harper Collins, New York, 1996, opening page.

[lxii] *HFT and the Computerization of Wall Street, Part 1: Seeds of Destruction*, Steve Wunsch, July 16 2013, TabbFORUM.com; *HFT and the Computerization of Wall Street, Part 2: A Bad Trade*, Steve Wunsch, TabbFORUM.com, July 22, 2013; *HFT and the Computerization of Wall Street, Part 3: Eliminating the Middleman*, Steve Wunsch July 31, 2013, TabbFORUM.com.

[lxiii] "The Founders would also have been aghast at President Roosevelt, who argued in Osawatomie that social justice was more important than property rights, as if these concepts were incompatible. He could easily have coined the No Justice, No Peace slogan, and certainly did what he could to promote it in principle, as has President Obama. Both presidents pushed with all their might to effect downward redistribution, considering it a moral obligation of government to counter inequality." *Nature's God*, Steve Wunsch, 2012, Amazon Kindle Direct Publishing, Kindle location 216, Amazon CreateSpace paperback, page 10.

[lxiv] *Capital in the Twenty-First Century*, Thomas Piketty, Belknap Press, Harvard University Press, Cambridge, Massachusetts, London, England, 2014. Kindle location 10124. Democratic debate and similar means of political cooperation are repeatedly referenced by Piketty to describe the process by which appropriate amounts and kinds of redistributive policies can be adopted, such as highly progressive income, inheritance or wealth taxes, preferably enacted on a globally coordinated basis, to counteract inequality before it becomes socially explosive. "This would contain the unlimited growth of global inequality of wealth, which is currently increasing at a rate that cannot be sustained in the long run and that ought to worry even the most fervent champions of the self-regulated market. Historical experience shows, moreover, that such immense inequalities of wealth have little to do with the entrepreneurial spirit and are of no use in promoting growth. Nor are they of any "common utility," to borrow the nice expression from the 1789 Declaration of the Rights of Man and the Citizen with which I began this book. The difficulty is that this solution, the progressive tax on capital, requires a high level of international cooperation and regional political integration."

146

lxv "In my AZX days I came across many people who believed that, on a truly level playing field, market making would be unnecessary and would disappear as investors provided liquidity directly to each other. And most of them believed that the electronic trading screens of NMS would create such a level playing field. Consequently they became fervent believers in the Commission's NMS mission." *Dark Pool Comment Letter*, Steve Wunsch, submitted to SEC January 14, 2010. Kindle location 296.

lxvi *HFT and the Computerization of Wall Street, Part 3: Eliminating the Middleman*, Steve Wunsch, July 31, 2013, TabbFORUM.com. "Exxon generally trades with a 2-cent spread, or a 1-cent cost one way, i.e., $10, or 1.3 basis points on $75,250. Even adding in an $8 commission, the total cost one way should be about $18, or 2.4 basis points. Trading at the open or close in the batch trade where everyone gets the same price and thus has no spread would bring the cost down to just the commission of $8, or 1 basis point. An individual who trades small size infrequently enough that his trades are random from the market's perspective can automatically get such results. An institutional trader that uses a simple randomizing algorithm that spreads out his market orders to look like retail can get close to the retail result, too, as long as he doesn't hurry to execute faster than the pace at which he can still pass for random retail."

lxvii With regard to *Dark Pools*, by Scott Patterson, this issue is discussed in *HFT and the Computerization of Wall Street, Part 3: Eliminating the Middleman*, Steve Wunsch, July 31, 2013 TabbFORUM.com. With regard to *Flash Boys*, by Michael Lewis, this issue is discussed in *The Tradeoff Between Fairness and Liquidity is an Old Story*, Parts One, Two and Three on April 10, April 17 and May 1, respectively, 2014, Steve Wunsch, TabbFORUM.com.

lxviii *The Price of Inequality*: How Today's Divided Society Endangers Our Future, Joseph E. Stiglitz, W. W. Norton & Company, 2012. We have already mentioned Piketty's *Capital in the Twenty-First Century*. Also in this category are *The Haves and Have-Nots*: A Brief and Idiosyncratic History of Global Inequality, Branko Milanovic, Basic Books, 2010; and *The Great Escape*: Health, Wealth, and the Origins of Inequality, Angus Deaton, Princeton University Press, 2013.

lxix *Capital in the Twenty-First Century*, Thomas Piketty, translated by Arthur Goldhammer, The Belknap Press of Harvard University Press, Cambridge, Massachusetts, London, England, 2014, Kindle location 417.

lxx *Capital in the Twenty-First Century*, Thomas Piketty, translated by Arthur Goldhammer, The Belknap Press of Harvard University Press, Cambridge, Massachusetts, London, England, 2014, Kindle location 1658.

lxxi *Capital in the Twenty-First Century*, Thomas Piketty, translated by Arthur Goldhammer, The Belknap Press of Harvard University Press, Cambridge, Massachusetts, London, England, 2014, Kindle location 1383.

lxxii *Capital in the Twenty-First Century*, Thomas Piketty, translated by Arthur Goldhammer, The Belknap Press of Harvard University Press, Cambridge, Massachusetts, London, England, 2014, Kindle location 6553.

lxxiii *Capital in the Twenty-First Century*, Thomas Piketty, translated by Arthur Goldhammer, The Belknap Press of Harvard University Press, Cambridge, Massachusetts, London, England, 2014, Kindle location 6466.

lxxiv *Capital in the Twenty-First Century*, Thomas Piketty, translated by Arthur Goldhammer, The Belknap Press of Harvard University Press, Cambridge, Massachusetts, London, England, 2014, Kindle location 6368.

lxxv *Capital in the Twenty-First Century*, Thomas Piketty, translated by Arthur Goldhammer, The Belknap Press of Harvard University Press, Cambridge, Massachusetts, London, England, 2014, Kindle location 6395.

lxxvi *Capital in the Twenty-First Century*, Thomas Piketty, translated by Arthur Goldhammer, The Belknap Press of Harvard University Press, Cambridge, Massachusetts, London, England, 2014, Kindle location 6395.

lxxvii I introduce this concept on the first page of *Nature's God*, which opens with an appeal to network scientists for help in applying their discipline to inequality issues and conflicts over redistribution. "First, as network scientists know, the concept they call *rich get richer*, or *preferential attachment* drives network formation throughout the universe. Simply describing this natural force more fully may help us rethink the premises that are causing so much conflict. Seeing that nodes in a network discriminate in their attachments between rich and poor -- between those with many links to others and those with few links to others -- may lead to an understanding that neither discrimination nor inequality is an appropriate concern of government." *Nature's God*, Steve Wunsch, 2012, Amazon CreateSpace paperback, p. 3, Amazon Kindle Direct Publishing, Kindle location 32.

lxxviii The Concise Encyclopedia of Economics, Google search on "Vilfredo Pareto."

lxxix "Two leading advocates of Republican reform, Michael Gerson, chief speechwriter for George W. Bush and a Washington Post columnist, and Peter Wehner, a senior fellow at the Ethics and Public Policy Center who served in the last three Republican administrations, wrote in the Winter 2014 edition of National Affairs that "many conservatives fail to see the extent to which equal opportunity, a central principle of our national self-understanding, is becoming harder to achieve. It is a well-documented fact that, in recent years, economic mobility has stalled for many poorer Americans, resulting in persistent intergenerational inequality. This phenomenon is more complex than an income gap. It involves wide disparities in parental time and investment, in religious and community involvement, and in academic accomplishment. These are traceable to a number of factors, including the collapse of working-class families, the flight of blue-collar jobs, and the decay of neighborhoods that once offered stronger networks of mentorship outside the home."" *What Makes People Poor?* Thomas B. Edsall, The New York Times, Sept. 2, 2014.

lxxx *The Righteous Mind: How Good People are Divided by Politics and Religion*, Jonathan Haidt, Pantheon Books, Random House, New York, 2012, Kindle location 106. "If you think that moral reasoning is something we do to figure out the truth, you'll be constantly frustrated by how foolish, biased, and illogical people become when they disagree with you. But if you think about moral reasoning as a skill we humans evolved to further our social agendas--to justify our own actions and to defend the teams we belong to--then things will make a lot more sense. Keep your eye on the intuitions, and don't take people's moral arguments at face value. They're mostly post hoc constructions made up on the fly, crafted to advance one or more strategic objectives."

[lxxxi] *Dark Pool Comment Letter*, Steve Wunsch, letter to SEC, January 14, 2010, Amazon Kindle, February 4, 2010, Kindle location 296. "It didn't take long when considering the issue while designing a call auction to realize the NMS was based on a false premise. It is only in a fixed time trade that such Nirvana is possible. In a perfectly ideal call auction, all buyers and all sellers would simultaneously trade directly against each other at an equilibrium midpoint price, thereby eliminating the need for intermediaries and their compensation at that point in time. The level playing field is a necessary condition, but not a sufficient condition, for Nirvana to occur. Without the competition at the known, fixed time, even on a perfectly level electronic playing field, there would still be some who were faster than others at processing the information on the screen or would somehow find relevant information that wasn't on the screen. A continuous market, therefore, cannot eliminate intermediation, no matter how level the playing field is, and no matter how powerful Congress makes the SEC."

[lxxxii] The most important of these studies came from the SEC and were the aforementioned Special Study Report in the early 1960s and the Institutional Investor Study in the early 1970s, for which the academics at the National Bureau of Economic Research (NBER) were hired by the SEC staff to do the background research. The academic justification for such disruptive reforms as the elimination of fixed commissions and the launching of the transparency and electronic trading of the National Market System (informally "NMS," but formally the 1975 Amendments, Section 11A, to the Securities Exchange Act of 1934) grew out of these studies. And all of these related antitrust-based reforms relied to one degree or another on the hope and belief that a properly structured and reformed Wall Street would either drastically reduce intermediation costs or eliminate them altogether. All of the reforms were set in motion shortly before or on Mayday 1975, although it took until 1997 in NASDAQ stocks (with the Order Handling Rules) and 2007 in NYSE stocks (with Reg NMS) for the full disintermediation dream of electronic high-frequency trading (HFT) to be realized.

[lxxxiii] *Dark Pools*, Scott Patterson, Crown Publishing Group, Random House, 2012, Kindle location 873: "The game had changed. Bodek became increasingly convinced that the stock market--*the United States stock market*--was rigged." Kindle location 882: "Ever the scientist at heart, Bodek decided to test the order types to validate the information he'd been given. Back at Trading Machines, he followed the advice he'd been given--he stopped using the sitting-duck limit orders and started using the insider orders. Immediately, his losses abated. His orders weren't getting abused time and again. Bodek felt as if he'd taken a gun that had been pointed at his head and aimed it at someone else. Someone was getting screwed. Just not Trading Machines." Kindle location 4615: "Was this the future for the U.S. stock market, whose purpose was to give companies the ability to raise money and investors the chance to tap into the growth of the global economy? The industry wouldn't stand a

chance, Bodek thought, if someone didn't stick his neck out and start taking on the madness. Riding the train home that night, he decided it might as well be him." Kindle location 4692: "To that end, in the summer of 2011, he hired a major law firm to help him use his understanding of toxic order types he'd gained from his exchange contacts while at Trading Machines, combined with the details of his understanding of high-frequency strategies he'd learned from the 0+ Scalping Strategy document, to lay out a road map. The road map detailed his argument that high-speed traders and exchanges had created a market that was hurting nearly all investors."

lxxxiv *'Spoofing,' a New Crime With a Catchy Name*, Peter J. Henning, The New York Times, October 6, 2014. "The indictment seeks to hold Mr. Coscia liable for trades executed in milliseconds by a computer, including one trade at 4:54 a.m. when he was probably asleep. The spoofing charges may send a chill through the high-frequency trading world because the evidence of fraudulent intent will come from a program that uses rapid-fire orders and does not depend on humans for its execution. So finding that Mr. Coscia engaged in spoofing may come down to a jury deciding whether one computer fooling another is a crime."

lxxxv In one of the most colorful images, Charlie Munger, who is Warren Buffet's partner in Berkshire Hathaway, on a CNBC interview with both of them, likened letting HFTs enter stock trading to "letting rats loose in a granary." Buffet apparently agrees with him and has said similar, if less colorful things.

lxxxvi *Auction Countdown-Calls for Reform*, Steve Wunsch, originally printed March 24, 1997 as a separate AZX Auction Countdown, included in *Auction Countdown*, Amazon Kindle, February 10, 2010, Kindle location 4617: "In fact, throughout the capitalist world -- including also Canada, the European countries, and Japan -- markets are being reformed with antitrust principles and laws, often styled as "deregulation." Given the wide acceptance of antitrust principles, and the fact that the laws based on them are in place, regulators are pretty much bound to enforce them. But stock markets present a primal challenge to antitrust theory and law. Every successful capitalist country has a stock market at its center, and every one of them is a cartel and a monopoly, usually formed that way long before the Sherman Antitrust Act of 1890. If antitrust theory is correct, how could these markets -- and the economies that depend on them -- have been so successful? Could it be that, just as transparency is not always good, cartels are not always bad? If cartels are always bad, as antitrust says they are, it seems to me that regulators have no choice but to continue the reform process. But this could already be having a negative effect on our ability to raise capital.

lxxxvii *Wall Street*, Walter Werner, Steven T. Smith, Columbia University Press, 1991, p. x.

lxxxviii *Adventure in Social Control of Finance: The National Market System for Securities*, Walter Werner, Columbia Law Review, Nov. 1975, p. 1244.

lxxxix As told to me in an email 12/10/14 confirming previous oral comments by Fred Siesel, an economic analyst who worked with Werner at the SEC, including on the Special Study Report. "Re unfixed commission rates: Walter was the first person at the SEC to suggest/propose, at least formally, that commission rates be "unfixed."

When he sent the memo to the Commission, I clearly remember [Associate Director of Policy Research] Gene Rotberg enthusiastically showing Walter's memo to anyone, and everyone."

xc *Adventure in Social Control of Finance: The National Market System for Securities*, Walter Werner, Columbia Law Review, Nov. 1975, p. 1238.

xci *Wall Street*, Walter Werner, Steven T. Smith, Columbia University Press, 1991, p. 152.

xcii *Adventure in Social Control of Finance: The National Market System for Securities*, Walter Werner, Columbia Law Review, Nov. 1975, p. 1285.

xciii *Wall Street*, Walter Werner, Steven T. Smith, Columbia University Press, 1991, p. 6.

xciv *Wall Street*, Walter Werner, Steven T. Smith, Columbia University Press, 1991, p. 206.

xcv *Adventure in Social Control of Finance: The National Market System for Securities*, Walter Werner, Columbia Law Review, Nov. 1975, pp. 1294-1295. "The agency's non-use of economic authority in practice invited a reading of Exchange Act principles that first excluded economic authority and then denied bases for the "economic regulation" inherent in reviewing reasonableness of fixed rates. The failure to act also led to extremes of agency behavior. Inaction swiftly became over-reaction: the remedy for failure to regulate market structure and assure reasonable fixed rates became abolition of fixed rates and creation of a new market system."

xcvi *The SEC as a Market Regulator*, Walter Werner, Virginia Law Review, May 1984. p. 763.

xcvii *Wall Street*, Walter Werner, Steven T. Smith, Columbia University Press, 1991, p. 42.

xcviii *Is Speculation "The Essential Native Genius of The Stock Market"?* Louis Lowenstein, Columbia Law Review, Vol. 92, No. 1 (Jan., 1992), pp. 232-246.

xcix *Wall Street*, Walter Werner, Steven T. Smith, Columbia University Press, 1991, p. 77.

c *Wall Street*, Walter Werner, Steven T. Smith, Columbia University Press, 1991, p. 5.

ci *Wall Street*, Walter Werner, Steven T. Smith, Columbia University Press, 1991, p. 115.

cii *Wall Street*, Walter Werner, Steven T. Smith, Columbia University Press, 1991, p. 118.

ciii *Wall Street*, Walter Werner, Steven T. Smith, Columbia University Press, 1991, p. 215, footnote 30 on Buttonwood Agreement section. "Almost half of those listed as brokers in Duncan's 1792 New York directory did not sign the Buttonwood Agreement."

civ *Wall Street*, Walter Werner, Steven T. Smith, Columbia University Press, 1991, p. 20. "On a spring day in 1792, twenty-four men signed the compact generally viewed as marking the birth of organized stock trading in New York. The Buttonwood Agreement, which takes its name from the legendary Wall Street trading beneath a buttonwood tree, asserts the fundamental principles that later shaped the New York Stock Exchange and other securities markets in the United States. "We the Subscribers, Brokers for the Purchase and Sale of Public Stock, do hereby solemnly promise and pledge ourselves to each other, that we will not buy or sell from this day for any person whatsoever, any kind of Public Stock at a less rate than one quarter per cent Commission on the Specie value, and that we will give a preference to each other in our Negotiations. In testimony whereof we have set our hands this 17th day of May at New York, 1792.""

cv *Wall Street*, Walter Werner, Steven T. Smith, Columbia University Press, 1991, pp. 190-191. "Broadside of Securities Trading Rules, September 1791. AT A MEETING of the DEALERS in the PUBLIC FUNDS in the CITY of NEW-YORK held at the COFFEE-HOUSE, on the 21st SEPTEMBER, 1791, it was agreed to be governed by the following rules." "[Rule] XIV. These rules shall take place on the 1st of October; they shall be subscribed by the several Dealers and Auctioneers--and the Dealers shall thereby pledge themselves not to do business with any Auctioneer who shall not have subscribed them."

cvi Wikipedia: Battle of Golden Hill.

cvii *1775, A Good Year for Revolution*, Kevin Phillips, Viking, Penguin Group, New York, 2012, p.137, Kindle location 2812.

cviii Wikipedia: Battle of Golden Hill.

cix *The Forging of the American Empire: From the Revolution to Vietnam: a History of U.S. Imperialism*, Sydney Lens, Pluto Press, London, 2003, p. 16.

cx *Wall Street*, Walter Werner, Steven T. Smith, Columbia University Press, 1991, p. 43.

cxi *Wall Street*, Walter Werner, Steven T. Smith, Columbia University Press, 1991, p. 43.

cxii *Wall Street*, Walter Werner, Steven T. Smith, Columbia University Press, 1991, p. 44.

cxiii *Wall Street*, Walter Werner, Steven T. Smith, Columbia University Press, 1991, p. 44. "Boston and other cities also had pools of capital to tap, and it is generally accepted that early in the nineteenth century, New York was not the country's leading market for raising investment capital."

cxiv *Wall Street*, Walter Werner, Steven T. Smith, Columbia University Press, 1991, p. 44. "The New York secondary trading market quickly absorbed the stock of railroad companies, at first those with a terminus in New York, but soon roads chartered and operating in other states as well. The new railroad stocks were financial assets that lent themselves admirably to the speculative capabilities of New Yorkers: they were the issues of a glamorous new industry made up of many entrants, some destined for success and profitability, others to failure and liquidation. Share prices and trading volume in New York were high. Speculation kept New York securities markets liquid. Buyers and sellers could execute their trades at short notice, often without substantial changes in price from the previous quote. Because trading volume gravitates to the market that assures best execution, Wall Street became the primary center for trading railroad shares."

cxv *Wall Street*, Walter Werner, Steven T. Smith, Columbia University Press, 1991, p. 45.

cxvi *The Dollar Trap: How the U.S. Dollar Tightened Its Grip On Global Finance*, Eswar S. Prasad, Princeton University Press, 2014, Kindle location 519. "The U.S. dollar has been the principal global currency for most of post-World War II history. In fact, the U.S. economy is estimated to have become the largest in the world in the 1870s. By the early 1900s it also accounted for the largest share of global trade."

[cxvii] *The Dollar Trap: How the U.S. Dollar Tightened Its Grip On Global Finance*, Eswar S. Prasad, Princeton University Press, 2014, Kindle location 542. "This has created a bounty for the U.S., often disparagingly referred as an "exorbitant privilege." The U.S. has lived beyond its means for an extended period, with its consumption and investment substantially exceeding the output it produces. The country has been able to borrow from the rest of the world, and the dollar's status has allowed it to finance this debt at cheap interest rates. What is more, because this debt is all denominated in dollars, the U.S. can in principle reduce its debt burden to other countries simply by printing more dollars and reducing the value of that debt in inflation-adjusted terms. Other countries have chafed at this privilege and yearned to move to a less dollar-centered system."

[cxviii] "The Second Industrial Revolution, also known as the Technological Revolution, was a phase of the larger Industrial Revolution corresponding to the latter half of the 19th century until World War I. It is considered to have begun around the time of the introduction of Bessemer steel in the 1860s and culminated in early factory electrification, mass production and the production line. The Second Industrial Revolution was characterized by the build out of railroads, large scale iron and steel production, widespread use of machinery in manufacturing, greatly increased use of steam power, use of oil, beginning of electricity and by electrical communications. The Second Industrial Revolution saw rapid industrial development, primarily in Britain, Germany and the United States, but also in France, the Low Countries and Japan." Wikipedia 12/24/14.

[cxix] *The Origins of English Financial Markets: Investment and Speculation before the South Sea Bubble*, Anne L. Murphy, Cambridge University Press, 2009, p. 220.

[cxx] *The Origins of English Financial Markets: Investment and Speculation before the South Sea Bubble*, Anne L. Murphy, Cambridge University Press, 2009, pp. 169-170. "Yet, we should not automatically assume that stock-jobbing was the same as broking. Contemporaries may have used the same label for the two individuals but they certainly saw a distinction between the two functions. Notably, the legislation passed in 1697 made it very clear that brokers were paid commission for bringing two parties with complementary needs together. Consequently, those who registered as sworn brokers risked prosecution by the City authorities if they were found to be dealing for themselves. Clearly that rule was not always strictly adhered to but it is interesting to note that after 1698 only a few of those who described themselves as brokers in the Bank of England's transfer books traded regularly enough to be also described as stock-jobbers." "Stock-jobbers, therefore, were not just acting as middlemen. Even if their activity was customer-driven at the outset, stock-jobbers accepted the risk of taking on a position without the immediate prospect of offsetting the trade. Because of the gap between purchase and sale, their profits were derived not from brokerage fees but from the differential between bid and offered prices and thus their chief concerns were whether the price at which they bought or sold was sufficient either to yield an immediate profit or to offer

protection until the position could be offset, or that a specific transaction made a positive contribution to a longer-term speculative position. In order to accomplish any of these goals, stock-jobbers undoubtedly at times resorted to the exploitation of naïve investors, something that brokers could not have done if they wanted to ensure long-lasting relationships with their clients. Broking and stock-jobbing, therefore, were not entirely compatible functions.

cxxi The original Industrial Revolution ran from about 1760 to sometime between 1820 and 1840. [Wikipedia]. 1760 would be seventy years after the roughly 1690 date at which the budding stock exchange in London called "Exchange Alley" was regularly talked about in financial and social circles and was providing financial support for new enterprises. "The years between 1685 and 1695 witnessed a revolution in public and private finance in England." [*The Origins of English Financial Markets: Investment and Speculation before the South Sea Bubble*, Anne L. Murphy, Cambridge University Press, 2009, p. 1] And 1760 would be fully forty years after the 1720 date at which Werner and Smith considered the exchange to have had "all the essentials" of modern markets. [*Wall Street*, Walter Werner, Steven T. Smith, Columbia University Press, 1991, p. 11] Exchange Alley would thus have had at least four and up to seven decades of new enterprise capital formation experience, plenty of time, in other words, to have ignited the sudden and surprising surge in new technologies and businesses known as the Industrial Revolution. ""Exchange Alley" in London boasted a thriving securities market at the beginning of the eighteenth century. By 1720, England had all the essentials of securities markets as they exist today." These essentials would have included active markets for trading and speculation by both professional and private individuals, which Werner and Smith demonstrate did not just accompany the formation of corporations, but in many cases actively facilitated it. "The trading market was of vital importance to public corporations, working its magic in several ways. Healthy trading of stocks in a particular type of venture stimulated promoters to organize new but similar ventures. The trading market allowed new businesses to raise capital even before they proved that they would be profitable. Speculators bought and held securities during the trial period, selling at a profit if the venture succeeded, and walking away with little loss if it failed." [*Wall Street*, p. 4] Although this passage refers to the U.S. market, one presumes that similar processes were at work in London a century earlier.

cxxii The Buttonwood Agreement, which the NYSE recognizes as its founding document, was dated May 17, 1792. But Werner and Smith describe earlier organizing broker meetings in February and March of 1792, and another document indicative of organizing intent similar to Buttonwood in 1791. [*Wall Street*, Walter Werner, Steven T. Smith, Columbia University Press, 1991, p. 26] They even suggest trading of some kind had been occurring "as early as the closing years of the conflict [the American Revolution]" in 1789 or even 1786. [*Wall Street*, p. 13, footnote 16] The NYS&EB, the original NYSE, was organized in 1817, but didn't really hit its stride until about 1820. "With the reporting and passing of the rules on March 8, 1817, the New York Stock & Exchange Board was born. Immediately, the new trading center began regular operations. Its first few years, however, can best be

154

characterized as a trial period. But after it passed the critical test of being useful to its members, the NYS&EB attracted more and more business. In 1820, a newly increased membership and a new constitution reinforced the organization, now thirty-nine brokers strong. In fact one contemporary argued that 1820 marked the true birth of the Exchange, as only subsequently did it become the vehicle for major stock transactions of the most active investors and brokers." [*Wall Street*, p. 28]

cxxiii *Wall Street*, Walter Werner, Steven T. Smith, Columbia University Press, 1991, p. 42.

cxxiv *Capital in the Twenty-First Century*, Thomas Piketty, translated by Arthur Goldhammer, The Belknap Press of Harvard University Press, Cambridge, Massachusetts, London, England, 2014, p. 86, Kindle location 1557. "The nineteenth century witnessed the first sustained growth in per capita output, although large segments of the population derived little benefit from this, at least until the final decades of the century. It was not until the twentieth century that economic growth became a tangible, unmistakable reality for everyone. Around the turn of the twentieth century, average per capita income in Europe stood at just under 400 euros per month, compared with 2,500 euros in 2010."

cxxv *The Haves and the Have-Nots: A Brief and Idiosyncratic History of Global Inequality*, Branko Milanovic, Basic Books, Perseus Books Group, 2011, Kindle Location 1225.

cxxvi *Comment: Productivity will make or break the next government*, Chris Giles, Financial Times, Dec. 18, 2014. "We are therefore left with the extremely unsatisfactory position that weakness in productivity growth is the most important known unknown for Britain's economy."

cxxvii *The Unsettling Mystery of Productivity: Since 2010 U.S. productivity has grown at a miserable rate. And no one, not even the Fed, seems to understand why*, Alan Blinder, The Wall Street Journal, November 24, 2014.

cxxviii *UK regulator to police seven more benchmarks*, Philip Stafford, Sam Fleming, Financial Times, Dec. 23, 2014. "The FCA plans tighter oversight of two of the WMBA's benchmarks -- Sonia (Sterling Overnight Index Average) and Ronia (Repurchase Overnight Index Average), which both serve as reference rates for overnight index swaps. The FCA also plans to regulate the WM/Reuters London 4pm closing spot rate; IsdaFix, the key rate for interest rate swaps; the London Gold Fixing; the LMBA Silver Price and the ICE Brent Index, which underpins one of the world's main crude oil futures contracts."

cxxix *U.K. to Criminalize Manipulation of Financial Benchmarks*, Katie Martin, The Wall Street Journal, Dec. 22, 2014.

cxxx Regulators have a long way to go to figure out how to reform these markets. In currencies, for example, relatively crude methods currently involving median prices over 30-second or 60-second periods set benchmarks that hold for from a half hour to an hour or two that govern prices at which dealers and customers trade until the next benchmark is snapped. But regulators will eventually discover, as I did when discovering the principles of fixed time trading versus continuous trading described in *Dark Pool Comment Letter*, that it actually is possible to eliminate all trading costs in fixings (unlike in continuous trading), by doing actual single price auctions where everyone trades at the same time and price, rather than mere surveys or snapshots of supposedly representative prices. This will set up an ongoing battle between the regulators and the banks that will play out in public as an attempt to eliminate banking profits in the public interest, just as the NMS did in continuous stock trading in the U.S. Today's headlines evidencing scandal, fines and reform efforts are therefore likely to continue for years as regulators grind the profits out of intermediation and simultaneously the confidence out of investors, just as happened with HFT in stocks. The dealers will want to keep it the way it is now, for which they are being fined billions. The Regulators will discover that there are better ways to do fixings, such as with single price auctions. Even if such auctions are never adopted, the fight over the theoretical value of costless methods and the desire of the banks to keep some profits, and their rigged methods, will give the public every reason to believe, as they do in U.S. stocks under HFT now, that the markets are rigged and will stay that way forever, even if they aren't. *JPMorgan Settles Investor Foreign-Exchange Rigging Lawsuit*, Bob Van Voris, Bloomberg Business, Jan. 5, 2015. "WM/Reuters rates are published hourly for 160 currencies and every 30 minutes for the 21 most-traded. They are the median of all trades in a minute-long period starting 30 seconds before the beginning of each half-hour. Rates for less-widely traded currencies are based on quotes during a two-minute window."

[cxxxi] *Wall Street*, Walter Werner, Steven T. Smith, Columbia University Press, 1991, p. 115.

[cxxxii] The original 1990 company was called Wunsch Auction Systems, Inc., or "WASI" by regulators. In 1992 with the support of the state of Arizona we moved our trading system to Phoenix and changed our name to the Arizona Stock Exchange, or AZX. We still kept several small offices after the change in other cities, including New York, where I remained.

[cxxxiii] "The Delta definition is relatively new, having grown out of the SEC's 1989 interpretation of the 1934 Exchange Act's definition of the word "exchange." The interpretation was made for the Delta case, in which the SEC was sued by two commodities exchanges for granting a no-action letter to Delta Government Options Corporation to operate an electronic "bulletin board" in over-the-counter options on Government securities. The judge in Delta objected to the Division of Market Regulation's previous practice of granting no-action letters without first saying whether a given system was or was not an exchange. After Delta, the Division could no longer grant no-action letters without determining that a system is not an exchange. If it is an exchange, the only options are a low-volume exemption or registration as a membership organization. The relevant part of the definition, taken from the 1990 order granting Delta temporary registration as a clearing agency, runs as follows: "What distinguishes an exchange from brokers, dealers and other statutorily defined entities is its fundamental characteristic of centralizing trading and providing purchasers and sellers, by its design (whether through trading rules, operational procedures or business incentives), buy and sell quotations on a regular or continuous basis so that those purchasers and sellers have a reasonable expectation that they can regularly execute their orders at those price quotations. The means employed may be varied, ranging from a physical floor or trading system

(where orders can be centralized and executed) to other means of intermediation (such as a formal market making system or systemic procedures such as a consolidated limit order book or regular single price auction."" *Auction Countdown - The Regulation of Calls - A Competitor's Perspective*, Steve Wunsch, first printed as a separate AZX Auction Countdown, May 23, 1995, included in *Auction Countdown*, Amazon Kindle, February 10, 2010, Kindle location 4514.

cxxxiv We had already been told that we would have to file for a "low volume exemption" to operate as an exchange, rather than get the usual "no action" letter from the SEC to operate as a broker dealer, which all of our nearest competitors, such as Instinet's Crossing Network or Jefferies' POSIT, had gotten. The practical effect of that choice by the SEC was to force us into an off-hours operating mode, since, as it was described to me, it would have been too politically uncomfortable for the Commission to approve our auction to operate at the same time that the main markets were operating, even though POSIT and Instinet's regular "real time" systems did. And the practical effect of the new definition was to make our banishment into the useless off-hours time slot much more likely to be permanent, rather than the temporary barrier I had hoped it would be when we were told to ask for the exemption. As it turned out, it was not completely permanent, but did last for about eight years, long enough to kill our business. The new definition got the SEC off the hook for cavalierly granting "no action" letters to brokers that wanted to compete with exchanges. But at the same time it put us *on* the hook, an effective scapegoat sacrificed to atone for the SEC's lax no action policy.

cxxxv "The term "exchange" is defined in Section 3(a)(1) of the Securities Exchange Act of 1934 as "any organization, association, or group of persons, whether incorporated or unincorporated, which constitutes, maintains, or provides a market place or facilities for bringing together purchasers and sellers of securities or for otherwise performing with respect to securities the functions commonly performed by a stock exchange as that term is generally understood."" *Auction Countdown - The Regulation of Calls - A Competitor's Perspective*, Steve Wunsch, first printed as a separate AZX Auction Countdown, May 23, 1995, included in *Auction Countdown*, Amazon Kindle, February 10, 2010, Kindle location 4492.

cxxxvi In regulatory jargon invented by the SEC in its rule making, the "first market" was the trading of NYSE-listed stocks on the NYSE floor or according to NYSE-authorized "upstairs" block trading rules. The "second market" was the over-the-counter, or OTC, trading of stocks that were not listed on the NYSE, which was the list that eventually became the NASDAQ list, the stocks of which traded in the NASDAQ dealer market via telephone. And the "third market" was the OTC trading of NYSE-listed stocks. "The Special Study started out by -- as I understand it - Milton Cohen saying, "We're going to divide this study into project one, which is the exchange market; project two, which is the over-the-counter market." And Dave Silver said, "There's this other market, which is the over-the-counter market, but in listed securities." So, that became project three, which became the third market. This was a nice thing, because it was easier to say than "over-the-counter market for listed securities."" Transcript of oral history of Don Weeden, interviewed by

Kenneth Durr, November 4, 2010, Securities and Exchange Commission Historical Society.

cxxxvii The 19c3 plan promoted and authorized by the SEC was intended to loosen the grip on listed trading at the NYSE by preventing any new stocks listed after April 26, 1979 from being subject to NYSE's normal restrictions against off-board trading. It worked. Eventually, the off-board trading model pioneered by 19c3 stocks became general for all listed stocks as the SEC progressively authorized the use of non-NYSE "print-shops," such as the regional exchanges and especially the electronic Cincinnati Stock Exchange, to get around rules such as NYSE Rule 394 and its final successor, NYSE Rule 390, that were meant to prevent such trading. Rules 394 and 390 were the last vestiges of the 1790s cartel that the exchange started with, which prevented members from trading with non-members outside the exchange. That agreement and its descendents, because they shunned trading with non-members, formed the core of the membership organization the SEC dedicated itself to breaking up, a mission at which the Commission has largely succeeded, thereby effectively outlawing the "stock exchange," as that term was generally understood.

cxxxviii In one famous incident, the NYSE-sponsored Martin Report on the future of the NSYE, which specifically looked into the problems allegedly caused by the third market, called for a ban on it, while offering, in a seeming quid pro quo, support for the SEC's idea developed in its Special Study of a transparent national market connecting all the exchanges electronically. In response, a letter from 19 famous academics defended both the third market and the national system. As Don Weeden remembers, "First, they tried to demean our business, to point out the inappropriateness of what we were doing; how we undermined the auction market, "the citadel of American capitalism." Then they tried getting rid of us through regulation. That was, of course, the whole purpose of the Martin (William McChesney Martin, former Chairman of the Federal Reserve) Report, which called for the "elimination of the third market." An extraordinary document, that got the proper reaction, which was almost overwhelmingly negative. One of the wonderful things that happened to us was Jim Lorie walking into our office. He was a very well-known economist with the University of Chicago, Graduate School of Business. He said, "What can I do to help?" We said, "Write a letter to the SEC." And he did, and he had nineteen signatures from the twenty-one top economists in the country. I mean, every name from Milton Friedman on the right, to Paul Samuelson on the left. Franco Modigliani was there, George Stiegler, nineteen names. It was a one-and-a-half page letter that just demolished the underpinnings of the Martin report." Transcript of oral history of Don Weeden, interviewed by Kenneth Durr, November 4, 2010, Securities and Exchange Commission Historical Society.

cxxxix The definition of "limited volume" in our exemption was often referenced as the nominal reason we were denied access to regular hours operation, and this term and the interpretations of it did change over the years in ways we paid close attention to, because they were always aimed straight at us and only us. During the years we operated, we were the only entity in the market that had the so-called Section 5 limited volume exemption. But there was nothing in Section 5 or Section 6, the sections of the Exchange Act law that governed how to apply the exemption that had anything to do with trading hours. Further, when we finally did receive regular hours permission many years after first asking for it, nothing in the language of the law or interpretations of it with respect to hours had changed. So we were left with the "political heat" explanation as the only reason that ever prevented our regular hours operation.

cxl Yes, it was a monopoly, not a duopoly (or tri-opoly) as it was often portrayed. The fact that there was only one dominant market for each stock meant that it was a monopoly, albeit one whose chores were divided by the lists of stock in which each market was the "primary" market. This arrangement would have probably met the test of "market division," a per se antitrust violation, if regulators had wanted to attack it on those grounds, although I have never heard of any cases where they did. They were probably too busy going after price fixing, manipulation, etc.

cxli "Turning and turning in the widening gyre The Falcon cannot hear the falconer; Things fall apart; the centre cannot hold; Mere anarchy is loosed upon the world, The blood-dimmed tide is loosed, and everywhere The ceremony of innocence is drowned; The best lack all conviction, while the worst Are full of passionate intensity." From the opening of *The Second Coming*, William Butler Yeats, 1919.

cxlii *Signs point to New York Stock Exchange going up for sale*, John Aidan Byrne, New York Post, Dec. 28, 2014. "The New York Stock Exchange is back in play -- and it may be sold, lock, "stock" and building as soon as next year, the Post has learned. Big Board owner Intercontinental Exchange, (ICE) is laying the groundwork. The latest all-out drive to make it more profitable, powered by better and faster technology -- and a regulatory overhaul to regain market share -- is pure window dressing, according to analysts and knowledgeable exchange watchers. This window-dressing could presage the once unthinkable: the closure of the Big Board's iconic trading floor."

cxliii *Alibaba's world record float gives US top slot*, Front Page, Financial Times, Dec. 19, 2014. "A last-minute rush of IPOs in Hong Kong raised more than $8bn in the past two weeks, but it was Chinese ecommerce company Alibaba's choice of New York for its stock market debut that gave the US its global lead in fundraisings. Alibaba's $25bn IPO on the New York Stock Exchange in September was a world record, and constituted more than a quarter of the $95.6bn raised in 285 US flotations this year -- the highest level since 2000."

cxliv *Germany weighs up the value of IPOs: The planned listing of retailer Zalando adds to signs that a suspicion of capital markets is lifting.* Alice Ross, The Financial Times, September 4, 2014. "News that the eurozone's largest online fashion retailer is launching an initial public offering has whipped up interest in Germany's normally stagnant equity markets. In one of the most anticipated IPOs this year, the Berlin-based start-up yesterday confirmed plans to raise up to 11 percent of its capital on the Frankfurt stock exchange. Its majority shareholder, Swedish investment group Kinnevik, has valued Zalando at 3.9 billion euros, with bankers estimating a value of up to 5 billion."

cxlv *Wall Street*, Walter Werner, Steven T. Smith, Columbia University Press, 1991, p. 77. "Overall, speculation in securities plays an important role in the mobilization of capital. Every project funded represents risks taken: the more risks taken, the more projects funded. Not only is speculation as important as investment in the new issue market, it also allows innovators to raise capital. It keeps the volume of trading high, which encourages investors who know that their investments can be converted to cash. High volume also tends to dampen the suddenness of market price swings. While speculation may distort trading prices in the short run, it also corrects them in the long run. It seems reasonable to conclude that investors in new issues have not been the only legitimate players in the securities markets. The indirect, less easily discernable roles played by speculators have been equally important to the market's success as an instrument for raising and allocating capital. The vital and positive contributions made by speculation and speculators are often overlooked, in particular by those who consider speculation a destructive practice at odds with beneficial "investment." The opinion--long held by earlier generations of historians and market analysts--that the securities markets' true function is only as an investment market has led many to view in isolation the role played by investors purchasing new issues. Other elements of securities markets have been discounted or ignored. Securities speculation in particular has been considered gambling, morally suspect at the least, and socially undesirable. Consequently, its significance has long been overlooked."

cxlvi Actually, these were coordinated actions by both agencies, and each involved several separate components. But Justice's actions hit a little earlier, such as in December 1996, while the SEC's actions hit a little later, such as in January 1997.

cxlvii "Prosecutors in the Justice Department's antitrust division are scrutinizing the price-setting process for gold, silver, platinum and palladium in London, while the Commodity Futures Trading Commission has opened a civil investigation, these people said. The agencies have made initial requests for information, including a subpoena from the CFTC to HSBC Holdings PLC related to precious-metals trading, the bank said in its annual report Monday. HSBC also said the Justice Department sought documents related to the antitrust investigation in November. The two probes "are at an early stage," the bank added, saying it is cooperating with the U.S. regulators. Also under scrutiny are Bank of Nova Scotia, Barclays PLC, Credit Suisse Group AG, Deutsche Bank AG, Goldman Sachs Group Inc., J.P. Morgan Chase & Co., Société Générale SA, Standard Bank Group Ltd. and UBS AG, according to one of the people close to the investigation. ... Previously launched investigations of the interest-rate and foreign-currency markets have led to billions of dollars in settlements from major financial firms. Related probes are continuing in the U.S. and Europe, with additional cases against firms and individuals by the Justice Department expected in the coming months, according to people familiar with the matter." *Big Banks Face Scrutiny Over Pricing of Metals*, Jean Eaglesham, Christopher M. Matthews, Wall Street Journal, Feb. 23, 2015.

cxlviii Frank Quattrone, who was probably the most successful and effective investment banker in the mid-1990s heyday of creating new technologies in the United States, was caught in the antitrust trap: "In 2003 Frank Quattrone, a CSFB star who handled high-profile IPOs during the dot.com boom, was charged by NASD with conflicts of interest between research and his investment banking activities. Quattrone, who was also reported to be under investigation by federal and New

York Prosecutors, resigned from the firm. NASD later permanently banned him from the securities industry, and Quattrone was convicted of federal obstruction of justice charges. The court verdict was later reversed, and the NASD action was overturned by the SEC." *Credit Suisse: Corporate Rap Sheet*, Philip Mattera, Credit Suisse Corporate Research Project. www.corp-research.org/credit suisse.

cxlix Some of these were quid-pro-quo understandings between bankers and their customers, either institutions who bought IPOs or companies that issued them. Spinning involved giving allocations in hot IPOs to top people at potential future IPO candidates to curry favor with them so they would be inclined to pick the bank that gave them the hot IPO shares when deciding which banks would be hired to do their own IPO. Laddering was an agreement by an institution that was granted a hot IPO allocation to buy more of the stock when it began trading so that its price would be supported and move higher. Other mentioned practices are straightforward per se antitrust violations. Price fixing and spread fixing were what the industry was caught doing via the "tacit collusion" revealed in the 1994 Christie-Schultz academic paper that resulted in the Order Handling Rules of 1997 and other antitrust reforms that produced electronic trading and HFT. The conflicts of interest that came from mixing investment banking and research were addressed by SEC rules against such mixing and a "Global Research Settlement" that requires separation of these functions and strict monitoring and supervision of the separate areas to make sure violations no longer occur. [Many say the lack of research coverage that the Tick Pilot is meant to address was caused by this separation, not decimals, and thus can't be solved by the Tick Pilot. I agree.] Other practices were meant to use the transparency of visible orders that are not expected to fill in order to manipulate prices in the opposite direction toward an order the manipulator wants to fill. Spoofing and layering, for example, are intended to manipulate market prices toward the price at which a trader has a resting order so that order will get filled. Front running and Manning violations involve trading ahead of orders that a trader has non-public knowledge of and/or a fiduciary duty to act as agent for. In the Manning case, a trader is prohibited from trading ahead of a customer if the trader's firm is at the same time acting on the same side of the market as agent on behalf of that customer. The most aggressive new prosecutions are gravitating toward classifying all of these, and even high frequency trading itself, as instances of "insider trading" on the grounds that HFTs know things the public doesn't, even if they are tiny in size and potential price movement and really "known" only for microseconds by a computer. The effect of this is that HFTs may soon face not just fines and banishment, but jail.

cl Although it may seem obvious to modern market observers that such practices should be illegal, it is necessary to point out that not one of them was illegal during the century prior to the creation of the SEC. As I said at greater length in a series of three TabbFORUM articles in 2013: "There were no laws against price fixing, monopolies, speculation, manipulation, insider trading, front running or any of the other unlevel playing fields of capitalism, nor would there be for a century. And the nation thrived." *HFT and the Computerization of Wall Street, Part 2: A Bad Trade*, Steve Wunsch, TabbFORUM.com, July 22, 2013. Further, as this piece points out, the success of the NASDAQ dealer market in creating the high tech advantage of the United States came about not in spite of its antitrust violations, but because of them. The piece concludes: "Stock exchanges that raise capital must violate antitrust to succeed. Therefore, either capitalism must go, or antitrust must go. Since capitalism is historically and still today the only potential source of our prosperity, if we decide to stick with the SEC and antitrust, our economic decline can only accelerate."

cli *Zero to One*, Peter Thiel with Blake Masters, Crown Publishing Group, 2014. Kindle location 930: "This extraordinarily stark pattern, in which a small few radically outstrip all rivals, surrounds us everywhere in the natural and social world. The most destructive earthquakes are many times more powerful than all smaller earthquakes combined. The biggest cities dwarf all mere towns put together. And monopoly businesses capture more value than millions of undifferentiated competitors. Whatever Einstein did or didn't say [about compound interest being "the most powerful force in the universe"], the power law--so named because exponential equations describe severely unequal distributions--is the law of the universe." Kindle location 952: "The power law becomes visible when you follow the money: in venture capital, where investors try to profit from exponential growth in early-stage companies, a few companies attain exponentially greater value than all others." Kindle location 1020: "Venture-backed companies create 11% of all private sector jobs. They generate annual revenues equivalent to an astounding 21% of GDP. Indeed, the dozen largest tech companies were all venture-backed. Together those 12 companies are worth more than $2 trillion, more than all other tech companies combined."

clii "From 1991 to 1997 nearly 80% of IPOs were smaller than $50 million. By 2000 the number of sub-$50 million IPOs had declined to only 20% of the market. The market for underwritten IPOs, given its current structure, is closed to 80% of the companies that need it." "The median IPO in the first half of 2009 was $135 million in size. This contrasts to 20 years ago when it was common for Wall Street to do $10 million IPOs and have them succeed." *Market Structure is causing the IPO crisis*, David Weild, Edward Kim, Grant Thornton, October 2009.

cliii $100 invested in Microsoft at its March 13, 1986 IPO would be worth over $55,000 today (11/7/14) at a price of $48 (after nine stock splits), for a total return of 65,729%. IPOROIcalc.xls.

cliv David Weild interviewed 12/18/14 by Larry Tabb, TabbFORUM.com, viewed Jan. 16, 2015. Weild claims that the IPO market should be producing at least 900 IPOs now, "GDP-adjusted" [instead of the less than 300 it produced in the supposedly good 2014 year], and that the difference between the 14,000 stocks we should have in our market by now if it had remained healthy [instead of being converted to HFT by the SEC's reforms] and the less-than 5,000 stocks we do have, means that the U.S. is missing 10 million or more jobs as a result.

clv *Nasdaq Leads U.S. Exchanges for IPOs in the Third Quarter of 2014*, John D'Antona, Jr., Traders Magazine, October 1, 2014. "The recent Alibaba IPO on NYSE isn't everything - although for a bit it seemed like the only thing. The IPO champ in the third quarter was Nasdaq, which welcomed 76 new listings in the third quarter, including 41 new IPOs. Nasdaq brought 140 IPOs to the market so far this year. This marks an 8 percent increase in listings compared to the same quarter last year. The combined proceeds raised by Nasdaq's IPOs year-to-date is approximately $16.7 billion. "This continues to be a record year for NASDAQ listings," said Nelson Griggs, senior vice president of listings at NasdaqOMS. "We've reached several important milestones so far, including surpassing both the 100 IPO mark and our 2013 total of 126 IPOs." According to Nasdaq, approximately 62% of all U.S. IPOs occurred on the bourse."

clvi *How Startups View Alibaba as an Active Investor*, Lizette Chapman, The Wall Street Journal, September 22, 2014.

clvii As Kevin O'Leary said on CNBC's "Squawk Alley" the morning of September 26, 2014.

clviii *Facebook Closes $19 Billion WhatsApp Deal*, Pammy Olson, Forbes, October 6, 2014. Jan Koum and Brian Acton are no doubt happy being multi-billionaires, and excited to work with Facebook's Mark Zuckerberg, who reportedly agreed to the high price only after overcoming Koum's seemingly sincere desire to stay independent. Whether it was a negotiating ploy or a true desire to stay independent, we'll never know. Nor will we know what WhatsApp could have done on its own.

clix Peter Thiel, PayPal co-founder, venture capitalist and author, interviewed by Wall Street Journal business editor Denis K. Berman at Wall Street Journal Digital Live conference, November 13, 2014. "[There were] maybe three hundred tech IPOs in the late nineties, maybe thirty now." Thiel also says in the interview that "I am very biased as an investor to be pro companies that are still led by their founders," as he discusses the reason for lagging innovation and productivity and why big companies can't innovate as well as small ones. When Berman notes that there are 59 pre IPO companies waiting to go public in the market today, Thiel says, "I think most of them won't go public until they are north of $10 billion."

clx His guess was a little low, but not much, and probably consistent with pre-IPO pricings and estimates. "The IPO raised $54 million for Amazon, giving it a market capitalization of $438 million." *Amazon.com IPO skyrockets*, Suzanne Galante, Dawn Kawamoto, CNET News, May 15, 1997.

clxi *The Great Escape: health, wealth, and the origins of inequality*, Angus Deaton, Princeton University Press, 2013, p. 186, Kindle location 2816.

clxii *The Great Escape: health, wealth, and the origins of inequality*, Angus Deaton, Princeton University Press, 2013, p. 230, Kindle location 3474. "Other rich countries have shared the slowdown in growth that we have seen in the United States. The decade of the 1960s was the postwar golden age, with an average growth rate of more than 4 percent a year, a rate that is high enough to increase incomes by a half in ten years. Growth fell to 2.5 percent a year in the 1970s, to 2.2 percent in the 1980s and 1990s, and to less than 1 percent in the decade up to 2010."

clxiii "The total number of dollar-a-day poor people in the world fell by three-quarters of a billion between 1981 and 2008 in spite of an increase in the total population of poor countries of about two billion. As a result the fraction of the world's population that lives below a dollar a day has fallen from more than 40 percent to 14 percent." *The Great Escape: health, wealth, and the origins of inequality*, Angus Deaton, Princeton University Press, 2013, p.44, Kindle location 791.

clxiv *The Great Escape: health, wealth, and the origins of inequality*, Angus Deaton, Princeton University Press, 2013, p. 178, Kindle location 2699.

clxv *A Wake-up Call for America*, David Weild, Edward Kim, Grant Thornton, 2009, p. 6. "Declines in the number of U.S. listed companies are much greater than those of other developed countries."

clxvi *Labor Market Fluidity and Economic Performance*, Steven J. Davis, John Haltiwanger, Jackson Hole, August 22, 2014. "While a more extensive set of international comparisons might tell a different story, the evidence here suggests that secular declines in U.S. labor market flows largely reflect forces and developments that are specific to, or more pronounced in, the United States."

clxvii *War On Wealth*, Steve Wunsch, Amazon Kindle, May 2, 2011. Kindle location 869: Appendix I: Articles on the Flash Crash.

clxviii *The Unsettling Mystery of Productivity: Since 2010 U.S. productivity has grown at a miserable rate. And no one, not even the Fed, seems to understand why*, Alan Blinder, The Wall Street Journal, November 24, 2014.

clxix The Financial Stability Oversight Council has ten members, consisting of the heads of the Treasury Department, the Federal Reserve, the Comptroller of the Currency, the Consumer Financial Protection Bureau, the Securities and Exchange Commission, the Commodity Futures Trading Commission, the Federal Deposit Insurance Corporation, the Federal Housing Finance Agency, the National Credit Union Administration Board, and an independent member with insurance expertise appointed by the President of the United States. "The Dodd-Frank Act provides the council with broad authorities to identify and monitor excessive risks to the U.S. financial system arising from the distress or failure of large, interconnected bank holding companies or non-bank financial companies, or from risks that could arise outside the financial system; to eliminate expectations that any American financial firm is "too big to fail"; and to respond to emerging threats to U.S. financial stability." Wikipedia: "FSOC" 11/20/14.

clxx Financial Times, November 13, 2014, "Front Page: Six banks hit with fines of $4.3 billion in global forex rigging scandal."

clxxi *Making Stock Markets Work to Support Economic Growth: Implication for Government, Regulators, Stock Exchanges, Corporate Issuers and their Investors*, Weild, D., E. Kim and L. Newport (2013), OECD Corporate Governance Working Papers, No. 10, OECD Publishing.

clxxii The best estimates are that HFTs make at most one tenth of a cent per share on an average executed trade and may make only half that (Rosenblatt, Dec. 2014), or $1.25 billion total for all HFTs combined per year. This relative pittance would be consistent with the visible costs on the screens that can be achieved with market orders, which, in the example I describe in *HFT and the Computerization of Wall Street, Part 3: Eliminating the Middleman* on TabbFORUM, (one cent one way on a two-penny spread stock) amounts to less than 3 basis points (including the $8 commission), and can be zero basis points (plus the $8 commission, or 1 basis point) if opens or closes are used where spreads disappear because everyone buys or sells at the same price. This compares to trading costs that used to be an average of two hundred basis points one way or more for institutions paying "net" (i.e., without paying a commission, but suffering large "spread," "market impact," "implementation shortfall," "delay" and other costs common to large orders (Plexus)), and more for individuals, who paid *both* the remnants of very high fixed commissions *and* one-way spreads of six-and-a-quarter cents or twelve-and-a-half cents (i.e., half the eighth or quarter tick) or more per share in most stocks. From the perspective of the average individual, whose small and instantaneously executed market orders are not predictable and therefore cannot be front-run, the only cost now is explicit commissions that average about $8 per trade, which compares to commissions that could exceed seventy-five or a hundred dollars per trade or more in the pre-NMS days. Spreads of a half-cent or one cent one-way in most active stocks are practically speaking already negligible for most individuals executing market orders, and can totally disappear if opens and closes are used, even for stocks that have larger spreads during regular continuous trading, leaving only the $8 commission, which would be 1 basis point on 100 shares of an $80 stock, or 2 basis points on 100 shares of a $40 stock.

clxxiii Good numbers were notoriously difficult to come by in the days before demutualization of the exchanges, because then all the major member firms were private partnerships, while the exchanges were not-for-profit corporations. Both of these circumstances tended to hide true profits. Further, because of the threat of pending NMS-style regulatory reform, the moral authority for which always presented Wall Street, the specialist system of the exchange, etc., as an unjustly wealthy monopoly, there was always an incentive to underplay profits.

clxxiv MIDAS is the SEC's Market Information Data Analytics System, bought from HFT firm TradeWorx, that allegedly will enable the SEC to keep up with HFTs in the marketplace. "The data and related observations address the nature and quality of displayed liquidity across the full range of U.S.-listed equities -- from the lifetime of quotes and the speed of the market to the nature of order cancellations." Two things should be said about MIDAS: First, it will not be useful to "average" investors at all, who will still have no idea what HFT means to them or how they should use the MIDAS information. Secondly real HFTs, in spite of the best efforts of TradeWorx and the SEC to update MIDAS, will always be ahead of them, and thus it will not provide anyone with the ability to compete with or otherwise deal with HFTs that would be different, or in any respect better than, simply using the market orders described above, which require no data analysis at all to get the benefit of. MIDAS, in other words, is something that benefits the SEC (by making it appear that the Commission is "doing something" about HFTs) (and TradeWorx), but will have no benefit at all for any investors.

clxxv *BATS Files Market Structure Reform Petition with SEC*, John D'Antona Jr, Trader's Magazine, Feb. 3, 2015. ""We certainly have strong thoughts on how to improve the highly efficient, fair and transparent U.S. equity market and the opinions of all participants are critical if there is to be true regulatory reform," [CEO] Ratterman said. "We urge everyone in the industry to engage in a formal, constructive dialogue with the SEC in order to drive incremental improvements for all investors." Under the BATS proposal, the company estimates that market-wide savings may exceed

$850 million annually for those accessing exchange liquidity in the 200 most actively traded U.S. stocks."

clxxvi *Obama: Income inequality "the defining challenge of our time,"* Rebecca Kaplan, CBS News, December 4, 2013. "President Obama pointed to a combination of growing income inequality and a lack of upward mobility as "the defining challenge of our time," arguing the government should take further steps to reverse a decades-long trend that has widened the gap between the nation's richest citizens and everyone else. "The basic bargain at the heart of our economy has frayed," Mr. Obama said. He repeated later in his speech that "the combined trends of increased inequality and decreasing mobility pose a fundamental threat to the American dream, our way of life, and what we stand for around the globe."

clxxvii *Fed's Yellen Says Extreme Inequality Could be Un-American; Central Bank Chief Says Income Inequality Could Be Impeding Economic Mobility*, Pedro Nicolaci Da Costa, The Wall Street Journal, October 17, 2014. "Ms. Yellen cited investments in education and opportunities for business ownership as key pathways for economic mobility, which she described as stagnant for several decades. "The past few decades of widening inequality can be summed up as significant income and wealth for those at the very top and stagnant living standards for the majority," she said."

clxxviii *Yellen risks backlash after remarks on inequality*, Robin Harding, Financial Times, October 18, 2014.

clxxix *Why Trading Floors Are Shrinking*, Gregg Wirth, Traders Magazine, October 1, 2014. "Still, the number of bodies on the floor of the NYSE, roughly 5,500 at its peak, has dwindled to a fraction of that, about 700 traders in all. The exchange's new owners, Intercontinental Exchange (ICE), have promised further renovations, including $80 million to modernize the interior of the building to encourage more open spaces and greater employee interaction. This tectonic shift didn't just happen at the NYSE, although because the 222-year-old institution is a bastion of American capitalism, the changes were just more noticeable. The enormous UBS trading floor in Stamford is now mostly filled not with active traders but with back-office personnel; the futures exchange the New York Board of Trade was shuttered (incidentally by ICE); and many Wall Street firms, like Morgan Stanley, have scaled back their trading floors and jettisoned legions of traders."

clxxx *Gingrich Calls GOP Budget 'Right Wing Social Engineering'*, David Chalian, PBS News.org, May 16, 2011. "The former House speaker broke from his party leadership on the Hill by stiff-arming the budget drafted by Rep. Paul Ryan, R-Wis., and passed last month in the House. "I don't think right wing social engineering is any more desirable than left wing social engineering. I don't think imposing radical change from the right or the left is a very good way for a free society to operate. I think we need a national conversation to get to a better Medicare system with more choices for seniors," Gingrich said."

clxxxi *Nature's God*, Steve Wunsch, 2012, p. 84, Kindle location 2125. "Why are all the proposals unrealistic, with little or no chance to move us back toward the Constitution or away from socialism? The reason is that the proposals are not meant to be realistic. They are only meant to be provocative and antagonistic. The Red Team proposals are picked for their ability to rally the Red Team troops around an anti-Blue Team agenda. They are mirror images of similarly unrealistic Blue Team proposals seeking to rally Blue Team members around an anti-Red Team agenda. The proposals of both teams are attractive for their capacity to show as sharply as possible how minor differences in the socialist programs of both parties might matter, even if they really don't. But while Republicans would fiddle with vouchers or medical savings accounts or shopping for insurance across state lines, while Democrats would fiddle with individual mandates or a single payer system, the end result will be socialized medicine just as much under Romney or any other Republican president as under Obama or any other Democratic president."

clxxxii *SEC Budget Increase Would Bolster Exams*, Security Traders Association of New York, Feb. 5, 2015. "The Securities and Exchange Commission's requested fiscal 2016 budget of $1.722 billion would allow the commission to hire hundreds of examination staff and step up enforcement, as well as help the muni office coordinate with self-regulators."

clxxxiii *Rushing to Cater to America's Rich*, Hiroko Tabuchi, New York Times, Feb. 7, 2015. "Since mid-2013, the number of millionaires in the United State has grown by 1.6 million, by far the biggest increase in the world and dwarfing the 90,000 Chinese who crossed the million-dollar mark since then, Credit Suisse estimates. In 2014, Americans with net wealth of more than $50 million outnumbered their Chinese counterparts eight to one." On an accompanying graph, China can be seen to have surpassed since 2007 all the other wealthiest countries except the U.S. in terms of their percentages of the global population of these individuals worth more than $50 million, all of which (Germany, Japan, Russia and Brazil) now have only about two to four percent of the these super-wealthy individuals, while China has 6 percent of them. But the United States has 49 percent of them.

clxxxiv *Gap Persists in Homeownership*, Lisa Prevost, New York Times, Feb. 7, 2015. "The rising tide of economic recovery is not lifting those most in need, according to an annual scorecard of financial security and opportunity put out by the nonprofit Corporation for Enterprise Development. Low- to moderate-income households and households of color remain far behind on a number of measures of financial well-being, especially when it comes to homeownership. "We are continuing to exclude an increasing percentage of Americans from our mainstream financial systems," said Andrea Levere, the organization's president. "This issue resonates quite profoundly in the conversations we're all having about income and inequality." While considerably more low-income individuals are obtaining the two- and four-year college degrees necessary for higher-paying jobs these days, the disparity in college attainment is still gapingly large. According to the scorecard, 54 percent of the richest 20 percent of adults have four-year degrees, compared with 12 percent of the poorest 20 percent. And poverty has not declined. The percentage of income-poor households -- defined as below the federal poverty threshold -- was 14.7 percent in 2013, compared with 12.3 percent in 2007."

clxxxv For more on this dynamic, see discussions in chapters 9 and 11 beginning on page 71 (Kindle location 1791) and page 84 (Kindle location 2105), *Nature's God*, Steve Wunsch, 2012. "While the Red Team wants to go back to America's constitutional roots, and the Blue Team places America's roots in the alleged fairness of Constitution-shredding traditions like the New Deal, the reality is these are both tropes, flourishes that shape an argument of the moment for either upward or downward redistribution. Like other seemingly unrelated issues -- cultural, moral, religious, defense, etc. -- the argument over whether America's true character lies in fairness or the Constitution is so remote practically speaking from the redistribution levers under debate, that it serves, as these other issues do, only as a marker of tribal loyalties and team allegiance designed to provoke emotion, righteous anger, action." Kindle location 1802.

clxxxvi *Capital in the Twenty-First Century*, Thomas Piketty, p. 515.

clxxxvii *Columbia Follows Piketty Plan in Raising Tax on Largest Fortunes*, Oscar Medina, Bloomberg Business Week, Sept. 9, 2014. "Columbia is seeking to increase taxes on the net wealth of its richest citizens in line with proposals laid out by French economist Thomas Piketty in his bestseller "Capital in the Twenty-First Century." The government will impose a 2.25 percent annual tax on wealth of more than 8 billion pesos ($4.1 million), Deputy Finance Minister Andres Escobar told reporters in Bogota last night. Smaller fortunes will pay lower rates, with capital of less than 750 million pesos paying nothing, Escobar said."

clxxxviii *Capital in the Twenty-First Century*, Thomas Piketty, Kindle location 4541.

clxxxix *Breaking up the estates*, Mure Dickie, Financial Times, Feb. 6, 2015. "The ruling Scottish National party wants land reform to revive local rural communities hit by depopulation, but critics say the plan smacks of class war and a further advance of an over-mighty state."

cxc *Progressive Kristallnacht Coming?* Tom Perkins, Wall Street Journal, January 24, 2014.

cxci Tom Perkins interview with Emily Chang, Bloomberg West, January 27, 2014.

cxcii Tom Perkins interview with Emily Chang, Bloomberg West, January 27, 2014.

cxciii *Nature's God*, Steve Wunsch, 2012, Amazon CreateSpace paperback, p. 75, Amazon Kindle Direct Publishing, Kindle location 1904. "A propaganda film, Der Ewige Jude, (The Eternal Jew) produced by Joseph Goebbels at Hitler's request, put the Jewish conspiracy at the top of German society and income in Berlin. According to the film, Jews were only 0.2% of common laborers, but were 15% of prosecutors, 23% of judges, 52% of doctors, 60% of lawyers, and had over 12 times the wealth of the average German (10,000 marks, versus 810 marks). Such inequality, according to Hitler and Goebbels, needed to be addressed by government."

cxciv *World On Fire: How Exporting Free Market Democracy Breeds Ethnic Hatred and Global Instability*, Amy Chua, Doubleday, 2003, Amazon Kindle, Anchor Books, Random House Digital, Inc., January 6, 2004, Kindle locations 3293 and 4900 ff. I discuss Chua's stance and suggestions in *Nature's God* (p. 110 and footnotes clxiii and clxiv on pages 138 and 139).

cxcv "Trayvon Martin could have been me 35 years ago," says President Barack Obama, cnn.com, July 19, 2013.

cxcvi "Rev. Fred Lucas, a Sanitation Department chaplain, startled some when he prayed for New Yorkers to be emancipated from 'the plantation called New York City' during his invocation at de Blasio's [inauguration] ceremony." New York Daily News, January 2, 2014.

cxcvii *L.I. thug to face charges in seven 'knockout' attacks*, Antonio Antenucci, New York Post, Dec. 17, 2013. "A Long Island man will be charged with punching out seven men as part of the "knockout" game, according to a spokesman for the Suffolk County Prosecutors office. Darryl Mitchell, 20, of North Amityville will be arraigned Wednesday in Suffolk County Criminal Court for allegedly slugging the victims -- two of them over 65 -- in confirmed incidents of the violent game, the spokesman said."

cxcviii *Man punched in the face in Union Square hate attack dies at Bellevue Hospital*, Rocco Parascandola, Tina Moore, New York Daily News, Sept. 9, 2013. "A white man who was punched in the face in Union Square by a black man who was spewing anti-white sentiment died early Monday at Bellevue Hospital, a police source said. Jeffrey Babbitt, 62, fell into a coma after he was randomly attacked Wednesday afternoon by a man who was yelling, "I'm going to punch the first white man I see!" Leshawn Martin, 31, was arrested on charges of misdemeanor assault in the attack. The unprovoked punch knocked Babbitt backward, and he hit his head on the ground."

cxcix Spike Lee explains expletive-filled gentrification rant, CNN, February 27, 2014.

cc "Of course, the Right is right in noting that if marginal tax rates were near 100 percent tax rates, incentives would be significantly weakened, but these examples show that we're nowhere near the point where this should be of concern. Indeed, University of California professor Emmanuel Saez, Thomas Piketty of the Paris School of Economics, and Stefanie Stantcheva of the MIT Department of Economics, carefully taking into account the incentive effects of higher taxation and the societal benefits of reducing inequality, have estimated that the tax rate at the top should be around 70 percent--what it was before President Reagan started his campaign for the rich." *The Price of Inequality*: How Today's Divided Society Endangers Our Future, Joseph E. Stiglitz, W.W. Norton & Company, p. 114, Kindle location 2663.

cci "Hitler declared that he knew nothing of bourgeois or proletarian, only Germans. *Volksgemeinschaft* [folk community] was portrayed as overcoming distinctions of party and social class. The commonality this created across classes was among the great appeals of Nazism." "A common Nazi mantra declared they must put "collective need ahead of individual greed"--a widespread sentiment in this era." "In his pamphlet, *State, Volk and Movement*, Carl Schmidt praised the expulsion of Jews from political life without ever using the term "Jew" and using "non-Aryan" only rarely, by praising the homogeneity of the people and the *Volksgemeinschaft* ensuing; merely *Gleichschaltung* [forcible-coordination] was not sufficient, but Nazi principles must continue to make the German people pure." "Among the goals of [*Gleichschaltung*] were to bring about adherence to a specific doctrine and way of thinking and to control as many aspects of life as possible." Wikipedia: "Volksgemeinschaft" and "Gleichschaltung," 1/9/15.

ccii "When he finally hit the streets of Bedford-Stuyvesant Saturday afternoon, he was hunting for cops to kill, and said moments before the fateful encounter that passersby should "watch what I'm going to do." He then pumped four shots into the squad car outside Tompkins Houses where Officer Wenjian Liu and Officer Rafael Ramos were having lunch while on an anti-crime patrol." *'Watch what I'm going to do:'* Cop killer Ismaaiyl Brinsley's chilling words before assassinations, Pamela Ng, Ayana Harry, PIX11 News, Dec. 21, 2014.

cciii *CCTV shows moment black teen, 18, raises and points loaded gun at St. Louis cop before being shot dead as mayor says this is 'different' to Ferguson shooting*, Darren Boyle, Lydia Warren, Jack Crone, Daily Mail, Dec. 24, 2014.

cciv *The New Jim Crow*: Mass Incarceration in the Age of Colorblindness, Michelle Alexander, The New Press, 2010, p. 17, Kindle location 532.

ccv *O'Reilly, Russell Simmons Clash on Black Crime: 'You Are So Desperately Wrong'*, Josh Feldman, MediaITE, Dec. 10, 2014.

ccvi *About a Boy*: Transgender surgery at sixteen, Margaret Talbot, The New Yorker, Mar. 18, 2013.

ccvii *The Scientific Quest to Prove Bisexuality Exists*, Benoit Denizet-Lewis, New York Times Magazine, Mar. 20, 2014.

ccviii *The End of Men*, Hanna Rosin, The Atlantic, Jun 8, 2010. "Earlier this year, women became the majority of the workforce for the first time in U.S. history. Most managers are now women too. And for every two men who get a college degree this year, three women will do the same. For years, women's progress has been cast as a struggle for equality. But what if equality isn't the end point? What if modern, postindustrial society is simply better suited to women? A report on the unprecedented role reversal now under way--and its vast cultural consequences."

ccix Confirming our own commitment to diversity and inclusion, President Obama favorably mentioned in his Jan. 20, 2015 State of the Union, making sure "a woman is paid the same as a man for doing the same work," and that "affordable, high-quality childcare" is available. He also enthused about marriage equality as a story of freedom: "I've seen something like gay marriage go from a wedge issue used to drive us apart to a story of freedom across our country, a civil right now legal in states that seven in ten Americans call home." And he talked about how defending our values makes us safer: "That's why we defend free speech, and advocate for political prisoners, and condemn the persecution of women, or religious minorities, or people who are lesbian, gay, bisexual or transgender. We do these things not only because they're right, but because they make us safer."

ccx *Inside Story: Foreign fighters and the lure of war abroad*, Ray Suarez, Al Jazeera America, October 19, 2014. A subsequent study was reported on the PBS News Hour 2/10/15 that said ISIS now has 20,000 foreign fighters from 90 countries, including 150 from the United States.

ccxi *After Terrorist Attacks, Many French Muslims Wonder: What Now?* Liz Alderman, New York Times, Jan. 11, 2015. "The situation is especially acute in the banlieues, the disadvantaged suburbs that ring Paris and other large French cities, and are populated by Muslims and people with Arab or Saharan family roots. In 2005 and 2007, violent riots broke out amid rising frustrations over social and economic inequality."

ccxii *Growing anger across the Muslim world over Charlie Hebdo magazine as hundreds of thousands march in Cechnya and Iranians chant 'Death to France' (but Pakistanis mistakenly burn the wrong flag)*, Ted Thornhil, Steph Cockroft, Reuters, Associated Press, Daily Mail, Jan. 19, 2015. "Scenes of chaos broke out across the Muslim world today as hundreds of thousands of protesters burned flags and effigies in anger over the French satirical magazine Charlie Hebdo. Protesters gathered in the main market square of Bannu, Pakistan, chanting 'Death to the government of France', before setting fire to dozens of French flags and an effigy of the former French President Nicolas Sarkozy."

ccxiii *Protests break out around the world against Charlie Hebdo*, Reuters, CBS News, Jan. 19, 2015.

ccxiv *The web is a terrorist's command-and-control network of choice*, Robert Hannigan [British spy chief], Financial Times Opinion, November 4, 2014. "The Islamic State of Iraq and the Levant (Isis) is the first terrorist group whose members have grown up on the internet. They are exploiting the power of the web to create a jihadi threat with near-global reach." "Isis has embraced the web as a noisy channel in which to promote itself, intimidate people, and radicalise new recruits. The extremists of Isis use messaging and social media services such as Twitter, Facebook and WhatsApp, and a language their peers understand. The videos they post of themselves attacking towns, firing weapons or detonating explosives have a self-conscious online gaming quality. Their use of the World Cup and Ebola hashtags to insert the Isis message into a wider news feed, and their ability to send 40,000 tweets a day during the advance on Mosul without triggering spam controls, illustrates their ease with the new media. There is no need for today's would-be jihadis to seek out restricted websites with secret passwords: they can follow other young people posting their adventures in Syria as they would anywhere else. The Isis leadership understands the power this gives them with a new generation."

ccxv *In New Era of Terrorism, Voice From Yemen Echoes as France Declares 'War'*, Qaeda Cleric, Killed in 2011, Is Invoked in New Attack, Scott Shane, New York Times, Jan. 11, 2015. "In the age of YouTube, Mr. Awlaki's death -- or martyrdom, in the view of his followers -- has hardly reduced his impact. The Internet magazine Inspire, which he oversaw along with another American, Samir Khan, has continued to spread not just militant rhetoric but also practical instructions on shooting and bomb-making."

ccxvi *Open Markets, but Maybe Not Open Minds*, Tyler Cowen, New York Times, Jan. 25, 2015. "Finally, the paper offers an intriguing result drawn from data on Muslims who responded to polling questions around the world: Compared with non-Muslims, they are much less tolerant of gay individuals but no less tolerant of difference across the races."

ccxvii *Inside Story: Foreign fighters and the lure of war abroad*, Ray Suarez, Al Jazeera America, October 19, 2014. A guest expert on the show, Mia Bloom, professor of security studies, University of Massachusetts, said that one of the appeals of Islamic State was its ability to offer a life without homosexuality.

ccxviii *The 'war on terror' is going backwards*, Gideon Rachman, Financial Times, Jan. 20, 2015: "A recent study by the Rand Corporation identified 49 Salafist-Jihadi groups operating around the world in 2013, compared with 28 in 2007. These groups staged 950 recorded attacks in 2013,up from 100 six years earlier." Or see *The Tragedy of the American Military*, James Fallows, The Atlantic, Jan.-Feb., 2015: "Although no one can agree on an exact figure, our dozen years of war in Iraq,

Afghanistan and neighboring countries have cost at least $1.5 trillion; Linda J. Bilmes, of the Harvard Kennedy School, recently estimated that the costs could be three to four times that much." "Yet from a strategic perspective, to say nothing of the human cost, most of those dollars might as well have been burned. "At this point, it is incontrovertibly evident that the U.S. military failed to achieve any of its strategic goals in Iraq," a former military intelligence officer named Jim Gourley wrote recently for Thomas E. Ricks's blog, Best Defense. "Evaluated according to the goals set forth by our military leadership the war ended in utter defeat for our forces." In thirteen years of continuous combat under the Authorization of the Use of Military Force, the longest stretch of warfare in American history, U.S. forces have achieved one clear strategic success: the raid that killed Osama bin Laden. Their many other tactical victories, from overthrowing Saddam Hussein to allying with the Sunni tribal leaders to mounting a "surge" in Iraq, demonstrated great bravery and skill. But they brought no lasting stability to, nor advance of U.S. interests in, that part of the world."

[ccxix] *The Age of Austerity*, How Scarcity Will Remake American Politics, Thomas Byrne Edsall, Anchor Books, Doubleday, Random House, New York, 2012, Kindle location 266. "Between 1939 and 1945, it is estimated, between fifty and sixty-six million people perished."

[ccxx] *Countdown*, Steve Wunsch, Amazon, Sept. 22, 2001, Amazon Kindle Direct Publishing, Jan. 26, 2010, Kindle location 25. "Government intervention to reallocate economic and social outcomes has undermined our infrastructure, set our people against one another, and caused our enemies to proliferate. Not only did this inattention to freedom open us up to the surprise attack on September 11, but the redistributionist ethos that brought us to this pass is pushing us even faster down the same road as we respond to it. As a result we could actually lose this war. Yes, the unthinkable is possible, -- indeed probable -- on our current course. Although we may still be more free than any other country, the backsliding on our principles must be checked and reversed quickly or we will find it impossible to maintain the moral and political cohesion on which our legitimacy to lead the world fight against terror depends. Moreover, without a return to freedom, the economic infrastructure that enables us to fight will rapidly erode. And most frightening of all, both the number and strength of our enemies will expand without limit unless we stand again for the principles our Founding Fathers enunciated two centuries ago."

[ccxxi] "He formed al-Tawhid wal-Jihad in the 1990s, and led it until his death in June 2006. Zarqawi took responsibility, on several audio and video recordings, for numerous acts of violence in Iraq including suicide bombings and hostage executions. Zarqawi opposed the presence of US and Western military forces in the Islamic world, as well as the West's support for the existence of Israel. In late 2004 he joined al-Qaeda, and pledged allegiance to Osama bin Laden. After this al-Tawhid wal-Jihad became known as Tanzim Qaidat al-Jihad fi Bilad al-Rafidayn, also known as al-Qaeda in Iraq (AQI), and al-Zarqawi was given the al-Qaeda title, "Emir of Al Qaeda in the Country of Two Rivers". Wikipedia: Zarqawi (3/2/15).

[ccxxii] *The Island at the Center of the World: The Epic Saga of Dutch Manhattan and the Forgotten Colony That Shaped America*, Russell Shorto, Vintage Books, Random

House, Inc, New York, 2005, Kindle location 184. "Its muddy lanes and waterfronts were prowled by a Babel of peoples -- Norwegians, Germans, Italians, Jews, Africans (slaves and free), Walloons, Bohemians, Munsees, Montauks, Mohawks, and many others -- all living on the rim of empire, struggling to find a way of being together, searching for a balance between chaos and order, liberty and oppression. Pirates, prostitutes, smugglers, and business sharks held sway in it. It was Manhattan, in other words right from the start: a place unlike any other, either in the North American colonies or anywhere else. Because of its geography, its population, and the fact that it was under the control of the Dutch (even then its parent city, Amsterdam, was the most liberal in Europe), this island city would become the first multiethnic, upwardly mobile society on America's shores, a prototype of the kind of society that would be duplicated throughout the country and around the world.

[ccxxiii] *The GenderBread Man*: Diversity Training, YouTube. Or see *About A Boy*: Transgender surgery at sixteen, Margaret Talbot, The New Yorker, Mar. 18, 2013. "Even for kids who are not "trans enough," the dream of finding the perfect niche endures. At a workshop called "Binary Defiance," at the True Colors Conference, the facilitator wrote specialized gender labels on the blackboard so fast that I practically sprained my wrist writing them down: "non-binary, gender queer, bigender, trigender, agender, intergender, pangender, neutrois, 3rd gender, androgyne, two-spirit, self-coined, genderfluid." These ever-narrower labels are meant to be liberating, offering people their own customized categories, but they often seem predicated on stereotypical notions about men and women."

[ccxxiv] *'Poor Door' in a New York Tower Opens a Fight Over Affordable Housing*, Mireya Navarro, The New York Times, August 26, 2014. "A 33-story glassy tower rising on Manhattan's waterfront will offer all the extras that a condo buyer paying up to $25 million would expect, like concierge service, entertainment rooms, and unobstructed views of the Hudson River and miles beyond. The project will also cater to renters who make no more than about $50,000. They will not share the same perks, and they will also not share the same entrance. The so-called poor door has brought an outcry, with numerous officials now demanding an end to the strategy. But the question of how to best incorporate affordable units into projects built for the rich has become more relevant than ever as Mayor Bill De Blasio seeks the construction of 80,000 new affordable units over the next 10 years."

[ccxxv] *Madison's Privacy Blind Spot*, Jeffrey Rosen, New York Times, January 19, 2014.

[ccxxvi] *The Dollar Trap: How the U.S. Dollar Tightened Its Grip On Global Finance*, Eswar S. Prasad, Princeton University Press, 2014, Kindle location 519. "The U.S. dollar has been the principal global currency for most of post-World War II history. In fact, the U.S. economy is estimated to have become the largest in the world in the 1870s. By the early 1900s it also accounted for the largest share of global trade."

[ccxxvii] *What Drives Success?* Amy Chua, Jed Rubenfeld, New York Times, January 26, 2014.

[ccxxviii] *Big Baby, Smart Kid*, David Leonhardt, Amanda Cox, The New York Times Sunday Review, October 12, 2014. "Crucial to the change has been a widely held belief that once fetuses pass a certain set of thresholds -- often 39 weeks of gestation and five and a half pounds in weight -- they're as healthy as they can get. More time in the womb doesn't do them much good, according to the thinking. For parents and doctors, meanwhile, scheduling a birth, rather than waiting for its random arrival, is clearly more convenient. But a huge new set of data, based on every child born in Florida over an 11-year span, is calling into question some of the most basic assumptions of our medicalized approach to childbirth. The results also play into a larger issue: the growing sense among many doctors and other experts that Americans would actually be healthier if our health care system were sometimes less aggressive. The new data suggest that the thresholds to maximize a child's health seem to be higher, which means that many fetuses might benefit by staying longer in the womb, where they typically add at least a quarter-pound per week. Seven-pound babies appear to be healthier than six-pound babies -- and to fare better in school as they age. The same goes for eight-pound babies compared with seven-pound babies, and nine-pound babies compared with eight-pound babies. Weight, of course, may partly be an indicator of broader fetal health, but it seems to be a meaningful one: the chunkier the baby, the better it does on average, all the way up to almost 10 pounds."

ccxxix *Big Baby, Smart Kid*, David Leonhardt, Amanda Cox, The New York Times Sunday Review, October 12, 2014. "Health costs have slowed sharply in the last several years, surprising nearly every expert. Remarkably, per-person spending on Medicare is on a pace to be about 6 percent lower this year than it was three years ago . . . The idea that we can be healthier with less health care is no longer just wishful thinking; it is a serious theory with growing evidence."

www.ingramcontent.com/pod-product-compliance
Lightning Source LLC
Chambersburg PA
CBHW080809180526
45168CB00006B/2380

* 9 7 8 1 5 0 8 7 2 2 4 8 9 *